THE HISTORY OF ARCTIC AND ANTARCTIC EXPLORATION

polar
REACHES

RICHARD SALE

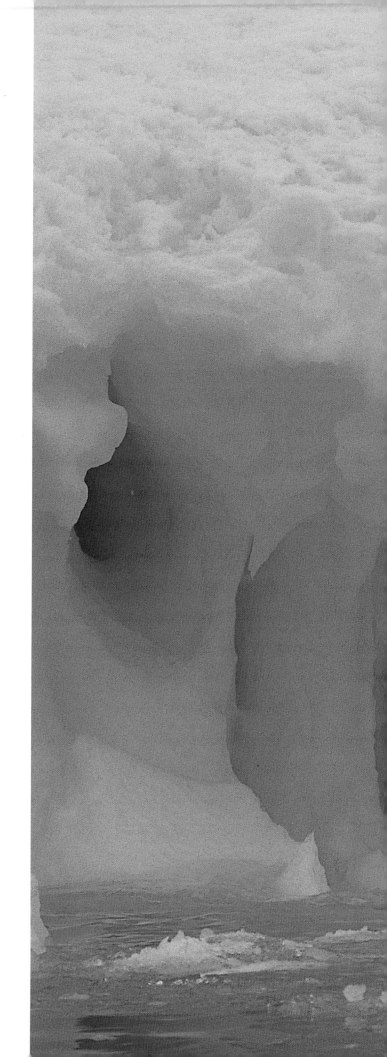

Dedication

To Susan
For consistently tolerating my absence in the Arctic on her birthday,
and allowing the Antarctic to routinely jeopardise Christmas.

Acknowledgements

I would like to thank the staff of libraries and museums, archives and
galleries all over the world for their kind assistance in providing
information and illustrations for this book.

I would like to thank Maria Gavrilo and Roald Potapov in St
Petersburg for their kind hospitality and assistance, and Eugene
Potapov in the UK for his help with my very poor Russian. Thanks are
also due to library, gallery and museum staffs too numerous to
mention individually in cities throughout Austria, Australia, Canada,
Denmark, Holland, Iceland, New Zealand, Norway, Russia, Sweden, the
UK and the USA. Particular thanks are also due to Alyson and Ian
Morris and Chris Bartle in the UK for their continuous assistance.

Equally importantly I would like to thank those who have made
journeys to the Arctic and Antarctic so rewarding over the years:
Harriet Backer, Susan Barr, Roger Francis, Chris Hamm and Nathan
Sale. And most particularly Per Michelsen and Tony Oliver for their
consistent companionship.

Finally I would like to thank Quark Expeditions (and Debra Taylor
in particular) for their help in getting me to a few of the more remote
sites in the southern hemisphere and the North-West Passage.

The Mountaineers Books
1001 SW Klickitat Way, Suite 201
Seattle, WA 98134
www.mountaineersbooks.org

©2002 Richard Sale

First edition, 2002

ISBN 0-89886-873-4 (North America)

Edited and designed by Blackingstone Books
Color origination by Colourscan, Singapore
Printed and bound by Printing Express Ltd., Hong Kong

Library of Congress Cataloging-in-Publication Data
A catalog record of this book is available at the Library of Congress.

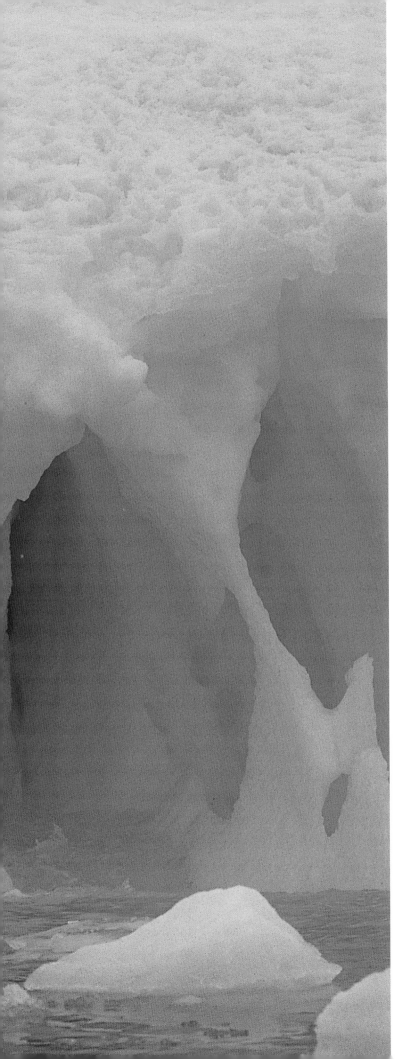

CONTENTS

Half title page top **Iceberg, Antarctica**
Half title page below **Midnight sun, Barrow Strait and Cornwallis Island**
Title page **Paradise Bay, Antarctica**
Left **Iceberg detail, Antarctica**
Richard Sale

Introduction

'People, perhaps, still exist who believe that it is of no importance to explore the unknown polar regions. This, of course, shows ignorance. It is hardly necessary to mention here of what scientific importance it is that these regions should be thoroughly explored. The history of the human race is a continual struggle from darkness towards light. It is, therefore, to no purpose to discuss the use of knowledge: man wants to know, and when he ceases to do so, he is no longer man.'

Fridtjof Nansen

The men who sailed the tiny wooden ships that explored the oceans of the medieval world faced cruelties almost beyond imagining. From harbour mouth to home again the ships were rarely still, their decks frequently washed by the waves. The sailors were constantly exposed to the elements, trimming sails and minding the wheel, tasks that could not wait for an improvement in conditions. Their clothes, usually inadequate rags, were invariably sodden. When they could retreat below decks they added their dampness to cramped living quarters that could be oven-hot in the tropics, perishing cold in high latitudes, and always squalid.

If they survived the storms (and many did not), or the ever-present risk of the tarred wood of the ship being rapidly consumed by flames from the cooking fire, they could succumb to starvation, thirst, disease or injury. Food could only be preserved by salting, a process that delayed, but could not eliminate, putrefaction. Anywhere a man could survive, fungus, mildew, cockroaches and rats could too, and usually much better. Four hundred years after the first ocean explorations those searching for John Franklin noted their provisions were 'discoloured, stinking and unfit' and had to be destroyed. One man wrote of the crossing of the Pacific on Magellan's round-the-world trip that 'we ate only old biscuit turned to powder, all full of worms and stinking of rat urine'. In the dark crevices of the ship the rats fed and bred, their populations reaching prodigious numbers. On Ellsworth's 1934 voyage home from Antarctica the rats killed and ate the

ship's cat. Elisha Kent Kane, the American Arctic explorer, wrote that if he were asked 'the three besetting curses of our Arctic sojourn, I should say RATS, RATS, RATS'. The rats carried leptospirosis and Weil's disease, salmonella, even plague.

And even without rats to infect the food and weaken the men through ill health, there was scurvy, which required no infestation or degradation of the food, but merely the absence of vitamin C. The disease's name derives from the Old English word for gnawing or shredding, a word which also meant contemptible or disgusting. All are descriptions which apply well to a disease which causes the gums to grow black and shrink until the teeth fall out, the skin to become covered with livid blotches, limbs to swell and joints to hurt. Scurvy caused old wounds to open and new areas to fail to heal, and there were few sailors who did not have an old wound, or several, for these were belligerent times and naval discipline was harsh. Without vitamin C scurvy is remorseless, and the bloated patient becomes covered in ulcers which ooze pus and blood. Gnawing and shredding, contemptible and disgusting. Secondary infections are likely, death inevitable.

Scurvy afflicted mariners for centuries. Long before the cause was established (memorably Edward Wilson on Scott's Discovery Expedition claimed that the clear symptoms of scurvy in the men were actually caused not by the disease, but by tobacco and the constant use of foul language) remedies were available: lime juice, fresh meat and vegetables. But the effectiveness of the former decreased with storage time (a fact not

Above **The *Endurance* in the Weddell Sea during Shackleton's most famous expedition. This shot, by Frank Hurley, was taken on a Paget plate, an early form of colour photography (see page 199).**
Mitchell Library, State Library of New South Wales, Australia

Below **The *Hecla* and *Fury* in winter quarters at Igloolik. The engraving illustrates that the British made considerable efforts to keep their sailors exercised and happy during the winter. During** Barents' expedition to Arctic Russia his men played golf, rather than the cricket the British clearly preferred. The line joining the ships across the snow bollards was to prevent men crossing between them becoming lost in winter's darkness, and was a feature of most expeditions. Illustrations from Nordenskiöld's book on his first transit of the North-East Passage show a similar arrangement linking the ship to the shore camp.
From William Edward Parry *Journal of a Second Voyage.*
Richard Sale Collection

understood at first), while supplies of the latter two could not be guaranteed. Ironically, as food ran short men were often forced to eat the rats that caused the shortage, so acquiring fresh meat. With the modern understanding of diet it is often assumed that scurvy was beaten centuries ago, but it probably contributed to the loss of Scott's South Pole team.

Water, too, was a problem, as a man dies quickly of thirst, only slowly of starvation. If a ship were becalmed water could run short and supplies often became brackish or stagnant. On Magellan's Pacific crossing the same informant noted that the water was 'impure and yellow'; it is not hard to imagine the source of the impurities and colour, and the likely effect on debilitated men.

Added to this list of known objective dangers were the subjective ones of loneliness and homesickness and, more importantly because it represented a collective dread, the fear of the unknown. It is fact, not myth, that the outer edges of ancient maps were inscribed 'here be monsters'. Hugeness is terrifying, ugliness is evil incarnate, so it is no surprise that unknown waters and lands were thought to be the home of monsters. And, often, what the mariners did find – whales, sharks, even turtles and sea snakes – were vast beyond their knowledge or understanding, and anything so monstrous could hardly be a portent of good: around the next cape, over the next wave, lurked Leviathan.

So why did they come, these brave frail men? It is usually said that the driving force was greed, a desire to find new lands to exploit, but a glance at history shows that to be too glib an answer. Before Europeans set out on their journeys of exploration the Chinese had reached India, Persia and east Africa, and the Arabs had sailed their dhows the opposite way. Yet neither contemplated the possibility of exploring further. It is true that developments in Europe – the stern rudder instead of the side-oar, lateen and square sails, better navigational instruments – allowed ships to sail ocean rather than coastal waters, but these inventions were driven by a need to innovate.

Geographically the Portuguese were the best placed of the Europeans for ocean voyages, their kingdom having a long Atlantic coast. In Dom Enrique (Henry the Navigator) they also had a prince who was interested in exploration, for a variety of reasons. One was undoubtedly economic: the fall of Byzantium to the Ottoman Turks had made trade with the east more difficult and so more expensive. But there was also the possibility of reducing the size and influence of the Muslim world.

The Christians had finally expelled the Muslims from Iberia, and the Portuguese were certainly interested in the possibility of outflanking the Turks. They were also intent on making contact with the legendary Christian Kingdom of Prester John so that the Muslim world might be encircled. The development of ships and the need and desire for exploration coincided with the invention of the printing press and the Renaissance. The former allowed mass communication, which further stimulated minds made fertile by the latter. The Portuguese, and later the other European nations, explored because they wanted to know.

This desire to know led to the discovery of Antarctica, the exploration of the North-West Passage and the journeys to the poles. In each case many of the pioneering voyages were made by the British. Though the search for the North-West Passage started with the Elizabethan privateer Martin Frobisher, the Golden Age of the search was the first half of the 19th century. This coincided with the end of the Napoleonic Wars, during which the society folk of Britain had been unable to travel to the Continent and had contented themselves with home-grown attractions such as the Tour of the River Wye where they sought the Picturesque, views of the natural world which could be admired and sketched. Gentle scenery was favoured, the wilder country of the English Lake District being seen as 'too horrid' to contemplate: it is claimed that some travellers drew the blinds of their carriages as they posted through the mountains, so fearful were they of the prospect. These notions passed easily to the Arctic: John Franklin's books on his land expeditions to the Mackenzie and Coppermine Rivers are full of romantic descriptions of the landscape and the horrors of the journey; it is no surprise that when Mary Shelley needed to exile to his doom the monster created by Baron Frankenstein she took him to the Arctic and its dreadful icy wastes. Romanticism and dread were also to condition later British expeditions.

The voyages in search of the North-West Passage, and then in search of Franklin's last expedition, also established the fact that the polar winter could be survived. Though scurvy was an issue and the problems of condensation and, therefore, ice in the ships made the winter a trial, the British proved that the polar winter could be tolerated rather than endured at some risk, the position which had prevailed during earlier attempts. This owed a great deal to the lessons learned earlier in the Royal Navy (who supplied the crews for the passage and pole attempts), lessons which were contemptuously dismissed or humorously reported (depending on the speaker) as 'rum, bum and concertina'. Given enough drink and entertainment, and a willingness to turn a blind eye to below-decks activity, a peaceful, if not necessarily wholly contented, atmosphere prevailed.

Franklin's expeditions were made before the Golden Age of polar exploration, the time when the North-West Passage was finally traversed and the South and North Poles reached ('perhaps reached' in the case of the North). By then the British Empire had expanded to include a significant proportion of the earth, and the British attitude towards polar travel reflected the national mood (or, at least, that of those who ran the country). Britain was then the world's most powerful nation and reacted petulantly when its view of the way things should be was challenged. When other nations began to take an interest in Antarctica the Marquis of Lothian spoke for the establishment élite as a whole when he said 'I should not like to see foreign names upon that hemisphere where all civilised points are inhabited by our countrymen and belong to this country', relegating at a stroke all the non-British countries of the southern half of the world to the league of uncivilised nations.

Yet for all the pomposity and arrogance of the British establishment the men at the sharp end exhibited a tenacity and spirit that was admirable. They sought to do great things, to establish British indomitability. Shackled by the amateurism of their leaders they were doomed to suffer and, often, fail, but there was something noble about their efforts. Scott's decision to use ponies and his failure to learn how to use dogs or skis was ludicrous, but reflected his superiors' view that 'derring-do will see us through' and that the British way – whatever it was – was innately superior. After Amundsen had beaten Scott to the South Pole, Helmer Hanssen, one of Amundsen's team, said of Scott that no one would ever do it that way (by man-hauling) again. Ironically, anyone using a method other than manhauling (perhaps with sail assistance) to reach either pole today would be considered to be operating outside the unwritten laws of modern polar trekking.

The Americans were latecomers to polar exploration. Their early expeditions included dramatic and agonising failures that mirrored the reckless enthusiasm of youth. Later, a nation whose ethos was (and is) based on rewards and glory being heaped on winners might almost be expected to have generated a debate such as that between Peary and Cook, the fact that neither might have actually reached the pole in 1909 reinforcing the point. That is unfair, as the debate (which went beyond normal argument into the realms of vindictiveness) and the rival claims seem to have been fuelled as much by personal animosity as by the facts; but the probable deception involved in Byrd's North Pole flight in 1933 makes the point again.

By contrast to the British and the Americans, the Norwegians, the third nation associated with the Golden Age of polar exploration, went about their expedition business in a methodical, professional way. Though their greatest men, Nansen and Amundsen, were not free of personal ambition, their expeditions were smaller and more democratic. When the *Terra Nova* met the *Fram* in the Bay of Whales the men of Scott's expedition were astonished to discover that the latter had individual cabins rather then separate quarters for officers and men. The Norwegians, on the verge of independence on Nansen's trips, newly independent on Amundsen's, were expressing that freedom by acting as a tightly knit group of friends.

But even as expeditions reflected national identities or moods, individual explorers can be glimpsed through society's veneer. What were these men like? Shackleton said that a polar explorer needed optimism, patience and physical strength. The great explorers had these three qualities in abundance, but it is neither a prerequisite nor a logical outcome of them that an explorer should be any less ambitious or greedy, or should not possess any other vices of ordinary men. Interestingly Shackleton's list does not include courage, which would seem, to ordinary mortals, to be a fundamental requirement. He did mention it, but thought it less important. Neither did he mention luck, which would also seem to have played a part in some of the most famous expeditions where men trod a thin line between success and failure. Shackleton almost died getting to within 160km (100 miles) of the South Pole, and probably would have done if the weather had been just a little worse. Nansen survived bear and walrus attacks on his trip from the *Fram*, but only just; and might not have survived at all had it not been for the chance meeting with Jackson. Many of the great stories of polar exploration involve survival against the odds, making heroes only of those that return.

It was the method of that survival that was the fascination because it explored the disputed borderline between life and death. Valerian Albanov, one of just two who survived the *Saint Anna* disaster in the Kara

Sea, spoke of how, with their ship frozen in the ice, the crew wrote letters to those who lived in the present while they, the writers, lived only in the past – before the ship was entombed – or the future, when life would start again. Only survivors have that future in which to tell their stories. At a bleak moment Albanov regrets that no one will know how he died. Perhaps some of the greatest polar stories are those untold and beyond telling, the heroism of men who did not survive, but died experiencing unimaginable horrors and terrors in a lonely, remorseless land.

Many of the men who went to the polar regions would have done so even if they had known the details of those desperate deaths, because they were driven by some inner demons. Their exploits were a vicarious thrill for the newspaper readers at the turn of the 20th century. In the main those people led static, humdrum lives, while the explorers pushed the boundaries of existance at the edge of the known world. Small wonder their exploits could fill the front pages for days on end. Today's reader is better travelled, and film and television have made the exotic commonplace. There are more diversions and so the exploits of the modern polar traveller – driven by the same demons – have been relegated to a few paragraphs on an inside page. Modern man – an adventurer rather than explorer as

invariably he/she knows what to expect, geographically – has much warmer, lighter clothing, better equipment, a global positioning system that requires no knowledge of navigation, and a radio to summon instant rescue or transport. He is flown to the start, flown back from the endpoint. It is a more sanitised adventure and, since it can be tried by anyone who has both the inclination and, more importantly, the money, it is more commonplace.

That is why the old explorers still command the greater coverage. Then if a man wanted to reach a pole he first sailed his ship across treacherous waters – a journey which took weeks, not the few hours of a plane ride. He had to overwinter as he could not reach his start point in time to trek the same year. He had to lay depots because his food was heavy and cumbersome, and he had to come back – no pole pick-up by ski plane. He was out of contact with his base for weeks at a time, giving his trip an imperative which is now largely lacking. The explorer can still die, but whereas safe return was once doubtful it is now highly probable.

Yet for all that, those pushing back the frontiers of the possible – Ousland, Gjeldnes, Larsen, Kagge, Dupre, Hoeschler – are from the some mould as Nansen, Amundsen and Shackleton, and it is likely that the polar regions will continue to attract such men.

The air tractor used during Mawson's Australasian Antarctic Expedition of 1911–14. The plane had crashed on its trial flight in Australia and, with its wings removed, was to be used to haul loads. It was not a startling success.
University of Adelaide, South Australia

The Arctic

Before the heroes came

From the first time man began to consider the night sky of the northern hemisphere, he probably realised that the stars circled one fixed star, and that while some stars rose and set others were visible at all times. This fact was first set down by the Chaldeans, who inhabited the south-eastern part of Babylonia – now southern Iraq – over 5,000 years ago. The Greeks realised that the further north the observer travelled the greater was the number of stars that were always visible. For observers in Greece itself, the circle in the heavens which defined the boundary between stars which were always visible, and those that rose and set, passed through the constellation of Arktos, the Great Bear. The Greeks therefore referred to this circle as the Bear's Circle, the Arctic Circle. The fact that the circle enclosing always-visible stars grew bigger as the observer went north meant that the earth was a sphere, that it rotated and that there was a northern pole to its axis of rotation. The Greeks understood this (in principal) but the information was lost in Dark Age Europe and took many centuries to retrieve. What was not lost was the name Arctic.

In the last third of the 4th century BC, perhaps about 330BC, when Aristotle was teaching at his school in Athens and his former pupil Alexander the Great was campaigning in India, a Greek named Pytheas set sail from Massalia (now Marseille), a trading port on the Mediterranean coast to the west of Italy. Pytheas was a gifted astronomer who had worked out the method of calculating latitude by measuring the shadow cast by a vertical pillar at a solstice. He probably wanted to travel north to confirm his method, perhaps even to reach the pole, which would have given him an exact fix. He may also have been an adventurer who wanted to visit Ultima Thule, the land where the sun neither set in summer nor rose in winter, word of which had reached Greece through traders. But it is likely that those who financed Pytheas' voyage were merchants who wanted more direct access to the tin and amber of northern Europe, goods which then reached the Mediterranean by land and river, and whose trade was controlled by others.

Pytheas sailed through the Gibraltar Straits and turned north. As far as Brittany he was probably following a known, if not well known, route, as it is thought that as early as 500BC the Carthaginian Himilco had reached the tin-mining area around Quiberon. Beyond that Pytheas was crossing waters unknown to the Greeks. He was away six years and exactly where he went has been the subject of debate ever since. Later Greeks and Romans who had access to his account dismissed Pytheas as a fraud, but modern experts are more sympathetic. It is likely that he followed the coast to the western tip of Brittany, then crossed to Britain; Cornwall, due north of Brittany, being another tin-producing area. Pytheas continued north, sailing around Britain to reach Orcas (probably the Orkneys, but some have suggested the Shetland Isles), then continued north again, sailing for six days to reach 'Thule' where the summer day was 21 or 22 hours long (too long for the Shetlands, thought by some to be the location of Thule). In Thule Pytheas heard that north again the sea stiffened or congealed. Some have suggested that he reached Iceland, but his Thule was inhabited and Iceland certainly was not at that time: Iceland is also further than six days' sail from Scotland. It is likely that Pytheas had actually reached Norway, a remarkable achievement, but one that so outpaced the understanding of the day that it was dismissed for almost 1,000 years.

Early Arctic dwellers

Of course, whether Pytheas' journey was real or fable, whether his Thule was Norway or the Shetlands, it was a voyage to a world which was already inhabited. Norway had been settled by Germanic tribes moving north, folk who eventually met and pushed north a people who were already living there. These were the Saami (the now-preferred name for an ethnic group formerly called Lapps) who herded their reindeer across the vast taiga (coniferous forest) and tundra of northern Scandinavia and western Russia. Like the Finns, the Saami had originated beyond the Urals, in the steppes of central Asia. As the ice sheets of the last Ice Age retreated the dwellers on the steppes had moved north behind them. At first the populations of the Arctic coast and the steppe could maintain contact, but ultimately the spread of the larch forests which now dominate Siberia isolated the tribes of the north, forcing them to take a different evolutionary path. The isolation created by the forest also allowed the gyr falcon, the world's largest falcon and the avian symbol

Above **Summer tents at Ammassalik in east Greenland. Photograph by Th N. Krabbe in September 1908.** Courtesy of the National Museum of Denmark, Department of Ethnography

Above **A reconstructed Inuit winter house at Resolute, Cornwallis Island, northern Canada. Animal skins were stretched over the bone framework as for the summer house. The houses were partially subterranean, the entrance crawl being lower than the house floor level to create a cold-air trap. The Inuit slept on the raised platform beneath which their few possessions would be stored.** Richard Sale

Above **Ancient tent ring on Ellesmere Island. Summer tents used skins stretched over a framework and held down with a ring of stones.** Richard Sale

of the high Arctic, to develop differences from its genetically almost identical cousin, the saker falcon of the Mongolian steppes. As with the humans of the Arctic and those of the temperate zone, the gyr and saker falcons can still cross-breed.

In 1947, while inspecting a mammoth graveyard at 71°N near the headwaters of the Berelekh River (on the Siberian mainland due south of the New Siberian Islands) Russian scientists found evidence of human habitation dating to perhaps 10,000 years BC, the oldest remains so far discovered north of the Arctic Circle. Sporadic finds from later periods indicate that these early Arctic dwellers were flint-using hunters who preyed on the mammoths and other animals which had migrated north as the climate warmed. Little is known of these folk, man emerging from the frosty mists of northern time only about 4,500 years ago. By then people with the generic name Palaeo-Eskimo were found all around the Arctic rim. They had crossed the land bridge which then existed between Asia and Alaska – though even without this the Bering Straits represented little barrier to a sea-hunting people – and the Nares Strait between Canada and Greenland which regularly froze in winter. Evidence of the earliest cultures – called Arctic Small Tool tradition from the size of the stone implements used – comes from sites as remote as Wrangel Island off eastern Siberia and Independence Fjord in Greenland's Peary Land. Depending on where these nomadic peoples lived they hunted sea mammals – seals, walrus, perhaps even whales – or land mammals, reindeer/caribou and musk oxen. They also hunted birds and polar bears.

About 2,500 years ago the Arctic became colder. The distribution of animals altered, necessitating changes in the peoples dependent on them. In the eastern Arctic a new tradition arose, known as Dorset Culture from its first identification near Cape Dorset on Baffin Island. The Dorset people hunted sea mammals, certainly whales as large as narwhal and beluga, almost exclusively. For this they used kayaks (from the Inuit *qajaq*) made by stretching animal skins over a simple wooden framework, a vessel which was light enough to carry and could be rolled if it capsized. They used tents made of animal skins stretched over driftwood or bone frames – the skins held down by a circle of stones – in summer, capable of rapid erection and packing. In winter the Dorset folk had fixed houses of stone and turf, again with roofs of frames and skins, heated and lit by burning blubber oil in soapstone heaters/lamps. They also cooked over blubber, the use of oil an indication of their efficiency in killing whales, seals and walrus. The Dorset folk could also build houses of snow (the word 'igloo' simply means house, its use to solely describe a hemispherical building of snow blocks being a modern, romantic idea). They had knives to cut snow blocks, harpoons, and crampons for moving on ice. They made carvings in ivory and soapstone. They also had an animalistic belief system which revolved around a shaman, a witch doctor/holy man who could bridge the gap to the spirit world. The Dorset Culture lasted 2,000 years before being replaced by a new tradition, the Thule People.

The origins of the Thule People are still debated. The conventional wisdom is that they developed on the east Siberian/west Alaskan coast and spread west in about the 11th century AD, though perhaps two centuries later, replacing or subsuming a people they called the Tunit (now thought to have been the Dorset Culture folk). It is conjectured that their westward expansion was driven by the search for the origins of the iron technology which the Norsemen had brought to Greenland, iron weapons and tools having been traded eastwards across the Arctic. The alternative view (strongly held by its proponents, but dismissed by mainstream historians) is that the Thule People originated in Greenland and were, in fact, the result of interbreeding between Norsemen left behind when the Greenland settlements were abandoned, and Dorset folk. That Norsemen who expanded into the Arctic possessed iron technology is indisputable. It is also true that the present-day Inuit (a short, stocky people) have legends of the Tunit that speak of their height and physical strength, a description which fits the Norsemen well.

Whatever the origins of the Thule People – and absorption of a limited number of Norse settlers would mean that their size would be lost over generations, only their technology prevailing – they, or their culture, spread rapidly across the Arctic to become the forerunners of the modern Inuit. Inuit, meaning simply 'the people', is now the preferred term for the indigenous Arctic people, Eskimo – which derives from the Athabascan 'eater of raw meat' – now being considered derogatory. Inuit is plural, a single person being an Inuk.

The Inuit still used tents for summer expeditions and stone and turf winter houses, with windows made of seal gut. They wore skin clothing and used skin bedding. The sealskin for their clothes and *kamiks* (waterproof boots that were ideal for use in kayaks) was prepared by scraping off the blubber, then sealing the skin in old urine until it became pliable enough to be stretched. This preparation, and the manufacture of clothes and kamiks, was women's work. From their kayaks the Inuit hunted sea mammals using a harpoon with a barbed point that detached from the throwing handle, but remained attached by rope – usually walrus leather, the strength of which amazed early Europeans by being greater than that of their ropes – to a sealbladder float. The float prevented the animal diving: it was then overtaken by the kayaker and dispatched at short range with a spear. Interestingly, the introduction of the rifle to the Inuit was not wholly successful. A dead animal might sink out of sight, a wounded animal escape: by contrast the harpoon and float took hold of the prey. The Inuit also hunted whales, perhaps initially by harpooning those which had been trapped by sea ice during the early winter. The term *savssak* refers to this entrapment. The animals, forced to breath through a hole of diminishing size, were an easy target. Later the Inuit also hunted bowhead whales – vast, but slow-moving – a hunt which, controversially in view of bowhead numbers, still continues. On land they used sledges drawn by dogs (originally domesticated wolves) to hunt polar bear and other animals with bow and arrow. In addition to kayaks the Inuit also had the

Above **Umiak and kayaks at Ammassalik in east Greenland. Photograph by Th N. Krabbe in September 1904.**
Courtesy of the National Museum of Denmark, Department of Ethnography

Right and below **Whale Alley originally consisted of about 60 bowhead whale skulls, mostly in groups of two and four, set upright, nose down, along the edge of the beach. There were also 'arches' of whale jawbones and curious structures of stone – stone rings and enclosures and well-formed meat stores. The skulls and jawbones were obviously brought to the site as no other bones have been found here. This remarkably impressive site is thought to be around 700 years old.**
Richard Sale

umiak or women's boat, a flat-bottomed boat, also made of skins over a wooden frame, rowed by two to six oars, depending on size. This was used to move the family between hunting grounds.

The Inuit cooked in soapstone, later iron, pots over a blubber-oil stove. But despite the apparent integration of the Inuit to the Arctic theirs was a precarious life. Failure of the caribou or whales to migrate along a normal route could mean starvation, as could a bad run of luck for a hunter. The Inuit were subsistence hunters, a fact which led to misunderstandings and appalling accusations at the time of Franklin's disappearance. The insecure nature of their lives coloured the rest of the world's perception of them. Shamanism envisaged all living creatures as having both human and animal, and spiritual and physical, qualities, a view reflected in their art in which humans and animals frequently transpose. The *angakok*, or shaman, was the man most able or most in tune with nature, a bridge between the real and spirit worlds, frequently taking the falcon or polar bear as his 'familiar'; the former because it was thought to be able to fly to heaven, the latter because it was feared and admired for its strength and hunting skills. The shaman would communicate with the spirit world, usually during a trance, in an attempt to promote successful hunting. This practice did not require fixed 'temples', though a remarkable find was made on Yttygran Island off the Bering Sea shore of Siberia's Chukotka Peninsula where about 60 bowhead skulls had been arranged in groups, together with stone pits which held mummified whale and walrus meat, and a stone shrine.

Norsemen move west

It was the Inuit that the first Europeans met when they reached Greenland and northern Canada, but it must be remembered that the Inuit are not circumpolar. In Europe the original Arctic dwellers were the reindeer-herding Saami, while in Russia there are several groups, similar to the Saami, including the Nganasans of the Taimyr Peninsula and the Chukchi of the Chukotka Peninsula whose lifestyles also depended on hunting and herding reindeer. The Inuit are also themselves divided into sub-groups.

The first Europeans to meet the Inuit were Norsemen from Iceland. Norse Vikings settled on Iceland in about AD870, fleeing – it is said – from the tyranny of King Harald. But Iceland was not uninhabited, the southern coast being home to Irish monks

who had probably arrived in *currachs* (cowhide boats) via the Faeroes a century or so earlier. These Irish monks have never been given the credit they deserve; many books on Iceland fail to note their pre-Viking settlement of the island, and other books on Arctic history ignore early journeys to the north. Abbot Brendon journeyed north of Iceland, meeting a 'floating crystal column' (an iceberg?) and seeing a 'smoking mountain rising from the sea' (Beerenberg on Jan Mayen?). On another journey north of Iceland a monk reached a place where the sea was frozen and, at midnight in summer, there was enough light 'to pick the lice off one's shirt'.

The Norse Vikings made journeys both north and west from Iceland. To the north they discovered Svalbard, meaning cold edge. For political reasons the Norwegians have claimed that this was the Svalbard archipelago, but most experts believe it was north-east Greenland. To the west they certainly saw the east coast of Greenland, Norsemen being blown off route and discovering a land of mountains at the end of the 9th century. The first landing on Greenland was by Eirik the Red in AD982 following his banishment from Iceland for murder. Eirik spent three years in exile in the land to the west, unable to return to Norway from where he had already also been banished for murder. He returned with tales of the lush, green land (a truism for the coastal plain, though it is now usually stated that Eirik's name – Greenland – was a propaganda exercise) and persuaded many to return with him in 986. Of the 35 ships which set out, 21 turned back or were wrecked, 14 reaching the safety of the fjords near Julianhåb (Qaqortoq). More Icelanders arrived in 987, two settlements being established: Østerbygd – eastern settlement – at Qaqortoq, and Vesterbygd – western settlement – at Godthåb (Good Hope, now Nuuk). The ruins of Eirik's own settlement of Brattahlid – across the Tunulliarfik (Eiriksfjord) from Narsarsuaq – can still be seen.

In AD986 Bjarni Herjolfsson was blown off route while returning to Iceland from the Greenland settlements and saw land to the west. However, it was another 15 years before Liefur Eiriksson, son of Eirik the Red and the man who brought Christianity to Greenland, set out to explore this new land, having bought Bjarni's boat. This was the first of at least three (perhaps as many as six) 'Vinland' voyages. The Icelandic sagas suggest that the Vikings explored southern Baffin Island, the Labrador coast and Newfoundland (where the ruins of a winter camp at

Above **The ruins of Eirik the Red's settlement of Brattahlid across the fjord from Narsarsuaq, south-west Greenland.**
Richard Sale

Right **The page of Eirik the Red's *Saga* which deals with the settlement of Brattahlid.**
Stofnun Árna Magnússonar á Íslandi,
Reykjavik, Iceland

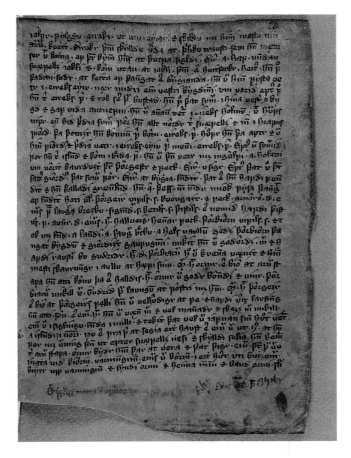

L'Anse aux Meadows is the only indisputable site so far discovered), and perhaps even the Cape Cod area of New England (if the vines of 'Vine-land' were really vines and not just berries). In the winter of 1002/3 Snorri Thorfinnsson was born in a Vinland winter camp, the first non-native American to have been born in the New World.

The Norsemen of Greenland certainly reached 73°N on the west coast, three cairns discovered north of Upernavik suggesting an overwintering. Inside one cairn a stone had been hidden: inscribed in runic it recorded the building of the cairns and the names of the builders. It is thought that the cairns date from the 14th century. Early in the next century the western settlement (which had a maximum population of 1,000 living in 90 farms, and four churches) disappeared. It is less clear when the eastern settlement (maximum population 2,000; 12 churches, a cathedral, a monastery and a nunnery) disappeared. The last known Bishop of Greenland died in 1377, and the last known ship to have sailed from Greenland left in 1410.

What happened to the Norse settlers is a mystery. The Norse certainly had contact with the Greenlandic Inuit: they called them *skrællinger*, possibly deriving from *skral*, small or weak, or from Karelia, a district of northern Finland/Russia whose native inhabitants were similarly short, stocky and dark. There were undoubtedly conflicts – Inuit legends recall skirmishes – but there was also trade and it is unlikely that the Inuit killed off the Norse. A change to a colder climate which made farming more difficult and animal husbandry marginal because of the lack of hay for winter fodder is more likely to have been the cause. The Greenlandic Norse supported 17 churches and two monastic houses, presumably with tithes. As agriculture failed life became untenable: those who could leave did, those who stayed probably died or were integrated into Inuit society. With the departure of the Norse the western Arctic was forgotten for a century or so, though a trade in the prized white gyr falcons continued and curiosities such as polar bears occasionally arrived in Europe. The other Arctic curio, the narwhal tusk, came a little later: a tusk was found on the shore of the Kara Sea in the mid-16th century. It was immediately thought to be from a unicorn and added impetus to the search for northern passages to

Above **Norse hood excavated at Herjolfsnœs, west Greenland.**
Courtesy of the National Museum of Denmark, Department of Ethnography

Right **This small soapstone statue was bought by the author from a Greenlandic carver who called it a 'Thuleman' and claimed it was an ancient design, a folk memory of the meeting of the Norsemen with the Inuit of north-west Greenland. The excitement this generated was somewhat tempered by other locals who claimed that the curious triangular head was modelled not on a Norse hood, but the parka hoods of US airmen who were stationed in north-west Greenland during the 1939–45 war!**
Richard Sale

the east, the merchants that sponsored them 'knowing that Unycorns are bredde in the landes of Cathaye, Chynayne and other Oriental Regions'.

But before the merchants sent vessels north another reason for heading that way arrived from a most unlikely source. The decree of the Catholic church that only 'cold' food could be eaten on Fridays had made fishermen wealthy, fish being considered cold as they lived in the cold sea. Cod, which when salted lasted a long time, was particularly prized. The Basques of the northern border country of Spain and France and the fishermen of Bristol, England, grew wealthy on cod. At first the Bristolians fished close to Iceland, but the Basque grounds were unknown, the Basques themselves too shrewd to reveal their secret. Eventually the Bristolians too found a new cod fishery. From it they returned with cod already salted, a procedure which required a land base. There is a legend in Bristol that before his westward journey Columbus visited the city and spoke to fishermen who, unlike the Basques, did not keep quiet about their finds. It is also said that Bristolian merchants wrote to Columbus after his voyage, complaining that he was taking credit for discovering what was already known.

Following Columbus' discovery, under the terms of the Treaty of Tordesillas in 1494 the Pope granted the Spanish the western hemisphere and Portugal the eastern, a situation intolerable to the English, French and Dutch, as it made them the buyers of the spices and other treasures of the east rather than the merchants. Shortly after the signing of the treaty a man arrived in Bristol offering to lead an expedition to Cathay. The man was Giovanni Caboto. Can it be entirely a coincidence that Caboto, who, like Columbus, was born in Genoa and at about the same time, chose Bristol to approach?

Passages to Cathay

Early voyages

Giovanni Caboto, now the honorary Englishman John Cabot, was given Letters Patent by Henry VII to explore for new lands and a passage to Cathay. Cabot's licence stipulated that he was to give 20 per cent of all profits from the voyage to the king and that no one was to disembark on any land discovered without Crown permission. Cabot left Bristol on 20 May 1497 in the *Mathew* (more likely named for Mathye, his wife, then the disciple) with a crew of 18. On 24 June he landed in Newfoundland, just a short distance from L'Anse aux Meadows. Finding evidence of inhabitants and fearing confrontation because of his limited numbers, Cabot took on water and left, exploring the local coast before returning to Bristol. On the next voyage Cabot (now the Grand Admiral Cabot, England's answer to Admiral of the Ocean Columbus) sailed with five ships, one of which soon returned after being damaged in a gale. The fate of the rest is a mystery. Sebastian Cabot, John's son, claims to have been on this trip and gives a plausible account of crossing the Arctic Circle, encountering 'monstrous heaps of ice swimming in the sea', days 18 hours long, and the entrance to a gulf heading west where many men died of cold. Kind historians wonder if he had sailed into Davis Strait and found Hudson Strait. Less generous folk claim that as Sebastian was a known storyteller he may not even have been on the expedition. Certainly he sheds no light on the fate of his father.

True or false, Sebastian Cabot's hint that he knew the secret of the North-West Passage kept him comfortable for the rest of his life, firstly in the pay of the Spanish (despite a disastrous trip to South America when he should have been heading north), and then the English. The latter gave him the title Grand Pilot of England and a fat salary. Trading on his title Cabot, now an old man and not fit to travel, persuaded London merchants to back a venture to find the North-East Passage (a curious decision if he knew the secret of the north-western route) and organised the first expedition to head that way. In 1553 three ships set out, following in the wake of the Norseman Ottar who, legend has it, sailed as far as the White Sea in the 9th century. Separated by a storm off northern Norway one, the *Edward Bonaventure* under Richard Chancellor (who carried, as did the other captains, a letter signed by Edward VI beginning 'Kings, Princes and Potentates

Above **The Letters Patent to discover new lands granted to John Cabot by Henry VII. The Letters were the authorisation warrant for Cabot's first voyage.**
UK Public Records Office

inhabiting the North-east partes of the worlde...'), made it to Archangelsk (Archangel). Chancellor discovered to his amazement that this was not in Cathay but Muscovy (Russia). He was warmly welcomed by officials of Czar Ivan IV (the Terrible) and taken the 2,400km (1,500 miles) to Moscow by sledge. At the capital he was equally well received and negotiated an Anglo-Russian trade treaty that made the London merchants (who formed the Muscovy Company) rich. Sadly on the return trip to England his ship, now carrying a Russian ambassador (Ossip Nepeja, the first such ambassador to England) was wrecked off Scotland. Chancellor died saving Nepeja's life.

The other two ships of the expedition reached the

Kola Peninsula where they decided to overwinter. Ill-prepared for the Arctic winter and with scout parties failing to find locals to help, all 66 men of the two crews died, probably from a combination of cold and scurvy: their bodies were found by Russian fishermen the following spring. A legend soon sprang up that the English sailors had been frozen to death as they worked, the commander at his desk, pen in hand, others carrying plates or cups, or in the act of eating. This seems absurd now, but the Arctic was an unknown, fearful land in the early 16th century and such things seemed all too likely: this version of the death of the crews formed the basis of the tale of *The Flying Dutchman*. After the Russian discovery the two ships were sailed back to England: to complete the disaster they were both wrecked en route.

In 1556 the Muscovy Company, emboldened by their trade agreement, put the miseries of 1553 behind them and tried again, Stephen Burrough sailing the *Searchthrift* to the Kara Sea where his progress was blocked by ice. Burrough overwintered at Kholmogory and returned safely, his gloomy pronouncements stopping further attempts until 1580 when, shortly after Frobisher's attempt to go west, the company tried one more time, this time with two ships, Arthur Pet commanding the *George* and Charles Jackman the *William*. The ships carried a vast inventory of tradable goods and 'a large Mappe of London to make show of your Citie' in order to impress the natives of Cathay. The expedition reached the Kara Sea where Pet, faced with a dispiriting mix of ice and fog, turned back. The *William* was never seen again.

Frobisher and Davis sail west

When the English (properly the British after the Act of Union between England and Wales) next tried to reach Cathay they headed north-west again. The expedition's leader was Sir Martin Frobisher, a Yorkshire-born pirate and slave-trader who had won his knighthood (as had his contemporary Sir Francis Drake) by presenting Queen Elizabeth I with the looted treasure of Spanish galleons. Unfortunately Frobisher had followed up the raid which won him his knighthood with one on a French ship carrying wine for an English merchant. Had it been a Frenchman's wine the capture would have brought him loud applause, but as it was he was thrown

Left **Sir Martin Frobisher by Cornelis Ketel.**
Bodleian Library, University of Oxford, UK

in jail and lost his fortune. Needing to restore his position he persuaded Michael Lok (brother of a slaving captain Frobisher had sailed with) to finance a trip to Cathay. Frobisher left London in June 1576 with the queen's blessing, with three tiny ships on a journey 'for finding of the passage to Cataya beyng a matter in oure age above all other, noteable' (as George Best, Frobisher's lieutenant, noted in his book on the trip). One ship, so small it was manned by just four sailors, sank off Greenland's southern tip, a second turning for home (where the captain reported the loss of Frobisher and his ship, the *Gabriel*, a premature obituary). Frobisher continued, finding Baffin Island and entering the bay which now bears his name. He sailed along it, convinced that to his right was Asia, to his left America.

In the bay Frobisher recorded two firsts: the first encounter with the Inuit (since the Vikings), and the first account of that merciless tyrant of the Arctic, the mosquito. The Inuit have an expression for these insects which swarm each summer and make life a misery for animals and man alike – *sordlo pujok*, like smoke. Frobisher noted that the insect was like 'a small fly or gnat that stingeth and offendeth so fiercely that the place where they bite shortly after swelleth and itcheth very sore', as good, and still valid, a description as could be conjured. Frobisher's meetings with the Inuit were, at first, less aggravating, with an exchange of gifts and attempts at an exchange of language; but then five of his men went missing. This reduced him to a crew of just 13 and enraged him – had they mutinied or been captured? If the latter, would they be eaten by these natives who had been seen eating raw fish and raw seal? In the end the worried Frobisher took a hostage (and his kayak) and sailed for home. There, in damp, chilly, autumnal London, the Inuk died, probably of pneumonia.

Above **The battle with the Inuit on Frobisher's expedition, by John White. Little is known of Elizabethan artist White, but it is conjectured that he accompanied Frobisher on his second voyage. Circumstantial evidence is supported by the authenticity of the painting – the uniforms, the setting and the incident itself.**
The British Museum

Right **John White's is one of the first paintings of Inuit. In 1654 a superior painting by an unknown artist was made of four Inuit who were taken to Norway and Denmark by Captain David Dannel. The painting is now in the Danish National Museum.**
Photograph by John Lee. The National Museum of Denmark, Department of Ethnography

Frobisher had brought back a lump of black rock, so like coal that Michael Lok's wife threw it on her fire. To her amazement it glistened. Retrieved and tested, it was, said Lok, gold ore of astonishing concentration. Three official assayers dismissed it as pyrite – fool's gold – but a glib-tongued Venetian alchemist resident in London convinced Lok's business associates that it was the real thing. In 1577, carrying the hopes of the 'Company of Cathay', famed to exploit the source, Frobisher was back in Frobisher Bay. This time the meeting with the Inuit was less cordial. Frobisher found some items of clothing from the five missing men in an Inuit tent, rekindling his fears of abduction. In trying to grab a hostage he was shot in the backside with an arrow, the incident precipitating a battle in which five Inuit were killed and one sailor badly wounded. Ironically, in view of Frobisher's fear of Inuit cannibalism, wounded Inuit threw themselves into the sea as they were convinced the English sailors would eat them. Frobisher captured a man, woman and child, loaded 200 tons of ore into his ship and sailed for home. Back in London the male Inuk entertained the queen by killing swans from his kayak, but all three Inuit soon died of pneumonia.

Despite expert misgivings over the gold ore Queen Elizabeth was convinced and underwrote a huge expedition of 15 ships which sailed under Frobisher in May 1578. By error the fleet reached Hudson Strait where ice destroyed one ship (and another fled home), but eventually worked its way back to Frobisher Bay. There on an island still called Koblunarn (White Man's Island) Frobisher built a stone hut and began mining the 'gold' ore. He took back almost 2,000 tons, but all attempts by the London alchemists failed to turn it into anything valuable. Michael Lok's backers turned on him and he ended up in Fleet's debtors' jail. Frobisher joined his old colleague Drake in raids on the Spanish West Indies: he died in 1594 from wounds received in the taking of the Spanish fort at Brest in France.

The next to try his luck was John Davis, who in June 1585 sailed with the *Sunshine* and the *Moonshine*. It could be argued that the latter was aptly named as the Elizabethan mathematician/alchemist Dr John Dee had been involved in the early discussions on the voyage. Born in Beguildy, Radnorshire, the Welshman Ieuan Ddu had been a famous local wizard before his brilliance as a scholar took him to Cambridge University and made him tutor to Elizabeth I. His fame as an astrologer and necromancer are said to have made him the model for Shakespeare's Prospero. Dee's spirit-world contacts had told him of a river that split America, leading directly to Cathay, and this had been one of the principal reasons for Sir Humphrey Gilbert's disastrous attempts to create a settlement in Newfoundland. The spirits also

Above '**A wonder in the heavens and how we caught a bear**' by Levinus Hulsius in Gerrit de Veer's *The Three Voyages of Willem Barents*. The wonder is a parhelion or sun dog caused by ice crystals in the atmosphere. The poor bear looks completely outnumbered.
Richard Sale Collection

Left **At the western end of Frobisher Bay, near Iqaluit.**
Richard Sale

guided Dee to form an alliance with John Davis and Adrian Gilbert, Humphrey's brother, but Davis, a shrewd, sea-hardened man, may have seen through Dee's occult posturings because the astrologer seems to have departed the scene before the expedition set out. Perhaps he foresaw failure...

Davis reached the east coast of Greenland, but could not land because of glaciers and icebergs (where was he?), then rounded Kapp Farvel (Cape Farewell) and reached the less desolate fjords the Vikings had settled. Here he met Inuit, the meeting being a joy of trade and mutual kindness. Pushing on, Davis explored the strait which now bears his name as far north as the Arctic Circle, then explored Baffin Island's eastern coast, discovering Cumberland Sound. He returned to Britain convinced that a North-West Passage was a reality – it was just a question of locating the right channel.

Davis returned north in May 1586, this time with four ships, two of which explored Greenland's east coast while Davis took the other pair to the west coast where the sailors took on the locals at long jump (victory for Britain, but only because of persistent foul play). Relations turned sour when the Inuit began to steal anything of iron they could find, including the

ship's anchor. Davis took a hostage against the return of the anchor, but when good weather arrived sailed with the Inuk still aboard; the man died before Britain was reached. Davis again explored the coast of Baffin Island, finding, as Frobisher had, that the 'muskyto... sting grievously' before heading home.

Davis sailed again in 1587 in the *Ellen*, a 20-ton ship that leaked so badly the crew almost lost heart. Despite this the *Ellen* reached 73°N, on the west Greenland coast, a new northing record, then crossed Baffin Bay, but was forced south by sea ice. Davis explored more of Baffin Island's east coast, then headed into Cumberland Sound again, reaching Pangnirtung where, in hot July sunshine, the crew went ashore and organised a foxhunt with the dogs they had taken with them as company. Further south Davis also reached the eastern end of Hudson Strait, but did not explore it.

Barents sails east

When Europeans next headed north for Cathay they were Dutch rather than British and sailed for the North-East Passage. Having recently thrown out the Spanish, the Dutch were keen to establish themselves on the world stage and, ignoring the English failures along the Russian coast (and that of Oliver Brunel, financed by a Belgian merchant, in 1584), sent two expeditions in May 1594. Willem Barents, born on the North Sea island of Terschelling, commanded the *Mercurius*, while Cornelius Nai commanded *De Swane* and, confusingly, another *Mercurius*. The plan was for Barents to attempt to round the northern tip of Novaya Zemlya (New Land), while Nai would attempt to penetrate the Kara Sea, either by sailing between Novaya Zemlya and Vaygach Island, or between the latter and the mainland. Barents pushed to about 77°N – a northing record – at the northern end of Novaya Zemlya, but from there all that could be seen was ice, with no glimpse or hope of open water. For several weeks he probed the ice but eventually had to admit defeat. When he rendezvoused with Nai he found him jubilant. Sailing through the Yugor Strait, Nai had negotiated the ice of the Kara Sea and found open water. Deciding that 'there is absolutely no further doubt that the passage to China is free and open' he turned around.

Back in Holland the delighted House of Orange and the Dutch merchants sent a fleet of seven ships out in 1595. Barents went again, but was not the leader of the expedition, merely master of the *Greyhound*. This time the strait to the Kara Sea, reached in late August, was blocked with ice. After several weeks of trying to break through, during which time two men were killed by a bear, the fleet sailed home. The Dutch, their fingers burned, decided not to organise another official expedition, but offered a substantial reward to anyone discovering the passage. A group of Amsterdam merchants took up the challenge, financing two ships which sailed in May 1596. The ships were commanded by Jacob van Heemskerk and Jan Cornelius Riip, much to Barents' aggravation. He was, however, offered a place on a ship and chose to go with Heemskerk. In what is now called the Barents Sea the Dutch chased a polar bear in a row boat, slaughtering it with muskets and axe.

Sailing north from Bear Island the Dutch passed icebergs (which, delightfully, a sailor new to the Arctic initially thought were huge swans) and a dead whale which 'stank monstrously' before reaching another island with an array of pointed mountains. These gave the island its name – Spitsbergen (though on their charts they called their discovery *Het Nieuwe Land* – The New Land). The Dutch had discovered – or, perhaps, rediscovered – Svalbard. Exploring the island's west coast they named Amsterdam Island and wondered at the plantlife, birds and warm days so far north. When the sun allowed a latitude calculation the Dutch had reached 79°49'N, the north-western tip of Spitsbergen.

Ice now blocked further progress and the Dutch returned to Bear Island where, after an argument with Barents, Riip decided to head home. Barents persuaded Van Heemskerk to head east and, dodging icebergs and floes, was able to go around the northern tip of Novaya Zemlya. But it was now early September and the sea ice soon blocked the entrance of the bay in which the Dutch had sheltered and named Ice Haven. The name was inappropriate, the ice soon tumbling in to crush the ship: the crew of 17 would be 'forced, in great poverty, misery and grief, to stay all that winter', while the noise of the ice 'made all the hair of our heads to rise upright with fear'. The Dutch built a hut of driftwood: when they put nails in their mouths before use they noticed that icicles formed on them before they could begin hammering them in.

Inside the hut were bunks and a bath, and a huge central fire over which they cooked food from the ship supplemented by the meat of local wildlife of which polar bears were particularly abundant. When the weather permitted they played a form of golf on a course between the hut and the ship about 3km (2 miles) away.

Above **The interior of the Barents' team hut on Novaya Zemlya. The engraving (by Levinus Hulsius in Gerrit de Veer's *The Three Voyages of Willem Barents*) makes the hut look quite inviting, a fact belied by the description of the dreadful winter the team actually spent.**
Richard Sale Collection

Below **Willem Barents. Barents' journey even inspired Shakespeare. In *Twelfth Night* Fabian, a servant of Olivia, tells Sir Toby Belch '...and you are now sailed into the north of my lady's opinion; where you will hang like an icicle on a Dutchman's beard...'**
Rijksmuseum, Amsterdam, Holland

The cold of the Arctic winter was so intense that all cracks in the hut were sealed, almost poisoning the men with fumes from the unventilated fire. To escape the cold the men huddled close to the fire, but often found that they smelled burning socks before their cold feet had registered they were too close to the flames. They also suffered from scurvy, despite the fresh meat. In all five of the 17 were to die from the disease, including Barents, whose death occurred during the homeward journey. The Dutch ship had been so battered by the ice it was unseaworthy, so two rowing boats were converted to sailing skiffs and used to sail south along the Novaya Zemlya coast as soon as the summer sun of 1597 had cleared the way of ice. Barents died on 20 June: five weeks later van Heemskerk and the other survivors met a group of Russian fishermen at the island's southern tip. Almost dead from scurvy, their gums so deteriorated that their teeth were falling out, and unable to eat solid food, the Dutch were nursed to health and taken to the mainland where they were met by Riip who had come to look for them.

Back in Holland the Dutch, still wearing caps of Arctic fox fur, each complete with a foxtail, were greeted as heroes. In Heemskerk's case it was a true reflection of the man: years later during a battle between the Dutch and Spanish, having lost a leg to a cannon shot, he held onto his sword and urged his men forward until he died of bloodloss. His monument in Amsterdam notes that he 'steered his way through ice and iron'. But Heemskerk returned from the ice empty-handed, while another expedition, which had gone around the Cape of Good Hope, was laden with cargo. The Dutch stared wide-eyed at these riches and forgot about the North-East Passage.

Whalers in the north

On 1 May 1607 Henry Hudson and his crew (of 11, one being John, Hudson's 14-year-old son) sailed the *Hopewell* out of Gravesend. The Muscovy Company was losing profits on its Russian trade to Dutch companies and had decided to try for Cathay again. Hudson's plan was simple: the north-east and north-west routes were ice-bound, but near the pole the sun was 'a manufacturer of salt rather than ice' and the sea should be clear, so Hudson was sailing due north, over the pole. Hudson reached the east coast of Greenland and headed north as far as Hold-with-Hope (73°N). From there he headed north-west, eventually reaching Barents' New Land and sailing north to a point where it became clear that the theory of salt rather than ice was wrong.

Heading south Hudson was pushed west where he saw a volcanic island which lay north of Iceland. He called it Hudson's Touches. Back in London he was able to tell his merchant-masters that while the route to Cathay had eluded him, the bays of Svalbard were home to vast numbers of huge whales.

The British merchants waited two years before following up Hudson's discovery, then sent Jonas Poole to check its accuracy. With Poole's confirmation the British decided to exploit the Svalbard whale stock. In this they were not alone. The Dutch remembered Barents' stinking whale carcass, and the Danes and French rapidly heard tales of whaling riches. The key to the successful plundering of the Svalbard stock were the Basques who had been hunting whales since at least the 12th century. Much of the terminology of whaling, for instance harpoon, was Basque, developed over the centuries of hunting the Right Whale in the Bay of Biscay. The British killed walrus on Bear Island (though not very expertly at first) but had to engage Basques – who were already whaling off the Labrador coast – to teach them how to kill Svalbard whales. The Basque technique was to establish a land station where the whale carcass was stripped and the blubber rendered to oil, and from which small boats took the catchers out to the whale. This was an especially good technique in Svalbard where millennia of trouble-free life had both increased the whale population and encouraged them to use sheltered bays close to shore. There was considerable ill-feeling between the British and Dutch over the whaling particularly after the Dutch took possession of Hudson's Touches, renaming it Jan Mayen after Jan Jacobsz May, a Dutch whaling captain. Jan Mayen (the name was retained by the Norwegians, who claimed sovereignty in 1929, as it had by then been in common usage for 300 years) was a particularly useful base as the whales migrated past it en route for Svalbard. On Svalbard the Dutch also had the best land station: Smeerenburg (Blubber Town) on Amsterdam Island. It is still common to see descriptions of Smeerenburg stating that it had a church, a bakery and a brothel, serving a population of several thousand, but the archaeological evidence does not support this delightful view of the Arctic Klondike town, suggesting a population of 200 at most housed in barrack-like rooms, and an absence of clergy and women.

The whale that the Dutch, British, French and Danes sought was the bowhead. As the trade increased the numbers of whales fell dramatically. It is estimated that the North Atlantic bowhead stock was

Above **Smeerenburg, a contemporary painting by Cornelius de Man.**
Rijksmuseum, Amsterdam, Holland

20,000–25,000 when whaling began, giving a sustainable annual yield of perhaps 500. The number actually taken exceeded this many times. By 1650 the Dutch had abandoned Jan Mayen: within another half-century Svalbard had been all but abandoned too, though ships continued to visit throughout the 18th century. By then whaling had also changed: the whales were not only less numerous, but more wary of the sheltered bays, and the Basque and American whalers were hunting different species in the open ocean. Land stations had always been cumbersome. They had to be set up each year, and hauling huge dead whales back to them was time- – and manpower- – consuming. The stations could be plundered when vacated, a fact which led to deliberate overwinterings. These were often disastrous: on Jan Mayen the seven men left in 1633 were found dead of scurvy in June 1634, and a similar fate befell a Smeerenburg party in 1634/5. Ironically, all eight Britons survived an accidental wintering in 1630/1.

The North-West Passage

Though the Muscovy Company checked Henry Hudson's account of the Svalbard whales they were obviously impressed enough with his journey to back him again, this time to try for the North-East Passage, again in the *Hopewell*. The journey was unsuccessful, the ship being stopped by the ice of the Kara Sea, but was significant for two reasons. Firstly the crew spotted a mermaid: 'From the navel upwards her back and breasts were like a woman's... Her body was as big as one of us, her skin very white... long hair hanging down behind, of colour black. In her going down they saw her tail which was like the tail of a porpoise and speckled like a mackerel'. An illusion created by a harp seal and months at sea in all-male company? Secondly, Hudson made a curious entry in his log to the effect that the return of the *Hopewell* was 'my free and willing return, without persuasion or force of any one of (my company)'. Many have speculated that this entry implies problems between Hudson and Robert Juet, his first mate. Hudson was an old man, already a grandfather. He was moody and capricious, his indecisiveness a burden to his crew. Juet was also elderly, an irritable trouble-maker whom many captains would have rejected, but who Hudson took on each of his journeys. They appear to have behaved like an old, grumpy married couple.

The Muscovy Company was less pleased with Hudson than they had been previously and declined to back a third voyage. So Hudson approached the merchants of Amsterdam who financed, in 1609, another trip to the Kara Sea, this time in *De Halve Maan* (The Half Moon). At the ice edge there was a mutiny (perhaps instigated by Robert Juet) as a result of which Hudson turned around and sailed across the Atlantic, discovering the Hudson River, Coney Island and Manhattan (the future site of New Amsterdam, later New York). The crew shot half-a-dozen native Americans for fun and fed alcohol to many more for the amusement of getting them drunk, behaviour which reflects badly on both Juet, who seems to have been the ringleader, and Hudson who not only allowed, but assisted, the folly.

Back in Britain Hudson's discoveries lit up the faces of the London merchants (while the activities of his crew barely raised an eyebrow) and in April 1610, with a crew of 22, he sailed the *Discovery* back to America. One of the crew was Henry Greene who seems to have usurped Robert Juet's place as Hudson's favourite. Juet's response was to become drunk and angry. Hudson calmed him, but the mood of the whole crew was then depressed by the journey through the violent waters of the Hudson Strait. Hugging the northern Quebec shore Hudson sailed between it and Digges Island to reach the vast, calm waters of what he was convinced was the Pacific Ocean. Turning south Hudson watched the Quebec shore waiting for the cities of Japan that would soon come into view; instead the bleak Arctic tundra held his eye all the way to the entrance to James Bay. There, at about 51°N, in Rupert Bay, the *Discovery* was frozen in as a distinctly un-Cathay-like winter took hold. In the dismay of not finding Java (where Hudson had told his crew they would spend Candlemas), Hudson replaced Juet, now openly sneering at his captain's hopes, with Robert Bylot. Juet nursed his grievance during a hard winter which saw several men succumb to scurvy, one dying of it. As the winter toyed with the men's minds Hudson picked a fight with Greene, his one-time favourite, then demoted Bylot. The pair joined Juet and others in plotting the takeover of the ship, reasoning that with so little food and so many sick with scurvy no one would escape alive without positive action. In June

1611 after the ship had been freed from the ice, Hudson was seized, and together with his son, four sick men and three others, was placed in an open boat. The ship's carpenter, whom the mutineers needed, chose to go with Hudson. The nine in the boat had only the clothing they wore, no water or food, no means of making fire and one gun. They stood little chance of surviving – and were never heard of again. The 13 mutineers sailed to Digges Island which they knew was rich in wildfowl. There, in a fight with the local Inuit, four men, including Henry Greene, were killed. Later Robert Juet died of scurvy leaving Robert Bylot, eventually the only man still capable of standing, to steer the boat into Berehaven in Ireland's Bantry Bay.

Back in London the eight survivors might have expected to be tried and hanged, their 'excuse' for mutiny hardly holding water, as in addition to the sick

Below **The documented verdict passed on the Hudson mutineers.**
UK Public Records Office

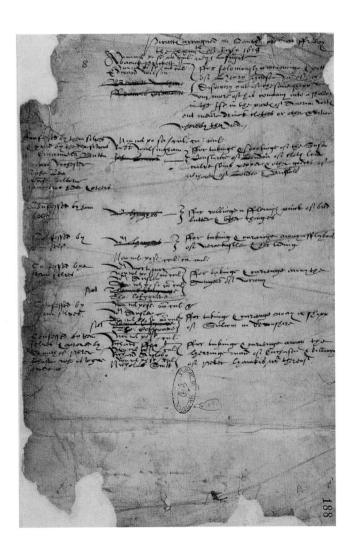

men they had also cast adrift healthy ones and the captain for no better reason than that they did not like them. But Bylot's claim to have found the North-West Passage allowed economics to triumph over the law of the land (and justice). Bylot, Prickett (a servant of Sir Dudley Digger, co-sponsor of the expedition – whose account of the mutiny is the fullest and, hardly surprisingly, exonerates him completely), and Edward Wilson, ship's surgeon, were soon heading back to Hudson Bay. When, eventually, four of the mutineers were tried for mutiny they were found not guilty.

The expedition of 1612 was commanded by Sir Thomas Button. Not only did it include some of the Hudson mutineers, it also used Hudson's ship *Discovery*. Bylot navigated it to Hudson Bay which Button then crossed, wintering at the mouth of the Nelson River (named for Francis Nelson, who died there, as did several others, of scurvy: five men were also killed by Inuit). He then headed north to reach Southampton Island and the Roes Welcome Sound (though the sound was not actually given that name until Foxe's expedition of 1631). Button thought the sound was the channel that would finally lead to the Pacific, but returned to England having done little more than nose the *Discovery* into it. In 1615 Bylot sailed again, now as master of the *Discovery*, with William Baffin as pilot. This time the northern coast of Southampton Island was reached, but Bylot and Baffin concluded that the Roes Welcome Sound was not the way to Cathay. On this journey Baffin calculated the longitude of the *Discovery* by taking a complete lunar observation on 21 June, a feat which earned him the admiration of all that followed him and that has led many of today's experts to consider him the greatest of the early Arctic explorers. It was in recognition of this that Sir William Parry named Baffin Island (close to which the observation was made) in his honour.

Baffin, lowly born and self-taught, had been on an expedition to West Greenland and two whaling trips to Svalbard before accompanying Bylot. He was clearly a better seaman and when the *Discovery* sailed again in 1616, though Bylot was still nominally master, Baffin was the real commander. Convinced that Hudson Bay was not the way to go, Baffin headed north through Davis Strait, discovering Baffin Bay, then Lancaster Sound, Jones Sound and Smith Sound, each named for an expedition backer. It was a masterful journey, one of the greatest of all in terms of discoveries, but ironically Baffin's maps were not published, and the details were soon forgotten. The man charged with publishing Baffin's data decided that the maps, and some tables, were too expensive to produce and so left them out. With the first phase of exploration of the Canadian Arctic coming to an end, it was 200 years before Baffin Bay was entered again. By then it was thought to be a new discovery.

The Danes and the race to Cathay

In the 17th century Denmark controlled what is now Norway, giving the Danes not only an Arctic seaboard, but also a perceived right to the legacy of the Vikings. It also gave them a duty to see if there were still survivors of the Viking settlements of Greenland, to which end Christian IV organised three expeditions (under the Scot John Cunningham and Englishmen John Knight and James Hall, all of whom were officers in the Danish navy) in the early years of the century. They found no Vikings, but did kidnap some Inuit. Next a Dane, Jans Munk, was dispatched to look for a North-East Passage in 1610. The voyage failed in the Kara Sea ice as had so many others before it. In May 1619 Munk set out again with two ships, the *Enhiorningen* (Unicorn) and *Lamprenen* (Lamprey). Munk reached and crossed Hudson Bay, wintering at the mouth of the Churchill River, now famous for its annual congregation of polar bears and bear-watchers. Sixty-five men overwintered, the illustration in Munk's book on the expedition – the first for a general readership, and one of the more charming examples – suggesting that conditions were not too bad. In reality they were grim: by early June all but three men were dead from scurvy and Munk, one of those remaining, wrote in his journal, 'Herewith, goodnight to all the world and my soul into the hand of God'. In fact he survived, and with his two companions sailed the *Lamprey* back to Denmark where Christian IV ordered him to go back and retrieve the *Unicorn*. Not surprisingly Munk failed to raise a crew and the second trip was abandoned.

The next attempt on the North-West Passage was in 1631 when two almost identical ships left London and Bristol, the most celebrated ports of 17th-century England. Each ship was 70 tons, square-rigged and manned by a crew of 22. They were named for Charles, the king of England, and his queen, Henrietta Maria. The master of the *Charles* was Luke Foxe, a self-taught Yorkshireman, a career seaman with an arrogant (but largely justified) opinion of his worth who called himself 'North-West' Foxe and had been trying for years to gain sponsorship for a voyage to discover the passage. Finally he had persuaded London merchants to fund

Above **Jens Munk's winter camp in Hudson Bay.**
From *Navigatio Septentrionalis*.
The Royal Library, Copenhagen, Denmark

the trip. Sir Thomas Roe, an ambassador of the king, agreed to act as patron and a renamed ex-Royal Navy ship was made available. Foxe boasted that his was the best ship in the world, though in reality it was a pensioned-off tub, barely seaworthy.

When the merchants of Bristol heard about Foxe's voyage they hastily gathered the money to mount a rival search. Whichever port controlled the trade with Cathay, with its priceless merchandise of silk and spices, would be the richest in England, and Bristol was not about to be second in that particular race. To captain their ship the Bristolians chose Thomas James, a Welsh-born barrister, a gentleman, but one of limited

experience of the sea and sailing, though he had once taken charge of a small fleet which sailed to clear the English Channel of pirates.

To avoid a charge of favouritism King Charles gave each man an identical letter. The winner of the race for the passage was to deliver it to the Emperor of Japan. The letters were in English as it was reasoned that the emperor, being both a king and a cultured man, would obviously speak the language. On the afternoon of 3 May 1631 James took the *Henrietta Maria* out of Bristol's harbour, to be followed two days later by Foxe and the *Charles*. Foxe caught and passed his rival at Resolution Island at the entrance to the Hudson Strait.

In Hudson Bay the two ships met by chance in late August, the two captains and their officers sharing a meal on the *Henrietta Maria*. It was not a happy occasion, Foxe writing that the time spent with James was 'the worst spent of any time of my discovery'. James, he noted, was a gentleman who 'could discourse of Art, but he was no seaman', recalling Macaulay's famous suggestion that the navy of King Charles comprised gentlemen and seamen, but the gentlemen were not seamen and the seamen were not gentlemen. James was no more impressed with Foxe, but he did try to persuade him that they should winter together. Foxe declined and sailed north, exploring the eastern coast of the bay as far as Southampton Island, and then exploring the vast bay, which now bears his name, between the island and Baffin Island. But before winter could take hold of his ship he turned west and sailed home to be greeted not by the congratulations of his sponsors as he had imagined, but their communal spleen-venting. James was overwintering and might discover the passage in the spring: where was the glory in returning empty-handed?

For his part James headed south, discovering James Bay and building huts on Charlton Island – which he named for the king – for overwintering. On nearby Danby Island he found a row of stakes driven into the shore, the only evidence ever discovered of the fate of Henry Hudson after the mutiny on the *Discovery* in 1610. James' crew spent an appalling winter. It was so cold frost formed on their beds, adding to the miseries of scurvy. When, finally, spring arrived so did the mosquitoes which plagued the men further. James, anxious to contact (hopefully friendly) Indians on the shore, climbed a tree to watch for a signal as his men set fire to brushwood. The fire spread rampantly through the tinder-dry island woodland, James being lucky to escape from his look-out and his long-suffering men escaping death only by fleeing to the ship. After months during which they had all but frozen to death, the closeness of death by burning must have seemed an ironic twist of fate. The survivors then sailed home without further incident.

Both Foxe and James wrote books. Foxe's is less polished but probably more honest. It begins with a plea (and a side-swipe at James' effort) 'Gentle Reader, expect not heere any flourishing Phrases or Eloquent termes, for this Child of mine begot in the North-West cold Clime, (where they breed no Schollers,) is not able to digest the sweet milke of Rethorick, that's food for them...', and goes on to note that Foxe had done his best 'with such Tackling, Cordage and Raftage as I had, to Rigge and Tackle this ship myself' which, if stretching the nautical simile to breaking point at least leaves the reader in no doubt about his view of himself as a master mariner. It must have been a great disappointment that James' *The Strange and Dangerous Voyage of*

Above **Captain Thomas James. whose account of his Arctic journey may have inspired the *Rime of the Ancient Mariner*.** Richard Sale Collection

Captain Thomas James became a classic: it is said to have inspired Coleridge to write the *Rime of the Ancient Mariner*.

The Hudson's Bay Company

In Britain the failure of Foxe and James ended thoughts of a North-West Passage, while the upheaval of the Civil War and the execution of Charles I banished thoughts of the New World for two decades. But with the Restoration the country turned its eyes outwards again.

French fishermen from St Malo had followed the Basques and Bristolians to the great cod-fishing grounds off Newfoundland, so it is no surprise that a Malouin also followed in the wake of Cabot's ship. Jacques Cartier made three journeys (1534, 1525 and 1541), discovering the St Lawrence River and naming

the country Canada. It is said that he got the name from a Huron Indian, asking him what the place was called and not realising the Huron had given him the name of his village. It is a plausible tale. Samuel de Champlain, who followed Cartier, named Quebec from the Huron *kebek*, 'a narrowing of the waters'. French enthusiasm for their new colony was based on cod-fishing and the trapping of beaver on the rivers that threaded the forests of Quebec. Beaver fur was waterproof, easily shaped and very durable, ideal material for hats, the Canadian animals being a lucky replacement for the European species which had been hunted almost to extinction to satisfy the trade. For half a century the French controlled the beaver trade, then in 1666 the restored English king, Charles II, was visited by two French trappers who enquired whether the king was interested in making himself (and them, of course)

Above **A north-west view of Prince of Wales Fort, Hudson Bay. The engraving is by J. Saunders from a drawing by Samuel Hearne. The Hudson's Bay Company set up many such forts across northern Canada. They offered protection from rival fur-trading companies and infuriated native Americans. The protection was needed: the company's initials, HBC, were later said to mean 'Here Before Canada', which is certainly how its early managers behaved. The company motto *Pro Pelle Curem* is difficult to translate accurately. It was claimed to mean 'a skin for its equivalent', suggesting the trading nature of the company. Later those on the management side suggested it meant 'we skin you before you try to skin us', while those on the trapping side preferred 'we risk our skins for your pelts'. More tragically, when alcohol had become a major trade item, the motto was translated as 'a skin for a skinful'.**
Hudson's Bay Company Archives, Provincial Archives of Manitoba, Canada

rich. Indeed he was, and an expedition was sent to Hudson Bay to see if the Frenchmen's tales were accurate. When the ship, the *Nonsuch*, returned loaded with furs the king granted his nephew Prince Rupert, son of the exiled king of Bohemia, jurisdiction over the fur-trapping lands. A group of merchants was assembled, the combination of prince and merchants being termed the Governor and Company of Adventurers of England Trading into Hudson's Bay, a title soon shortened to the Hudson's Bay Company. The company was granted 'sole trade... of all those Seas Streightes Bayes Rivers Lakes Creekes and Soundes... that lye within the entrance of... Hudson's Streightes...'

In his monarchical way King Charles dismissed both the claims of the native peoples and the French to the land he had given away. The French were eventually ousted by force while the Huron, Cree and other native tribes were just ignored. The Hudson's Bay Company established a series of forts around the southern shores of Hudson Bay, employees rarely venturing out of them to explore the local area. The lack of initiative in aiding the search for a North-West Passage was criticised in

Much more significant than the Hudson's Bay Company's explorations of western Hudson Bay was James Cook's voyage in the *Discovery* and *Resolution* (1776–80) to the northern Pacific to investigate the western end of the North-West Passage. Cook arrived late and was unable to travel very far north because of the ice of the Beaufort Sea, though he did satisfy himself that Asia and America were not joined north of the Bering Strait, following the Alaskan shore as far as Icy Cape. He found a safe anchorage on the Alaskan shore at the end of an inlet he explored – now the town of Anchorage on Cook Inlet – and sailed up an eastward heading arm that he discovered was just another blind alley. His almost tangible weariness is reflected in the name he gave it – Turnagain Arm. Cook then turned south, landing in Hawaii in December 1778. Two months later he was murdered in a confrontation with the locals over a stolen boat. It was a sad end for one of the greatest explorers of any age.

UK National Maritime Museum

Above **The sea ice of the Beaufort Sea. Driven chiefly by wind, the ice in the Beaufort circulates clockwise, the motion – the Beaufort Gyre – being the main ice movement of the Canadian Arctic.**
Richard Sale

Britain, but with profits from fur-trading being so high the criticism at first fell on deaf ears. Eventually in 1719 the company provisioned an expedition of two ships commanded by John Knight to explore the inlets of western Hudson Bay. The expedition of 40 men disappeared. Later explorers found their wintering quarters on Marble Island, near Rankin Inlet, and there were Inuit stories that men had survived until at least 1721 before succumbing to hunger and disease. In 1741 the company, responding reluctantly to suggestions that it was deliberately avoiding finding, perhaps even covering up the existence of, the passage – the first accusation was undoubtedly true, though the second was not – allowed one of its captains, Christopher Middleton, to lead another expedition. Middleton discovered Wager Bay but was accused of having actually discovered a channel not an inlet, an accusation which ruined him and resulted in a second expedition, in 1746, under William Moore, which confirmed Middleton's findings and also discovered Chesterfield Inlet.

But although they had been involved in these seaborne expeditions, not until 1769 did a company man set out to explore the wilderness that lay west of Hudson Bay. The man was Samuel Hearne, and though

the company's main aim was to see if there was any truth in the Indian rumour that a river flowed between banks of solid copper, the London-born Hearne was also travelling for its own sake. He was a keen naturalist, a good artist, and loved to camp out in the wilds beyond the walls of Fort Prince of Wales, set at the mouth of the Churchill River where he was employed. Hearne's first two attempts to find and follow the legendary river failed due to incompetent guides and poor equipment, but when he set out for a third time in December 1770 he was guided by a group of Chippewyan Indians led by a brilliantly resourceful man named Matonabbee.

Despite occasional severe hardship – the explorers lived off the land and on one occasion when hunting failed to provide food for the seventh day in succession an old pair of boots were boiled and chewed – the group eventually reached and followed the river to its

Above **Samuel Hearne carved his name into a rock at Sloop Cove near Churchill.**
Richard Sale

Left **Samuel Hearne. An engraving from 1796 by an unknown artist.**
Hudson's Bay Company Archives, Provincial Archives of Manitoba, Canada

mouth. There to Hearne's horror the Chippewyans massacred a group of Inuit. One badly wounded Inuit girl clung to Hearne's knees begging for help, but when he pleaded for her life the Chippewyans ignored him and speared her to death as she lay at his feet.

Hearne found one piece of copper ore and visited an Indian mine from which limited metal was extracted. At the mouth of the river, the imaginatively named Coppermine, Hearne erected a cairn and claimed all the local land for the Hudson's Bay Company. He was the first European to have seen the ocean between Hudson Bay and the Siberian coast, though there are still some who doubt if he actually reached the coast, believing much of his account was concocted from Indian tales. Hearne's woefully wrong positioning, in latitude and longitude, of the river mouth, does not help his cause.

Back at Fort Prince of Wales Hearne, now its commander, was eventually forced to surrender it to a French gunboat: Hearne was captured and the fort destroyed. Matonabbee, believing Hearne and the other Englishmen killed, hanged himself as his own position among the Chippewyan had depended on the company's existence. In fact Hearne survived captivity, was released and regained the governorship. Eventually he went back to England where he died, aged 47, virtually penniless. He died awaiting the cheque for £200 from a publisher for his classic book *A Voyage from Prince of*

Wales' Fort... to the Northern Ocean...: for comparison, 20 or so years later Jane Austen was being offered £10 for her first novels.

Three years before Hearne's death another man set out westward. Alexander Mackenzie was born on the Hebridean island of Lewis, his burning ambition to succeed likely emanating from the poverty of his childhood. Orphaned by the age of 16, Mackenzie joined the North-West Fur Trading Company (a rival to the Hudson's Bay Company, though later the two merged) and rapidly rose through its ranks. In the North-West Mackenzie met Peter Pond, a tough Connecticut-born American who had explored west of Hudson Bay and discovered Lake Athabasca. Pond told Mackenzie of native stories of a river which flowed west from the Great Slave Lake (discovered by Samuel Hearne) to the sea. Hoping that the river might be navigable and the sea the Pacific Ocean, Mackenzie left Fort Chippewyan on the southern shore of Lake Athabasca on 3 June 1789. With him were four French-Canadian *voyageurs* (expert paddlers), an Indian guide called English Chief (named because he was a chief and spoke English!), a German and an assorted bunch of women and Indians. The group travelled in three canoes which were paddled and portaged north to the Great Slave Lake. Here ice made progress difficult and mosquitoes made life virtually intolerable, but the team pressed on, reaching, and then descending, the legendary river. Travelling at a remarkable rate (an average daily progress of 40km/25 miles) the party headed west, then north-west.

Mackenzie's account of the journey is a curious mix of styles. He is sometimes eloquent about the sheer beauty of the landscape through which they passed. He is also interesting when talking about the native peoples they met (though often disapproving of their habits and lifestyle). But on his companions he is almost silent. Mackenzie was clearly driven by his ambition to reach the Pacific, his men merely the means of achieving that end – hardly worth mentioning except to occasionally complain about them. As the expedition moved further north the Indian fear of Inuit (a strange, and mutual, loathing with no apparent historical cause: the two peoples, and the various tribes within them, regarded each other as enemies just because they existed, almost as though there was a natural order) meant that local guides were difficult to obtain. Mackenzie got around this by kidnapping – nothing was allowed to prejudice his great exercise.

Eventually Mackenzie reached the river's huge delta, a complex of narrow channels, swamp, taiga

Above **Sir Alexander Mackenzie by Sir Thomas Lawrence.**
National Gallery of Canada, Ottawa

Left **Three days after sighting the Pacific Ocean, in a mixture of vermilion face-paint and bear grease, Alexander Mackenzie wrote an inscription on a rock beside the Dean Channel. The North-West Company had yet to merge with the Hudson's Bay Company and as a good North-West Company man Mackenzie wrote that he had arrived from Canada, not Hudson's Bay.**
Archives of British Columbia, Canada

islands and pingos. He resolutely tried to force a way through this chaos and on 12 July he camped on what most experts now believe to be Garry Island (at 69°29'N, 135°35'W). That night the team had to move because the water lapping the shore rose into their camp. Mackenzie thought this was due to the wind, but two days later realised it was a tide: he had reached the sea. Mackenzie hurriedly climbed to the high point of the island and looked north. All he could see was ice – this was not the Pacific Ocean.

Mackenzie called the river he had explored Disappointment. He returned along it, regaining Fort Chippewyan on 12 September. Today the river is called the Mackenzie. It is North America's second longest (after the Mississippi/Missouri complex, though it is longer than either, draining 20 per cent of Canada). Though his employers were unimpressed – he had returned with neither furs nor a route to the Pacific – Mackenzie's journey is now seen as one of the greatest in Canadian history. It was not his last. Sharing his employer's frustration he headed west again in 1793, following the Peace and Parsnip Rivers, then the Bella Coola to the sea. On 19 July Mackenzie notes, 'I could perceive the termination of the river and its discharge into a narrow arm of the sea'. He had reached the Pacific Ocean. He was the first European to gaze at the ocean from the American shore; the first to have crossed the continent.

The Royal Navy tries for the North-West Passage

The Napoleonic Wars removed all thoughts of exploration from European minds in the late 18th/early 19th centuries, but their legacy provided the new impetus for British searches for a North-West Passage. Britain was now the major world power, its pre-eminence based on naval might. But such status brings fears as well as benefits and these were, in part, exploited to persuade the British Admiralty to use naval ships to search for an Arctic seaway. Russia, a likely competitor on the world stage, lay at the other end of such a passage and seemed intent on expanding into America. The Russians had taken the Aleutian Islands and Alaska; Otto von Kotzebue had discovered Kotzebue Sound; and one reason for Bellingshausen's Antarctic journey had been to look for naval bases, a point hardly likely to have been lost on the British. But it is too simplistic to say that the maintenance of their superpower status was the only reason for the search. John Barrow, Second Secretary to the Admiralty (and the senior civil servant, as opposed to politician or

Above **William Scoresby was not only a man of courage and intellect, but also possessed a withering stare, capable of turning the strongest man to jelly. It is claimed that he once stared at a ship's ferocious guard dog and that the dog, in panic, jumped overboard and drowned.**
Richard Sale Collection

naval officer, there) is usually, and rightly, identified as the major influence on the decision to use naval ships. Though he undoubtedly understood the need to maintain an active navy and a complement of experienced officers, Barrow was also a geographer and historian with a number of published articles. He was interested in exploration for its own sake, and the naval expeditions of which he was the architect went not only to the Arctic but to Africa and Antarctica.

Barrow's enthusiasm for exploration coincided with a sudden break-up of the Arctic ice, icebergs spilling down into the Atlantic – and cooling Europe – as the Arctic Ocean unfroze. This change (due to one of the earth's periodic temperature shifts) was noted by William Scoresby, a Whitby-based whaler. Whitby, on the Yorkshire coast of England, had a fleet of Arctic whalers which made a good living during the late 18th/early 19th centuries and Scoresby was one of the most successful whaling captains. But he was much

Above **The first communication with the Inuit of Prince Regent Bay, as drawn by John Sacheuse. The wholly incongruous scene was to be mirrored over and again as the British failed to learn the lessons of Inuit survival in the Arctic and, later, the Antarctic.**
From John Ross *A Voyage of Discovery... in HM Ships* Isabella *and* Alexander.
Richard Sale Collection

more than a sea captain: he was also a scientist and surveyor and, later, a social worker and clergyman. His observational science in the Arctic has led many to call him the Father of Arctic Science, and his book *An Account of the Arctic Regions* has been called 'one of the most remarkable books in the English language'.

Noting the melt of Arctic waters Scoresby sailed beyond 82°N (probably a record northing at the time) and wrote to Sir Joseph Banks, President of the Royal Society, suggesting that the lack of ice made it an ideal time for a renewal of the quest for a northern sea route to the Orient. Scoresby was hoping that he might lead a British expedition, but when Barrow heard of his suggestion he chose naval men. Barrow organised two expeditions in 1818: John Ross and William Edward Parry were to search for the North-West Passage, David Buchan and John Franklin were to sail over the North Pole. The two expeditions were then to meet off the Siberian coast. That it was still thought possible that a

route over the pole might exist despite the evidence to the contrary seems ridiculous now, but at the time there were many scientists, some of them eminent, who believed in a temperate polar ocean (the perpetual sunlight of summer melting the ice) whose currents forced a ring of ice southwards: if the ring was breaking up, the ocean might be reached.

Buchan in the *Dorothea*, and Franklin in the *Trent*, fared badly. A violent storm forced them to shelter in Spitsbergen's Magdalenafjord, then pack ice, probably pushed south by the storm, imprisoned and threatened to crush their ships. Once extricated (by another storm which broke up the ice), Buchan abandoned the expedition and sailed home. Ross and Parry, in the *Isabella* and *Alexander*, had a more interesting time. They were heading north to seek the passage, as the land expedition of Hearne (see below) had shown that the sea at the mouth of the Coppermine River was still frozen in July. Northwards, of course, if the science was correct, the sea would be open. The crew included James Clark Ross, John's nephew, Edward Sabine, a Royal Artillery officer, and a south Greenlander John Sacheuse (who had reached Britain as a stowaway on a whaler) who would interpret during the first encounter between the Inuit of north-west Greenland and Europeans since the Vikings.

That meeting, in Prince Regent Bay, was remarkable for two reasons. The Inuit had been isolated from

their fellow Greenlanders to the south for generations by a minor ice age. They had come to believe they were the only people on earth, and what Ross seems to have thought were friendly greetings, Sacheuse was able to interpret as shouts of 'Go away'. But more importantly the meeting resulted in an image which, behind its amusing depiction of the event, was to be a mirror of later British polar expeditions. On the right are fur-clad Inuit, on the left British naval officers in dress uniform – tailed coats, buckled shoes, cocked hats – a bizarre scene.

Apart from making contact with the Inuit, Ross discovered red snow, a phenomenon caused by growth of the unicellular plant *protococcus nivalis*. He also rediscovered Baffin Bay (which at the time was believed mythical) and the entrance to Smith, Jones and Lancaster Sounds. He ignored the first two, but sailed a short distance into Lancaster Sound. Then he stopped, sighting a mountain range which, he said, clearly showed the sound was a bay. Parry could not see these mountains (as he was several miles behind Ross this is not surprising) and urged him to continue, but Ross declined and returned to Britain where he was damned for his timidity both privately and publicly. That red snow was the only discovery of the expedition, and the fact that the men pulling their noses violently (supposedly an Inuit greeting) provided fodder for newspaper cartoons, did not endear Ross to Barrow. When Ross offered his services for future expeditions, he was declined, though his naval superiors obviously did not entirely share the view of the civil service as they promoted him.

The man who ate his boots

When Barrow tried again in 1819 it was Parry who commanded, in the *Hecla*, accompanied by Matthew Liddon in the *Griper*. Parry had been unmerciful in his condemnation of Ross' decision to turn back in Lancaster Sound. Parry was 29; most of his crew, which included Sabine, were younger. This youthful, energetic team were intent on pushing forward: it is said that the crew cheered when Parry decided to enter the sound despite heavy pack ice and numerous icebergs. Parry pushed west through what is now called the Parry Channel (comprising Barrow Strait and Melville Sound), discovering and naming Devon, Somerset, Cornwallis, Bathurst and Prince of Wales Islands. As they sailed Sabine noted that the compass needle pointed south – the expedition was north of the North Magnetic Pole.

Parry headed south into Prince Regent Inlet, but was stopped by ice, then continued west to Melville Island. From there he could see (and name) Victoria and Banks Islands, but further progress into what is now called McClure Sound (but was then Banks Strait)

Above **Cutting into Winter Harbour. The engraver has given the impression of the cut channel being a sinuous British stream, but it is more likely that the exhausted sailors took a direct route.**
From William Edward Parry *Journal of a Voyage for the Discovery of a North-West Passage.*
Richard Sale Collection

Below **Surgical tools from Parry's first expedition found at Winter Harbour.**
Vancouver Maritime Museum, Canada

Below **Parry's ships** *Hecla* **and** *Griper* **in Winter Harbour, Melville Island, 1819–20. The starry night, camp fire and snug-looking ships – and Parry's description of the winter – are almost certainly at odds with the hardships the men faced.**
From William Edward Parry *Journal of a Voyage for the Discovery of a North-West Passage.*
Richard Sale Collection

was impassable because of ice. Parry had reached 110°W and was therefore able to claim a prize of £5,000 offered to anyone who could reach that longitude north of the Arctic Circle: he shared the reward among his crew. He may have guessed that beyond the McClure Sound was open sea: if he was correct, he was within 160km (100 miles) of open water and had found the northern North-West Passage (not that traversed by Amundsen) though it would be many years before that would be proved. On Melville Island Parry sought shelter in Winter Harbour. There he overwintered, his ships de-rigged and covered with wagon cloth to form an exercise yard. Bread was baked, beer brewed and a reasonable, scurvy-free winter was passed. In June 1820 Parry explored Melville Island while waiting for the ice

to free his ships, adding musk ox, caribou, hare and birds to the menu. In August the ships were finally freed and the expedition returned to Britain where Parry became the most famous man in the country (until Franklin arrived). His expedition had been an undoubted success. John Barrow thought that success in finding the passage was now just one journey away, a view which Parry endorsed publicly, though privately he was much less certain.

Parry's seaborne journey had been supported by a land expedition led by John Franklin which was intended to survey the north American coast east and west of the river mouths reached by Hearne and Mackenzie. Franklin had no experience which fitted him to command such an expedition, but then neither did any of the other candidates available to Barrow. With Franklin were John Richardson, surgeon and naturalist, George Back, Robert Hood and John Hepburn. Accompanied by four Orkney islanders collected on the way to Canada, Franklin headed west in late August. The expedition landed at the Hudson's Bay Company's York Factory on the south-western shore of the bay, then moved inland to Cumberland House, a company post, where the Orcadians turned back. Richardson and Hood overwintered at the house, but Franklin, Back and Hepburn continued to Fort Chippewyan on Lake Athabasca. The cold was intense, temperatures so low that their tea, left to brew in best English tradition, froze before they could drink it.

At Fort Chippewyan Franklin found he had walked into a bloody feud between the rival Hudson's Bay and North-West fur-trading companies. He could avoid the conflict, but it prevented him from buying the supplies he had banked on. So when his team, escorted by guides, voyageurs and assorted camp-followers headed north in 1820 it was poorly provisioned and too big to service easily by hunting. Starting in July and going by way of Fort Providence on the Great Slave Lake, Franklin was forced to overwinter in the Fort Enterprise which he built close to the source of the Coppermine River. From this log-built camp Franklin's team were forced to shuttle supplies from Providence and Chippewyan through the winter.

In June 1821 Franklin finally started down the Coppermine, but problems continued: at Bloody Falls (named for the massacre of the Inuit on Hearne's journey: skulls and bone were still visible when Franklin arrived) the Indian guides/hunters deserted, fearful of reprisals. Then the voyageurs expressed fears about using their fragile, birch-bark canoes on the sea. But

Below **One winter journey from Fort Providence, all the way to Fort Chippewyan, on Franklin's land expedition, was led by George Back, sent by Franklin to avoid a possibly murderous conflict that had arisen between Back and Hood over a beautiful Indian girl named Greenstockings by the British after a particularly striking part of her costume. The two men had actually fought a duel over the girl, another officer having the foresight to remove the powder from their pistols to avoid bloodshed. After the incident Franklin was left with no choice but to separate the men. Hood, a gifted artist, painted this portrait of Greenstockings and her father, from which it appears that they might have been the models for Garry Trudeau's *Doonesbury* characters. Greenstockings bore Hood's child, so it would seem that he was the winner in the midshipman escort competition.**
National Archives of Canada

Above **The expedition encamped at Point Turnagain, 21 August 1821.**
From John Franklin *Narrative of a Journey to the Shores of the Polar Sea.*
Richard Sale Collection

Franklin persevered, becoming the first European to reach the river's mouth since Hearne. From the mouth, with a depleted party, he set out east along the coast. The plan had been to reach Repulse Bay, but by late August, with both supplies and men almost exhausted, Franklin was forced to admit defeat. He named his furthest east Point Turnagain; then, after wasting time wondering whether to overwinter, headed back towards the river. The weather was atrocious, the sea threatening to destroy the canoes; in desperation the team landed and started to trek across the tundra. The country was devoid of life and almost barren of vegetation and as their food ran out, despite abandoning their canoes to save weight, progress slowed to a crawl. Surviving on *tripe de roche*, a lichen scraped from rocks, and the leather of their boots and jackets, the party finally reached the Coppermine River. There Richardson almost died trying to swim across with a line, and precious days were lost in building a canoe to replace those they had abandoned.

Once over the river Back and the three strongest voyageurs headed off for Fort Enterprise: one man died before it was reached. The Indians who had fled from Bloody Falls were supposed to have stocked the fort with food hunted and gathered locally, and to have waited for Franklin, but they had done neither. Finding Enterprise empty Back started out after the Indians. In the main party Franklin was forced to abandon Hood who was too weak to move: Richardson and Hepburn stayed with him while Franklin continued slowly behind Back. Two men died and four tried to return to the river camp. Only one arrived, a half-Iroquois, half-European called Michel Teroahauté. He brought meat he claimed to have been cut from the body of a wolf, but his curiously healthy appearance and odd behaviour convinced Richardson the meat was human flesh. His fears that Teroahauté had killed the other three men were, he felt, confirmed when Hood died of a single gunshot wound. Teroahauté, the only one present at the time, declared it had been suicide – but the wound was in the back of Hood's head. When the three men set off for Fort Enterprise, Richardson and Hepburn feared for their own lives when Teroahauté claimed to have stopped to gather *tripe de roche* but returned without any. To Richardson it was clear that he 'had halted for the purpose of putting his gun in order with the intention of attacking us'. To forestall this Richardson shot the heavily armed Teroahauté.

At the fort Franklin and his team were in the last stages of starvation. More men died, and the rest were only days from death when the Indians found by George Back arrived with food. The hint of cannibalism, the murders and the general horror of the trip made Franklin a hero in Britain, where he was known as the 'man who ate his boots'. His book on the trip sold out and second-hand copies were said to have changed hands for much more than the cover price. It is no surprise: the book is a fine one, the copy at the British Library being inscribed, in an unknown hand, 'this is one of the most affecting narratives ever written.'

Franklin and Parry again

Despite his misgivings Parry agreed to lead another expedition in 1821, the *Fury* replacing the worn-out *Griper*. This time Parry went to Hudson Bay, a decision which seems curious in the light of the string of early failures there, but reasonable when considered against his opinion that the ice at the western end of the Parry Channel would prove a consistent bar to progress. Parry hoped that the ice would be less severe in the south and intended to find a westerly route out of the bay to the north of Southampton Island.

Parry confirmed Middleton's discovery that Repulse Bay was not the way west. Parry overwintered on Winter Island at the mouth of Lyon Inlet. His choice of names indicates a lack of romance – if he was not honouring a nobleman who might return the favour at a later date he was stating the obvious: on Melville Island he had wintered at Winter Harbour, this time it was on Winter Island. Here the British made friends with a group of local Inuit, one of whom, a woman called Iligliuk, drew a map which led Parry to a strait which he named Fury and Hecla after his ships. During the summer of 1822 Parry navigated the strait to its western end, but was unable to break out into what he called the Polar Sea (the Gulf of Boothia). This was a remarkable feat: not until 1948 was the strait navigated from the gulf to Foxe Basin, and not until 1956 the other way – the way Parry attempted it – both journeys requiring an icebreaker. Parry then wintered on Igloolik, an island close to the mouth of the strait. He tried to get through the strait again in 1823, but failed, and returned to Britain.

Parry went north again in 1824, this time trying to find a route by way of Lancaster Sound and Prince Regent Inlet, avoiding both Fury and Hecla Strait and the exit from Parry Channel, but hoping to forge a route from the western end of the strait. The attempt was doomed: the British had not discovered just how far north the Boothia Peninsula reached. That year there was also heavy ice in Baffin Bay and it took Parry all summer to reach Lancaster Sound, much of the time spent in hauling the ships (*Hecla* and *Fury* again) through the thick ice by the back-breaking work of anchoring a hawser to a floe far ahead and heaving on it. The sound itself was almost free of ice, allowing Parry to reach Port Bowen on the eastern shore of Prince Regent Inlet where he wintered. In July 1825 when ice freed the ships Parry went south along the inlet's western coast, but a sudden storm pushed ice against the ships pinning them against the shore. *Fury* was damaged beyond repair and abandoned (at Fury Beach), Parry retreating for home with everyone on board the *Hecla*.

There had been a second expedition in 1824, and another in 1825 linked to Parry's third voyage and a second land expedition of John Franklin. In 1824 George Lyon sailed the *Griper* northwards with the intention of reaching Repulse Bay and then sledging across the narrow peninsula (the Rae Isthmus) at its back, which Iligliuk had shown on her map, to reach the sea beyond (Committee Bay), perhaps linking up with Parry. It was a good plan, but heavy ice and appalling weather in Roes Welcome Sound so badly damaged the *Griper* that Lyon did well to get the ship back to Britain at all: he had not even reached Repulse Bay. The next year Frederick Beechey, who had been Franklin's lieutenant on the *Trent* in 1818, took the *Blossom* to the Bering Strait in the expectation of meeting Parry when he exited the passage, or Franklin when he reached the strait overland. Beechey waited in vain: Franklin reached Foggy Island, just 250km (156 miles) away, but Parry was half a continent away, battling the ice of Prince Regent Inlet.

Given the horror of the earlier land journey it is intriguing why Franklin was willing to lead another in

1825 and why Richardson and Back were prepared to go with him. But go they did. This expedition was better equipped, supplies being easier to obtain now the fur-trade war was over. The men followed the Mackenzie River, easier to navigate than the Coppermine, and with fur-trade forts spaced at intervals along its length so that the journey was hardly similar to that of Alexander Mackenzie. The expedition did descend into horror as the previous one had, but was remarkably successful. At the river's delta mouth Franklin led one team west in two boats, *Lion* and *Reliance*, passing Herschel Island, which he named for the Herschels, father and son, famous British astronomers. Had his team not been halted by thick fog, they would have reached Point Barrow and met Beechey's expedition: Franklin stopped just 250km (156 miles) short. At the same time Richardson led a team eastwards in *Union* and *Dolphin*. Richardson named Franklin Bay for the expedition leader as a mark of the 'respect and regard' he had for him, and the strait between the mainland and Victoria Island for his two boats on his way to the Coppermine River. When Franklin returned to England in 1827 the North American coast from near Point Barrow to Point Turnagain had been mapped.

The North Magnetic Pole
The failures drained the Admiralty's resolve, and with the public's enthusiasm turning to apathy there was no incentive for the government to invest more money, particularly as it had been clear since the outset that even if a passage existed it would not be useful. In the latter stages of the American moon-landing programme in the 1970s public apathy followed such a series of successes that it had become routine. Interest was only rekindled by the near-catastrophe of Apollo 13. For the British of the first third of the 19th century apathy followed a series of failures, many of which did not even have the benefit of a horror story. What was needed to

Above **The Smoking Hills of Franklin Bay. The cliffs of the western side of the bay are of bituminous shale which ignited (probably as a result of a lightning strike) several thousand years ago and have been smouldering ever since.**
Richard Sale

revitalise public interest was a major success – or a major tragedy.

The North-West Passage was to supply the latter. But first a private individual, Felix Booth, Sheriff of London and gin bottler, stepped forward to finance another attempt. Booth's commander was John Ross, ignored since 1818 for his timidity, but a man with an interest in steam navigation who had tried, unsuccessfully, to persuade the Admiralty to let him take a steamship to the Arctic. So keen on the idea was he that Ross part-financed the trip from his own pocket. Ross' nephew, James Clark Ross, who had been on all of Parry's voyages as well as John Ross' first Arctic voyage, was to go with him. Booth's plan was for the ship to make for Prince Regent Inlet, following its western shore to find a channel that opened westward. Ross' ship was the *Victory*, a paddle steamer: when the expedition set out, in 1829, *Victory* was the first steam-driven ship to head north-west. The engine and fuel store were so vast that another ship was needed to carry the expedition's supplies. Worse still the steam engine gave the ship a speed barely above walking pace, the boilers leaked (despite dung and potatoes being put in them on the manufacturer's instructions) and the boiler room was so hot the stokers could only work for short periods before becoming exhausted and fainting. Fortunately when the paddles were lifted out of the water the *Victory* sailed well and Prince Regent Inlet was eventually reached.

Ross sailed south of Parry's Fury Beach – the beached *Fury* had gone – naming the Gulf of Boothia and Boothia Felix (now the Boothia Peninsula) for his patron. Ross overwintered in Felix Harbour in Lord Mayor's Bay (also named in Booth's honour: he was also remembered in Sheriff Harbour, to round off a fine bag of dedications), the steam engine which had so enthralled him being dismantled and manhandled on to the shore as so much rubbish. During the winter of 1829/30 *Victory* was visited by Inuit who told Ross that there was no westward channel to the south. This influenced Ross' later explorations, though it was not finally confirmed that Boothia Felix was a peninsula until Rae's trip of 1846.

The spring of 1830 did not release the *Victory* and James Ross decided to trek – with dog- and manhauled sledges, and with Inuit guides – across Boothia Felix to see what lay to the west. He discovered King William's Land (now King William Island), reaching its northern tip which he called Cape Felix, naturally. At the cape James Ross noted 'the pack ice... that had... been pressed against that shore, consisted of the heaviest masses that I had ever seen in such a situation... the lighter floes had been thrown up, on some parts of the coast... having travelled as much as half a mile beyond the limits of the highest tide-mark'. It was this ice pressure that was to trap and destroy Franklin.

Ross now turned south-west and continued to Cape Victory: he was only about 350km (220 miles) from Point Turnagain, but was out of food and had to return to Felix Harbour. It had been a significant journey, but the most significant discovery was missed: Ross did not explore southwards on the west side of King William. Had he done so he would have found that his Poctes Bay was not a bay and that King William was an island, not a peninsula. Many have argued that this lack of knowledge contributed to the loss of Franklin. He chose to go down King William Island's west edge because he believed – as Ross did – that the eastern side was a bay. It is an easy excuse for the failure of Franklin's final expedition, particularly as Amundsen did go to the east of King William Island on his successful transit. But even had Franklin known King William was an island he would still have failed, as his ships had too deep a draft to negotiate the shallow waters of the eastern coast and of Simpson Strait to the south of King William. There is evidence that Franklin did indeed try the eastern side before trying, fatefully, the western side.

During the summer of 1830 the *Victory* could be moved only 6.5km (4 miles) to Sheriff Harbour where the following winter was spent. When summer 1831 came the ship remained entombed and James Ross set out on another sledge trip. He recrossed Boothia Felix and headed north along the Boothia Felix coast. At 8am on 1 June at 70°5'17"N, 96°46'45"N magnetic measurements showed that Ross had reached the North Magnetic Pole. His team raised a cairn and a jackstaff, since 'nature had erected no monument', from which fluttered the Union Flag as Ross solemnly claimed the territory for the British Crown.

Later, back at the ship, this act of possession took on a surreal aspect when the British attempted to explain to the Inuit that the local area no longer belonged to them. Since the nomadic Inuit did not understand the concept of land ownership their baffled response dealt with the lack of seals that year and the need to acquire more fish-hooks. It would have made just as much sense to them if Ross had told them that Britain owned the sky.

The *Victory* was finally freed from the ice in late summer, but managed to gain just a few miles northward before being entombed again. During the winter

Above **James Clark Ross at the North Magnetic Pole. A charming engraving from Robert Huish's book *The Last Voyage of Capt John Ross*. It almost certainly caught the imagination of the public despite its errors. The Aurora Borealis can only be seen at night and Ross travelled during the continuous daylight of the Arctic summer; the telescope is highly fanciful as the magnetic pole is discovered with a dip circle and does not require the 'conquering' of a mountain. In fact the pole was discovered at sea level (more or less).**
Richard Sale Collection

of 1831/2 the crew began to show signs of scurvy, despite John Ross' intelligent use of fresh meat to keep it at bay. Ross therefore decided to abandon the ship, hauling boats and supplies north to Fury Beach where there were still supplies from Parry's last voyage. Fury Beach was reached in July and a hut (Somerset House) built. But before the boats could be rigged for a voyage to Lancaster Sound winter set in again. During this fourth winter one man died of scurvy. With most of the crew now ill, many weeks in 1833 were spent transporting supplies to the ice edge. Finally, on 15 August, the boats were launched. To the men's joy

Above **George Back followed the Great Fish River to Chantry Bay, camping on Montreal Island in the bay. Years later the island was almost certainly visited by survivors of Franklin's last expedition, but they, unlike the man in the foreground, probably were not carrying suitcases.**
From George Back *Narrative of the Arctic Land Expedition.*
Richard Sale Collection

Lancaster Sound was open water. On 25 August, to even greater delight, a sail was sighted. The ship lowered a boat and rowed towards the expedition. When Ross asked what ship it was he was told it was 'the *Isabella* of Hull, once commanded by Captain Ross'. The ship had been John Ross' first Arctic command in 1818 and was now a whaler. Ross noted that when he told the *Isabella*'s mate (who had brought the boat across to them) that he was the same Captain Ross, 'with the usual blunderheadedness of men on such occasions, he assured me I had been dead two years'.

Back in Britain John Ross was knighted, James Ross promoted. The only sour note was Sir John Barrow's unfair review of John Ross' book; he had still not forgiven what he saw as the cowardice of 1818. But now, as then, Barrow's article was published anonymously. Not that there was much need for secrecy, as John Ross was at war with just about everyone, including his nephew James. Ludicrously, John was claiming to have discovered the North Magnetic Pole while James was claiming to have commanded the *Victory*.

In 1832, nothing having been heard from John Ross for nearly three years, people in Britain began to clamour for a search expedition. Ross' having been a private venture the government and Admiralty were not keen to finance a search, but eventually some private money

was also raised and George Back, veteran of the two Franklin overland expeditions, returned to Canada with instructions to follow the Great Fish (now Back) River to the sea and then to head north to Fury Beach where, it was assumed, Ross would head if he ran low on food. The assumption was correct, though the search was far too late, few having much hope that Ross could have survived four winters. That he had is likely to have influenced the Admiralty when there was an equal clamour to search for the missing Franklin expedition.

Back established a base on the shores of the Great Slave Lake and overwintered. During the winter he met Greenstockings (see page 40) again, immediately recognising her because she had retained her beauty. She now had a number of children, one of whom, presumably, was Robert Hood's though, not surprisingly, Back makes no such comment. In April 1834 news arrived that Ross had

Despite the failure of John Ross to find the passage, the expedition had aroused sufficient interest to persuade the Admiralty to send George Back northwards again in 1836, though his instructions were to survey the last section of uncharted coast, southwards from the Fury and Hecla Strait to Point Turnagain. To do this Back sailed the *Terror* to Repulse Bay with the intention of crossing Melville Peninsula on foot. But the *Terror* was trapped in the ice, squeezed and battered for ten months. When she was eventually released she was almost unseaworthy and Back sailed for home immediately. He just made it to Ireland's west coast, beaching the ship to prevent her sinking.

UK National Maritime Museum

returned safely to England, but Back continued with his trip, though on a reduced scale, following the Great Fish River to Chantry Inlet. Ice and lack of time prevented more than just a survey of part of the bay's shoreline, marking another point on the map of the mainland.

Dease and Simpson, and Rae

Following the overland expeditions of Franklin the missing sections of the North American coast were filled in by men from the Hudson's Bay Company. Between 1836 and 1839 Peter Dease, a senior company official, and Thomas Simpson, cousin of company governor George Simpson, made a series of journeys. Though Dease was nominally in charge it was Simpson, a young man of burning ambition and amazing stamina, who was the driving force. Simpson's abilities were remarkable: he could travel up to 80km (50 miles) daily on foot, sometimes in winter, for day after day, and shrug off conditions which would have repelled ordinary men. On the pair's first expedition, to fill in the gap between Franklin's Foggy Island and Point Barrow, Simpson and five others left Dease and the rest of the

Above **Thomas Simpson – date and artist unknown.**
Hudson's Bay Company Archives, Provincial Archives of Manitoba, Canada

team and pushed west across dreadful country, wading freezing cold rivers up to their waists and being cold day and night. Borrowing an Inuit umiak for the last stage of the trek they finally reached Point Barrow.

Next Dease and Simpson made for the coast east of Point Turnagain. In 1838 Simpson descended the Coppermine River and pushed east over ice, passing Turnagain and discovering an island he named for the young British queen: Victoria Island. Halted by the conditions he returned in 1839 and sailed two boats, *Castor* and *Pollux*, all the way to Back's Chantry Inlet, discovering en route that King William was an island, not a peninsula: the channel separating King William Island and the Adelaide Peninsula is now called Simpson Strait.

Now Simpson's ambition seems to have overcome him. He wrote, 'Fame I must have, but it must be alone.' Fed up with Dease, his senior, Simpson walked to the Red River settlement (Fort Garry, now the site of Winnipeg), a journey of almost 3,200km (nearly 2,000 miles) which he completed in 61 days, on foot, in winter. He was happy there would be a message at the fort telling him to continue his explorations by linking Chantry Inlet to Fury and Hecla Strait. There was no message. Certainly disillusioned, probably furious, he headed south, intending to reach a US port and a ship for Britain. Just after he left the instructions he craved arrived. But it was too late: Simpson was dead. He had started his journey with four other men. The survivors told how Simpson, enraged by the injustices of life, shot dead two of them, the other two fleeing in terror. When they returned to camp Simpson had shot himself. Perhaps that tale is true – but why go back to a camp occupied by a murderous companion? The events surrounding Simpson's death are still debated. What is clear is that a major explorer had died without fulfilling his potential. He was 31 years old.

The last big piece of the jigsaw was finally fitted in 1847 when Dr John Rae, later to discover Sir John Franklin's fate, crossed the isthmus from Repulse Bay to Committee Bay (which he had already crossed in 1846) and headed north along the bay's western shore. Rounding what is now called the Simpson Peninsula Rae headed north, looking for a channel that separated Ross' Boothia Felix from the mainland. When he reached Lord Major's Bay he realised there wasn't one. Boothia Felix was the Boothia Peninsula, and the coast of Canada had been mapped.

Franklin's last expedition

In 1845 Sir John Barrow was in his 81st year. He had occupied the same post for 41 years, and felt the time had come to retire. James, now Sir James, Ross had returned from Antarctica with the news that there was little to encourage the British to go there again, a fact which may have encouraged Barrow to remember the unfinished business in the north. He wrote to the Admiralty pointing out Britain would be a laughing stock if, having found the eastern and western ends of the North-West Passage, she did not explore the part in the middle. The Admiralty agreed, making *Erebus* and *Terror*, Ross' Antarctic ships, available.

But who should command? James Ross declined: he was, he said, too old at 44. John Ross was, of course, still beyond the pale. Parry could not be tempted out of retirement and Back's health had not recovered from the excesses of 1836/7, while Sir John Franklin was not only old but had just been dismissed from his position as governor of Van Dieman's Land (Tasmania).

Nominally the dismissal followed an unseemly row with a junior, though it was actually engineered by a vested interest on the island who feared Franklin's humanitarian view of prisoner treatment might affect the profits they made from prison labour.

Franklin had had a distinguished service career. He had fought at the Battle of Copenhagen when he was just 15. He had been a signal officer on the *Bellerophon* at Trafalgar: the ship was the most heavily engaged in the battle. Franklin emerged unscathed, but was later wounded at the Battle of New Orleans where Packenham's army was routed by Andrew Jackson. But despite all this he was not promoted. He was, it seems, amiable and competent, but dull, and the governorship of a prison colony was his only reward. After his dismissal Franklin returned to Britain looking for both justice and a job. He was almost 60 and overweight, clearly not suited to what might be an exhausting command. But his second wife, Lady Jane Franklin, campaigned relentlessly on his behalf, seeing the expedition as a way of allowing her husband to regain the prestige cruelly robbed by the unfair dismissal from Tasmania. Eventually the Admiralty succumbed to her pressure.

Franklin was given two ships for the expedition, *Erebus* and *Terror*, the pair James Clark Ross had taken south. They were strengthened to withstand pressure from the ice and fitted with railway locomotive steam engines which turned screw propellers, a radically new idea. Sir John Barrow reasoned that the ships, reinforced at the bow and powered from the stern, would plough through the Arctic ice. John Ross had his doubts and also worried about the crew size. The compliment was 133 men and Ross noted how hard it had been to feed one-sixth that number when the *Victory* had been lost. But Barrow was hardly likely to listen to John Ross. The ships were being stocked with tinned food, a revolutionary new idea which promised to eliminate both hunger and scurvy. The canned meat and vegetables were supplied by Stephen Goldner, the man with the lowest tender, but a production line that left much to be desired in terms of the quality of the food and the cleanliness of his production methods. It was said that the only part of the pigs that did not go into Goldner's cans was the squeal, and that with slaughtering of pigs, sheep and cows being carried out on the premises and within sight of other animals the filth that also reached the cans was indescribable. Goldner's cans arrived only hours before the ships sailed, too late for samples to be checked for quality, or the can seals examined.

Above **A daguerreotype of Sir John Franklin.**
UK National Maritime Museum

Below **Goldner cans from Franklin's expedition on Beechey Island.**
Richard Sale

On 19 May 1845 the *Erebus* and *Terror* were made ready to depart the River Thames. Just before sailing a dove flew down and perched on a mast. The commander and crew were cheered by this obvious happy omen. On 26 July the two ships were seen by a whaler, moored to an iceberg on Baffin Bay, close to the entrance to Lancaster Sound. After an exchange of greetings the whaler sailed away. It was the last time that either ship or any of the crew – reduced to 129 after four men had been sent home from Greenland – were seen by European eyes.

History had taught the British not to be too concerned if nothing was heard of Arctic expeditions for several years, but by 1848 James Ross (now Sir James after his southern success) was demanding a rescue mission. That year Ross took two ships to Somerset Island where he was forced to overwinter before retreating in the face of heavy ice. At the same time two more ships were dispatched to the Bering Strait. Despite sledge journeys eastwards (ironically following one of Franklin's land routes) no trace was found of Franklin. During his trip Ross tried the ingenious idea of trapping Arctic foxes and fitting them with collars that carried a message of hope to Franklin, then releasing them. It was the first of many ideas for contacting the beleaguered crew, one of the more entertaining being that of releasing thousands of message-bearing balloons.

During the decade that followed the first rescue attempts more than three dozen expeditions set out in search of Franklin or clues to his disappearance. Many of these were official expeditions from Britain, but some were private. Of the latter, most were at the instigation of Lady Jane Franklin. Jane Griffin had met Franklin when he married her friend Eleanor Porden, marrying him after Eleanor's death and after several chaste dalliances of her own, most notably with Peter Roget, author of the famous thesaurus. Lady Jane was a formidable woman who campaigned relentlessly on behalf of her lost husband, badgering the Admiralty into further searches and spending a fortune on her own. She also wrote to Zachary Taylor, president of the United States, asking for help. That request failed to elicit an official response, being defeated by procrastination in the government, but it did result in a semi-official one when congress backed and part-funded an expedition set up by Henry Grinnell, a New York shipping magnate. The 'First Grinnell Expedition' was also the first American expedition to the Arctic, igniting a public enthusiasm which was to lead, ultimately, to the tragedies and successes of Greely, Cook and Peary.

Charles Francis Hall, another American, also went north on a Franklin search. Hall was a curious man whose later death is the subject of one of the Arctic's most enduring mysteries. Hall believed he had been chosen by God to lead Franklin survivors (who had sought refuge with the Inuit) back to civilisation. Hall actually murdered one travelling companion whom he thought was inciting mutiny, so intent was he on his crusade and so deep was his paranoia that mankind was seeking to stop him. Yet Hall's notes of his interviews with the many Inuit he met form the basis of a coherent story of what exactly did happen to Franklin and his crew. Hall also retrieved the skeleton of one of Franklin's men, and took it back to the US: the skeleton, believed to be that of Henry Le Vesconte, an officer on the *Erebus*, was eventually taken back to Britain and buried at Greenwich. Another skeleton, thought to be that of John Irving, an officer on the *Terror*, was also repatriated and buried in Edinburgh. Le Vesconte and Irving were the only two of Franklin's men to return to Britain.

The Franklin search filled in almost all the gaps in the map of the Arctic coast and the islands close to it. The numerous expeditions also gathered such evidence as existed on the fate of Franklin and his men. There were too many searches to cover them all adequately, but several were too important to exclude.

In 1850 Richard Collinson in the *Enterprise* was given command of an expedition of two ships – Collinson in the *Enterprise*, Robert McClure commanding the *Investigator* – which sailed to the Bering Strait to

Opposite above **Noon, midwinter at Port Leopold on James Clark Ross' expedition in search of Franklin. The original painting was by W.H. Browne who accompanied the expedition.**
Richard Sale Collection

Opposite below **The Arctic Council by Stephen Pearce. The council was a group of the great and the good of British Arctic exploration, formed to offer advice to the Admiralty on the conduct of the Franklin search. They probably did not meet as a group, as depicted here, but the painting does illustrate all the main players in the Royal Navy's quest for both the North-West Passage and Franklin. On the wall are (left to right) portraits of John Franklin, James Fitzjames and Sir John Barrow. The others are (left to right) George Back, William Edward Parry, Edward Bird, James Clark Ross, Francis Beaufort, John Barrow Jnr, Edward Sabine, William Hamilton, John Richardson and Frederick Beechey.**
By courtesy of the UK National Portrait Gallery, London

Above **The sledge party leaving HMS *Investigator* under the command of Lt Cresswell. This is one of a series of sketches by S. Gurney Cresswell, an officer on McClure's ship *Investigator*. Cresswell was involved in sledge trips in Prince of Wales Strait as well as leading one retreating party from the *Investigator* to Melville Island.**
Richard Sale Collection

search eastwards. Probably by design, the ambitious McClure found himself ahead of his commander, and instead of waiting headed east. He reached the mouth of the Mackenzie River and sailed eastward towards the Coppermine. On hearing from local Inuit that they had not seen a ship like his before he reasoned that Franklin had not followed the mainland coast, and headed northeast. McClure entered a waterway (which he named for the Prince of Wales) between Victoria and Banks Islands and, to his growing excitement, realised that he was

heading directly for Parry's Barrow Strait and Winter Harbour. When he was finally stopped by heavy ice McClure was only 50km (30 miles) from Barrow Strait and sent out a sledge party which found that the Prince of Wales was a strait, not a sound: McClure had discovered the North-West Passage, a fact which he promptly noted in a cairn he built. *Investigator* spent the winter in the ice of Prince of Wales Strait, then sailed south around Banks Island, McClure intending to reach Barrow Strait by going north along the island's west coast. He rounded the northern tip of Banks, but was forced by heavy ice to overwinter in Mercy Bay, so called because the finding of such a comfortable harbour seemed an act of providence. But though providential as a winter quarters, the bay was a trap from which *Investigator* was never to escape.

McClure sledged to Winter Harbour, proving that a passage existed north of Banks Island as well, then waited for the ice to free his ship or rescue to arrive.

When neither happened, and with his crew dying of scurvy and starvation, he decided that in the spring of 1853 two parties would set out by sledge, one east towards Port Leopold on the north-eastern tip of Somerset Island where James Ross had left supplies in 1848, the other south-west to, and up, the Mackenzie River. These teams were to comprise the sickest men and carry few supplies. McClure and the fitter men would overwinter again in the hope that *Investigator* would be freed and could sail east to complete the passage. That McClure was intending to send men to their deaths is obvious from the comment of Johann Miertsching, a Moravian missionary who accompanied the ship as interpreter. Miertsching, who was to go with the Mackenzie team noted, 'How many of us will in this way see Europe? The answer is "No One".'

But before McClure could carry out his ridiculous plan Lt Pim arrived at the ship from the *Resolute*, one of the ships of Belcher's 'Arctic Squadron' which had sailed west along Lancaster Sound looking for both Franklin and McClure. The *Resolute* had wintered on Dealy Island (off Melville Island), finding a note McClure had left at Winter Harbour which gave the position of Mercy Bay. McClure returned with Pim to the *Resolute* where its commander, Henry Kellett, a senior officer, effectively ordered him to abandon his plan and the *Investigator* and to bring his men to the *Resolute*. In doing so McClure's crew completed a transit of the passage from west to east, but in two ships and by sledge between them. Back in Britain McClure received a knighthood and claimed – and was given – the government reward for discovering the passage: he had actually found two passages, completing both by sledge. But McClure declined to share the reward with Kellett on the grounds that he had ordered the abandonment of the *Investigator* which, McClure complained, could have been freed and so completed the journey. Kellett, presumably amazed and appalled, gave money for the relief of McClure's still sick crew who also got nothing from McClure, receiving only the Arctic pay that was due to them.

Trailing his second-in-command, Collinson, in the *Enterprise*, unwittingly followed McClure up Prince of Wales Strait, finding his note on the discovery of the passage, and then up the west coast of Banks Island, though ice prevented him from reaching Mercy Bay. Collinson then sailed south again before turning east. He sailed between Victoria Island and the mainland, overwintering in Cambridge Bay. Had it not been for his timidity it is possible Collinson would have reached Victoria Strait, perhaps discovered the remains of Franklin's expedition (if Inuit reports on the movement of the *Erebus* are correct Collinson might even have found the ship), perhaps even – though more doubtfully – sailed north and reached Lancaster Sound. But Collinson did not push too hard into doubtful country, so much so that one of his officers noted, 'Poor Sir John. God help you – you'll get none from us.' However, sledge parties from the *Enterprise* explored the east coast of Victoria Island proving that there was another North-West Passage to the south of McClure's. Collinson then returned to Britain. Interestingly, during this sledge journey along the Victoria coast Collinson's men found a cairn erected by John Rae and, beyond it, three further cairns. Exactly who had built these has never been satisfactorily explained, but Collinson chose to ignore them. They also found a piece of washed-up door frame which almost certainly came from one of Franklin's ships. Again the find was ignored. It is true that his expedition's only interpreter was with McClure and so he could not properly question the local Inuit who may well have had information on Franklin's fate (they actually drew a picture of a ship trapped in ice, but Collinson did not realise its significance: he did attempt to sledge across the ice of Victoria Strait to King William Island – had he succeeded he would have discovered what happened to Franklin – but did not complete the journey). Collinson's journey to Cambridge Bay was a masterpiece of navigation in such a large ship – a fact acknowledged by Amundsen – but his decision not to follow up clues probably relating to the main objective of his trip delayed discovering the fate of Franklin for several years.

The first trace of where Franklin had gone after the whaler had left *Erebus* and *Terror* in Baffin Bay was found in 1850 when a whole fleet of ships had gathered at Beechey Island prior to searching from the Arctic's eastern end. The Americans De Haven and Kane from Grinnell's first expedition were present, as were several Royal Navy ships and John Ross on a private search mission. While many of the commanders were conferring on the island men from the *Assistance*, a Royal Navy ship commanded by Horatio Austin, who had already found some naval stores and meat cans at Cape Riley on nearby Devon Island, found three graves. They were of William Braine and John Hartnell of the *Erebus*, and John Torrington of the *Terror*. All three had died in early 1846, Torrington the first on 1 January. Clearly Franklin had spent the winter of 1845/6 on Beechey Island. But though the discovery was welcomed, it offered no clue.

In Britain Lady Jane Franklin, dismayed at the lack of positive news, was financing her own expeditions. One of these, in 1851 in the *Prince Albert*, led by William Kennedy, included Joseph René Bellot, a handsome Frenchman who captured the hearts of every lady in England, not least by offering to work for nothing in such a noble cause. The trip discovered nothing about the fate of Franklin, but did find the narrow strait separating the Boothia Peninsula from Somerset Island. This – Bellot Strait – was sledged, but at its far side the party crossed Peel Sound rather than exploring southwards. On a later expedition Bellot disappeared when a crack opened in an ice floe.

Left **The graves of the three Franklin expedition sailors at Beechey Island. The headstones are replicas of the originals which have been removed to the museum in Yellowknife. A narrow causeway links the 'island' of Beechey with Devon Island, in the background.**
Richard Sale

Below **'The Departure of the South-West Division', an engraving in Edward Belcher's *The Last of the Arctic Voyages.* During his expedition Belcher sent sledge parties out in many directions to search for Franklin, but apart from the graves on Beechey Island had little to show for his efforts.**
Richard Sale Collection

The *Resolute* which rescued McClure and his crew was part of the 'Arctic Squadron' of five ships commanded by Sir Edward Belcher which sailed in 1852 to search from Lancaster Sound. Belcher was a tyrannical man, intensely disliked by his junior officers, and with dissension causing his expedition to disintegrate, he ordered all the ships that were sealed in ice to be abandoned, transferring all the crews to the one free ship (and two supply ships which had fortuitously arrived). To comply with the order to desert the *Resolute* Kellett, though appalled by the decision, closed up his ship, his and McClure's men sledging to Beechey Island. In a curious sequel, in 1855 an American whaler discovered the *Resolute* drifting undamaged in the ice of Davis Strait, having travelled 1,600km (1,000 miles) eastwards through the Parry Channel. It is claimed that when they boarded the Americans found unspilled wine glasses still on the messroom table. The ship was towed back to the US where it was refitted (even pictures and books being carefully restored or replaced) and returned to Britain as a gift to Queen Victoria. It was a fine gesture, but the Admiralty failed to live up to it: in 1880 the *Resolute* was broken up. From her timber a writing table was made and presented to the American president. The table later languished in the White House basement for many years until it was rescued and used by John F. Kennedy. Later still the table achieved a moment of notoriety when it became an important prop in a 'meeting' between President Bill Clinton and Monica Lewinski. Belcher had abandoned five ships and was court-martialled for the offence by a furious Admiralty. Though his reputation was shredded he was found not guilty because he was able to show that his orders had been sufficiently vague to allow the interpretation he had chosen to find in them.

The next news of Franklin's fate came from Dr John Rae, a Hudson's Bay Company surgeon. Rae was an Orkney islander who rapidly learned that the adoption of Inuit methods made survival much easier than it was for those naval officers who insisted on maintaining naval method in an environment for which it was entirely unsuitable. This idea – 'going native' as the British establishment contemptuously called it – almost certainly added to the venom with which Rae's news was greeted. In 1853, on a second overland journey in search of Franklin (and with a secondary purpose of surveying small sections of unexplored coast to confirm that Boothia was a peninsula) Rae met Inuit who told him of their meeting with a large group of (perhaps 40) white men who were dragging a boat along the western shore

Above **Dr John Rae, an engraving from a portrait by Stephen Pearce. Rae was a consummate Arctic traveller, learning from the Inuit and putting what he had learned to good use. Not only did he complete the map of Canada's Arctic shore but he has a strong claim to being the discoverer (if not the traveller) of the North-West Passage. Rae also discovered the fate of Franklin, telling a story for which the British establishment never forgave him.**
Hudson's Bay Company Archives,
Provincial Archives of Manitoba, Canada

of King William Island. By sign and pidgeon Inuit they learned that the white men had abandoned ships crushed in the ice and were looking for caribou and birds to hunt. Later the Inuit had found the remains of many men close to the Great Fish River. Some were in a tent, others under an overturned boat and, as Rae reported, 'from the mutilated state of many of the bodies, and the contents of the kettles, it is evident that our wretched countrymen had been driven to the last dread alternative – cannibalism – as a means of sustaining life'.

Rae brought back relics which he had traded from the Inuit. These proved beyond doubt that the men were Franklin's; and, given the size of the party, they could not really have been anyone else's. But these

Above **The inhospitable terrain of King William Island. With its frost-shattered rocks, minimal shelter and limited vegetation and animal life, King William was a desperate place for the Franklin survivors.**

Richard Sale

offering by the Inuit 'to their barbarous, wide-mouthed, goggle-eyed gods.' Having demolished the Inuit testimony Dickens went on to note that 'it is in the highest degree improbable that such men [Franklin's] would, or could, in any extremity of hunger, alleviate the pains of starvation by this horrible means'. Dickens also noted that as Franklin's men had no fuel and so could not light fires they could not have practised cannibalism, not being able to cook the meat: the Inuit ate raw meat, but they were savages of course, not civilised Englishmen.

The reaction to Rae's news is a lesson in Victorian values. The belief in the innate superiority of the Briton to any native, and even to anybody from a civilised country, is manifest (the upper classes in Britain also put the working class in much the same category as the 'savages' they so despised). The logical extension of this xenophobia (perhaps racism would be a better word) was that the British officer class had nothing to learn from natives and everything to teach them. It was an attitude that had sent men in dress uniforms to the Arctic and would, in not so many years, send others equally unprepared to Antarctica.

The controversy hurt Rae immensely. He felt humiliated, a feeling heightened when the government did not honour him with the knighthood they had bestowed on much less deserving individuals, and quibbled over the payment of the reward for finding the fate of Franklin, Lady Jane Franklin consistently lobbying against him.

Lady Jane Franklin chose not to believe his story and pressed for another search expedition. The Admiralty and government were reluctant: too many ships and lives had been lost already; it was now ten years since Franklin had sailed away, and the Crimean War had begun. The Admiralty's publication of Rae's story – it was they, not he, that had told *The Times* – was an effort to call a halt to further expeditions. Despite public pressure and Lady Franklin's moral blackmail they stood firm, forcing Lady Jane to finance the final search herself.

In 1857 Francis McClintock, already a veteran of several search missions and a sledging expert, took command of the *Fox*, a small, but highly manoeuvrable ship, and headed north. The *Fox* almost failed to make a search at all, heavy ice sealing her in. The ship drifted south for eight months before being released and did not make Lancaster Sound until July 1858. McClintock found Peel Sound closed by ice and in desperation went down Prince Regent Inlet in the hope

positive finds were all but washed away by the wave of public indignation that followed the publication of Rae's account of cannibalism, particularly as the account was based on Inuit testimony; Rae had not visited the campsite and seen the kettles for himself. *The Times* thundered that no one could take this seriously as the Inuit 'like all savages are liars'. Charles Dickens was equally outraged. Egged on by Jane Franklin, who orchestrated a campaign against Rae and his account, Dickens published articles in his magazine *Household Words*. Speaking for much of the country he claimed that the story was bound to be false as it was based on the word of 'the savage' and 'we believe every savage to be in his heart covetous, treacherous and cruel'. Dickens went on to hint that it was more likely that the Inuit had murdered Franklin's men and that if there was indeed human flesh to be found in kettles it was an

The McClintock note is actually made up of two, written one year apart on an official form that requested, in six languages, its return to the Admiralty or local British consul. The first note, signed by Lt Graham Gore and Charles Frederick Des Voeux, mate, was written in May 1847 and states:

HMS Ships Erebus *and* Terror *28 May 1847 wintered in the Ice in Lat 70°5'N, Long 98°23'W. Having wintered in 1846–7 at Beechey Island in Lat 74°43'28''N Long 91·39'15''W after having ascended Wellington Channel to Lat 77° and returned by the west side of Cornwallis Island. Sir John Franklin commanding the Expedition. All well. Party consisting of 2 officers and 6 men left ship on Monday 24th May 1847.*

The date of the wintering on Beechey is wrong – it was 1845/6 – but the remarkable information is that Franklin had sailed around Cornwallis Island finding open water in Wellington Channel but presumably being stopped by ice at about 77°N. What was the condition of the ice in the Parry Channel? Could he have sailed west from Cornwallis and gone beyond Melville and Banks islands towards Alaska?

The second message reads:

(25th April) 1848 HM Ships Terror *and* Erebus *were deserted on the 22nd April 5 leagues NNW of this (hav)ing been beset since 12th Sept 1846. The officers and crews consisting of 105 souls under the command (of Cap)tain FRM Crozier landed here – in Lat 69°37'42'' Long 98°41' (This) paper was found by Lt Irving under the cairn supposed to have been built by Sir James Ross in 1831 – where it had been deposited (4 miles to the northward) – by the late commander Gore in June 1847. Sir James Ross' pillar has not however been found and the paper has been transferred to this position which is that in which Sir J Ross pillar was erected – Sir John Franklin died on the 11th June 1847 and the total loss by deaths to this date 9 officers and 15 men.*

Right **'The Franklin Message'.**
From Francis McClintock's *The Voyage of the Fox in the Arctic Seas.*
Richard Sale Collection

This note was signed by 'James Fitzjames, Captain HMS *Erebus*'. It was also signed 'FRM Crozier, Captain and Senior Offr', Crozier adding a postscript 'and start on tomorrow, 26th, for Backs Fish River'.

Despite its brevity the note reveals a great deal. The two ships had left Beechey in summer 1846 and headed south, presumably through Peel Sound, becoming beset off King William Island in September and being abandoned two years later. Lt Gore (who left the first message) was dead, as were 23 others (three on Beechey, 20 later, including Franklin), a much higher death rate than on any previous expedition. A later discovery of the likely grave of Lt Irving at Victory Point suggests that if he was the man who went to Ross' cairn he was fit enough to have survived for some time after the suggested journey south towards the Great Fish (Back) River.

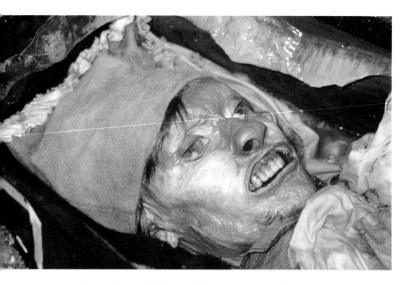

Above **The almost perfectly preserved bodies of John Hartnell, top, and John Torrington, are revealed after the Beechey Island exhumations.**
Richard Sale Collection

McClintock almost reached Starvation Cove on the Adelaide Peninsula before turning north along King William Island's west coast. Along the shore he found remnants of the expedition including an almost intact skeleton. Ahead of him Hobson was finding the only note ever discovered from the Franklin expedition as well as a boat (pointing north) holding two skeletons and many other items, and the vast pile of supplies at Victory Point. The fate of the Franklin expedition had been discovered, though the manner in which it came about was, and still is, a matter of conjecture.

The conventional scenario, established 30 to 40 years later, is that with *Erebus* and *Terror* beset and food and fuel running low, the men abandoned the ships and started south, intending to use boats to follow the Great Fish (Back) River to a Hudson's Bay Company outpost. Overcome by hunger and (perhaps) scurvy they died one by one, the last groups perishing at Starvation Cove on the Adelaide Peninsula and Montreal Island in Chantry Inlet. This story is now challenged, in part by analysis carried out on bones from King William Island and autopsies on the three corpses at Beechey Island, and also by close examination of Inuit testimony gathered by Charles Hall. The bone analysis shows high levels of lead as well as distinct signs of scurvy. High lead levels are also present in the Beechey corpses, though their deaths were from natural causes.

The finding of significant levels of lead has led to Professor Owen Beattie, the leader of the teams which carried out the analyses, to suggest that lead poisoning from the solder used to seal the food tins carried by the expedition was a factor in crew deaths. Canning was a new technique in the 1840s and the lethal potential of lead was not understood. A more recent suggestion has been that the food within the cans was contaminated on account of poor hygiene at Goldner's canning factory. One writer has even suggested botulism as a cause of death. Certainly the death rate was very high and the preponderance of officer deaths also suggests a can-based mechanism: as a rule officers fed better than crew, and the cans might have been considered the better fare. Roald Amundsen relates a story told to him by Inuit he met at Gjøahaven during his journey through the passage. This maintains that Inuit retrieving cans of food from the Franklin trip died after consuming the contents. It is also the case that hundreds of empty cans were left on Beechey Island, seemingly more than could have been consumed in a single winter. Were many found to be bad and abandoned? However, against this hypothesis is

that Bellot Strait was navigable. He pushed through the strait but was unable to exit its western end and retreated to overwinter close to the eastern end, spending the dark months laying down supply depots for sledge journeys in the spring.

In April 1859 three teams set out. One headed north-west, while McClintock and Lt William Hobson headed south to explore King William Island.

the fact that without modern medicines botulism has a very high mortality rate, perhaps 75 per cent. The cans were large and many men would have eaten from each one opened. How can so many men have survived so long if many cans were contaminated?

An alternative scenario, one supported by Inuit stories and now gaining credibility, suggests that with men dying, perhaps from a combination of contaminated food and scurvy, Crozier (in command after Franklin's death) decided to abandon the ships. He brought as much as possible ashore, then set out south. At first his crew managed to shoot a lot of game (after Franklin the Inuit abandoned King William Island because its animal life had been exterminated) but eventually food runs out. One group of men now try to regain the ships, some dying along the way – this scenario would explain why the discovered boat was pointing north not south – while others continue south, driven eventually to cannibalism. One ship appears to have broken free of the ice and was probably sailed to Kirkwall Island off Adelaide Peninsula's western coast where it was beset again. This ship sank when Inuit cut into it to plunder its contents.

This latter account seems much more plausible. But there are certainly some mysteries in the Franklin story: why did Crozier go south when Fury Beach, where there were still supplies, was closer? Why were so many luxury items hauled by a sick, starving crew? Who was the giant with long teeth the Inuit claimed to have found on the ship near Kirkwall Island? Why did the survivors, if they were heading for the Great Fish River, choose to cross Simpson Strait at its widest point rather than at its narrowest? The latter offers the intriguing possibility that the very last survivors may have been heading for Repulse Bay, and there are tantalising Inuit tales of white men surviving for many years and even that some almost made it to Hudson's Bay Company forts. Quite whether the still-unsolved (and probably unsolvable) mysteries warrant the suggestion of extra-terrestrial intervention of a recent theory seems unlikely.

When McClintock returned Lady Jane Franklin used her formidable powers of persuasion on his behalf, using him as a final weapon against Rae. She lobbied for McClintock to receive a knighthood, which he did, and for his name to be placed on her husband's memorial in Westminster Abbey, which it was. She also ensured that the memorial, and another in Waterloo Place, bore inscriptions which stated that Sir John Franklin was the discoverer of the North-West Passage. If the discovery requires only the identification of a waterway then it was John Rae who did that, in 1846. Franklin's expedition did not discover a complete waterway until after his death (and may not even have done so then – though if a ship really was sailed to Kirkwall Island then they may have, without realising it). McClure's discovery post-dated both. If the requirement is to have completed a navigable route rather than merely identifying it, then Amundsen wins the race.

Right **The Franklin Monument on Beechey Island. The monument was erected by Edward Belcher. Beside it are the ruins of Northumberland House, a timber depot built during the Belcher expedition.**
Richard Sale

The passage completed

After the disastrous loss of the Franklin expedition and the costly and exhausting searches, the British gave up the idea of a North-West Passage. It was clearly of no commercial value, the need to keep naval officers and ships occupied had slackened, and given a choice between national honour and the national exchequer pragmatism won. Not until 1902 did an expedition return to the Canadian Arctic when Otto Sverdrup sailed in the second *Fram* expedition. A few years later the North-West Passage was finally completed by ship.

The Norwegian Roald Engebreth Gravning Amundsen was born on 16 July 1872 and grew up, a pugnacious boy, on the outskirts of Oslo (then Christiania), acquiring early the skills of skiing and seamanship. Having obtained his master's certificate, chiefly by working on sealing boats, Amundsen served his polar apprenticeship on the *Belgica*. By 1901 he felt ready to take command of his first expedition. As a teenager Amundsen had been inspired by the books of John Franklin: not the tragic events surrounding his disappearance, but the accounts of the overland journeys to the shores of the Arctic ocean. Most of all Amundsen wanted to be the first to complete a transit of the North-West Passage.

Amundsen had learned much from the early accounts of the British in the Arctic. He realised that safety lay in small ships which were highly manoeuvrable and had shallow drafts; that it lay in fewer men as the land could only support a limited number; and

that it lay in adopting Inuit methods of dress. In 1901 he bought *Gjøa* (pronounced 'you-ah'), a tiny (47-ton) herring-fishing boat. The ship was refitted, the hull sheathed against ice and a small engine installed. At midnight on 16 June 1903 Amundsen and his crew of six (including Adolf Lindström, who had been with Sverdrup on *Fram*'s second voyage, and Helmer Hanssen, who would later accompany Amundsen to the South Pole) took *Gjøa* out of Oslo fjord. On 25 July Amundsen stopped at Nuuk in west Greenland to add ten dogs to those he already had. In Greenland he met the Danes Rasmussen and Mylius-Erichsen, men whose names are prominent in the history of Greenland exploration.

Leaving Greenland *Gjøa* made good progress, going through Lancaster Sound to reach Beechey Island on 22 August. Now, faced with a choice of routes, Amundsen headed south-west, then south through Peel Strait. This choice, rather than west towards Banks Island, was probably due to Amundsen's wish to reach the North Magnetic Pole (or at least to study magnetic variations close to it) as he had been concerned that without some scientific purpose his trip would be dismissed as a mere adventure. Making amazing progress through open water *Gjøa* reached the entrance to Sir James Ross Strait (between Boothia and King William Island) on 30 August.

As Amundsen soon found – and Franklin had, perhaps, already found – Sir James Ross Strait is shallow and shoal-filled. *Gjøa*, despite her limited draft, ran

aground early on 31 August, damaging her keel. After getting the ship afloat again, fire broke out in the engine room and threatened to engulf the fuel tanks. The fire was put out quickly, but Amundsen was left in no doubt about what could have ensued. Soon after *Gjøa* grounded again on a reef, this time much more seriously as it happened at high tide. The next high tide failed to refloat the ship which was then battered by a storm which threatened to haul her along the reef, tearing her bottom out. Amundsen decided to abandon ship, but Anton Lund, ship's mate, suggested jettisoning cargo to reduce the draft. This worked, the ship floating free: *Gjøa* and the expedition were saved.

Continuing south, *Gjøa* rounded the southern tip of King William Island. Amundsen could see that Simpson Strait was ice-free, but it was now mid-September and he preferred to overwinter in a natural harbour where the ship would be protected and could be anchored just metres from shore. There was, too, the need to stay close to the North Magnetic Pole – the passage could wait a little. The chosen anchorage was named Gjøahavn, now Gjøahaven, a Canadian historic park.

At Gjøahavn the crew were visited by the local Inuit and Amundsen learned all he could from them on dog-driving, sledging (particularly how to coat sledge runners with ice so they slid more easily), clothing, igloo building and survival techniques, lessons that proved invaluable later in Antarctica. He set out on a sledge journey to find the magnetic pole on 1 March,

but it was too cold for both men and dogs. Forced to retreat, the men had to help haul the sledges, showing Amundsen that manhauling was 'futile toil' (something the Royal Navy had failed to learn despite dozens of lessons). But Amundsen failed to appreciate the lesson of starting too early and made the same mistake again in Antarctica. When he did finally go again he took just one companion, Peder Ristvedt. The two reached Sir James Ross' cairn and found that the pole had moved, the first proof that it migrated. The two men circled the area, but though in his book on the passage journey Amundsen claims to have passed over the 'new' pole he did not in fact approach closer than 50km (30 miles) of the new site. It is not clear why Amundsen did not reach the pole, and the miss rankled with him for the rest of his life.

The sledging took most of the summer; winter came early and the expedition stayed at Gjøahavn. The next summer Ristvedt and Helmer Hanssen explored the east coast of Victoria Island by sledge. Then, on 13 August 1905, *Gjøa* left her harbour and became the first ship to navigate Simpson Strait. After four days the ship had reached Collinson's most easterly point: a North-West Passage had now been fully explored. On 26 August *Gjøa* met the US whaler *Charles Hansson* off Nelson Head, the southernmost point of Banks Island. Further east, at King Point near Herschel Island (west of the mouth of the Mackenzie River) ice stopped *Gjøa*, forcing the crew to overwinter for a third time. In

Above **The crew of *Gjøa* photographed when the ship arrived in Nome, Alaska.**
USA Library of Congress

Below **Dawn, Herschel Island. The island was named by John Franklin for the British father-and-son astronomers.**
Richard Sale

Right **On 6 March 1897 men from whalers moored at Herschel Island were playing baseball on the ice in a temperature of 20°C beneath a blue sky. Within seconds a storm arrived, dropping the temperature to –20°C and creating a white-out. The men scrambled to find cover, any cover, but the next day five bodies, all frozen to death, were found. Eight years later Amundsen arrived at the island. It was from Herschel that Amundsen headed south with the news that he had completed the North-West Passage.**
Richard Sale

Above **The eastern end of the Bellot Strait. At its narrowest the strait is barely 300m (1,000ft) wide, but over 600m (2,000ft) deep. On its southern side is Zenith Point, the most northerly point of the American mainland. Though discovered and sledged in the winter of 1851/2 by Joseph René Bellot, the strait was not navigated until 1942.**
Richard Sale

Above **The SS *Manhattan* nears Point Barrow during the first commercial transit of the North-West Passage.**
US Navy Historical Centre

October, using dog-sledges, Amundsen, two Inuit and William Moys, captain of a shipwrecked US whaler, travelled south to Eagle City where Amundsen formally announced his completion of the passage. Technically, of course, that was not completed until 1926 when, with Amundsen back on board but one crewman, Gustav Wiik, having died, *Gjøa* was sailed around Point Barrow and through the Bering Strait. The ship reached San Francisco on 19 October 1906 where it stayed until 1972 when it was returned to Norway to stand close to *Fram* on Oslo's Bygdøy museum's site.

Not until 1940 was Amundsen's traverse repeated, and then in the opposite direction, the Canadian Henry Larsen skippering the *St Roch* from west to east, over-wintering at Cambridge Bay and Sir James Ross Strait. In 1942 *St Roch* went through Bellot Strait (the first transit by ship) to reach Lancaster Sound rather than following *Gjøa*'s route. In 1944 Larsen took the *St Roch* west again, following the northern passage – west from Lancaster Sound, then south-west along the Prince of Wales Strait. The journey was completed in 86 days, *St Roch* becoming the first vessel to complete the passage in both directions and the first to complete it in one season. In 1962 the USS *Skate* made the first submarine transit, travelling east–west, then in 1969 the 155,000-ton US tanker *Manhattan* made the first commercial transit, using the northern route, escorted by the Canadian icebreaker

John A. Macdonald. Eight years later, in 1977, Dutchman Willy de Roos piloted the 13m (42¹⁄₂ft) ketch *Williwaw* east–west, the first singled-handed transit.

Knud Rasmussen had followed the passage over land (with dog-sledges) as early as the 1920s, a feat which was repeated by the Japanese Naomi Uemura in 1974/6. In 1991/3 the young Spaniard Ramón Hernando de Larramendi followed in their dog tracks, but actually went further. Starting at Narsarsuaq – and travelling with three colleagues, though none of them completed the full journey, joining Larramendi for certain stages – he kayaked Greenland's west coast to Ukkuisissat, then used a dog-sledge to reach Siorpaluk, crossing Smith Sound and Ellesmere Island (to Eureka) before turning south to follow the passage down the Boothia Peninsula's east coast, then along the mainland coast to Inuvik. The team kayaked to Kotzebue and then used dog-sledges to reach Anchorage. A similar, but shortened, journey from Prudhoe Bay to the Gulf of Boothia was made solo by kayak and dog-sledge by Jonathan Waterman in 1997/9.

In 1984 and 1985 the first commercial passenger transits were made east–west, then west–east. Today there are regular passenger trips and, with the possibility of the Arctic ice reducing due to global warming, there are again whispers that a commercial route might become a reality.

The North-East Passage

The conquest of Siberia

In 1533 the three-year-old Ivan IV inherited the title of Grand Prince of Muscovy from his father. Ivan's grandfather, Ivan III, had freed Muscovy from the rule of the Mongol Golden Horde and had expanded the princedom as far as the Urals. In 1547 Ivan was crowned Czar, the first Russian to hold the title. Six years later he established a relationship with western Europe by signing his trade agreement with Richard Chancellor. Ivan IV has become known as Ivan the Terrible, his cruelties being considered gross even during a period of history not noted for the benign treatment of those considered enemies of the state. Ivan's reign of terror, aided by disease, ill-considered military campaigns and, most particularly, a drying up in the supply of furs, had brought Russia to the edge of disaster. The sable, a member of the marten family with a much-prized thick coat, had been all but exterminated in northern Muscovy: without new sources of supply Ivan faced economic ruin. He therefore encouraged (or, at least, failed to discourage: Ivan's support was vague and ambiguous) the Stroganovs, one of Muscovy's most powerful mercantile families (and claimed as the source of the original beef stroganoff), to probe eastwards beyond the Urals where it was known that there was a seemingly limitless supply of furs.

Across the Urals, traditionally the boundary of Europe and Asia, lay Siberia, named from the Mongolian *siber* meaning beautiful and pure or, perhaps, from the Tartar *sibir*, which translates as 'sleeping land'. The sheer scale of Siberia is breathtaking. Trains on the Trans-Siberian Railway take eight days to chug their way from Moscow to Vladivostock, six of those days spent east of the Urals. East of the Europe/Asia obelisk the train crosses five time zones. East of Vladivostock, a traveller would cross three more as he edged around the Sea of Okhotsk and continued to Bering Strait. Siberia stretches from the Arctic Ocean to the Mongolian Steppes: it covers almost 8 per cent of the world's land area. The whole of the United States of America, including Alaska, together with all the countries of Europe (apart from European Russia) could be fitted into Siberia; an area three times the size of Italy would remain uncovered. Lake Baikal, Siberia's largest lake is, by volume, the largest freshwater lake on earth, holding one-fifth of the world's fresh water. Each of its three great rivers – the Lena, the Ob and the Yenisey –

drains a basin bigger than western Europe. But the size of Siberia is modern knowledge: when Ivan took an interest in the area the Russians knew only that it extended as far as Lake Baikal.

It is usually written that it was to this majestic wilderness that the Stroganovs sent Vasily Timofeyevich, a notorious cossack and Volga pirate known as Ermak. In reality Ermak crossed the Urals – hauling boats over the mountains so he could make use of the rivers beyond – to attack the Mongolian khanate of Siberia, which at that time comprised only what is now the south-western corner of modern Siberia. Ermak was a leader in the Ivan the Terrible style, anyone foolish enough to question his authority being tied in a sack along with a bag of sand and dumped in the nearest river. He seems to have been driven by the chance of plunder rather than only expansionist zeal, but the vast wealth in furs he 'liberated' from the control of avaricious middlemen led to a massive Russian expansion eastwards. In that sense Ermak can be seen as having led the Russians into Siberia. Ironically, in view of his preferred method of disposing of his enemies, Ermak died by drowning during a river crossing, weighed down by his massive armour.

At first, despite his tacit support for the Stroganov initiative, Ivan was appalled by the reprisal raids Ermak's incursions generated on Russia's southern border. His mood soon changed when the first batch of furs, thousands of sable, arrived. Within a century the Russians had reached Kamchatka, leaving only the extremities of Taimyr and Chukotka beyond the Czar's grasp. In Moscow the arm of government which administered Ermak's first conquest was called Sibirskiy Prikaz, the Siberia Department, which had administered the khanate during the Mongolian rule of Russia. As Russia expanded eastwards the department took over the administration of all the land east of the Urals, but the name remained the same and so the modern Siberia came into being. In view of the source of the name it was a fortunate accident, for Siberia really is the most beautiful land.

The fur trappers and, to a lesser extent, the religious dissidents who followed them, explored Siberia by water rather than land. In this they were not only applying common sense in so vast a land, but following a tradition which was centuries old. The aboriginal peoples of northern Russia close to the White Sea were land-dwellers herding reindeer in much the same way as their Saami cousins to the west. These folk were displaced, in part at least, by migrants from central

Above **A model of *Mangazeya* in the Arctic and Antarctic Institute's museum, St Petersburg. Mangazeya was built at the mouth of the Ob in 1601, one of the first fortified Russian towns in Siberia. The town was built entirely of wood; even the streets were paved with logs. Within a few years Mangazeya was the richest, most important town in Siberia, an equal to the 19th-century gold-rush towns of Alaska, but its fall was equally spectacular. As the Russian conquest of Siberia expanded, the town's fortunes rapidly declined: by 1672 it had been abandoned.**
Richard Sale

Above **The ancient peoples of the White Sea coast were once known as Samoyed. The name is now considered a term of abuse, akin to Eskimo. Originally the word was thought to mean 'self-eater' and Samoyeds were widely believed to be cannibals. It is probable that the word actually derives from Saami, the now-preferred term for Lapps as the folk were closely related to the Saami of the Kola Peninsula. Today the people call themselves Nentsy. During his journey through the area in 1893 Frederick Jackson, whom Nansen met on Franz Josef Land, drew this picture of a now long-gone Nentsy ritual site on Vaygach Island. The site consisted of one large and many small carved wooden effigies and a vast heap of reindeer antlers and polar bear skulls. This illustration of the site is from Frederick Jackson's *The Great Frozen Land*.**
Richard Sale Collection

Russia. Documentary evidence shows that as early as the 12th century the newcomers were using the river systems which feed the White Sea in order to trade.

By the 15th century the area around the White Sea was being called Pomary (from *po mor* – by the sea) and its inhabitants were famous as hunters who travelled the ice and seas of the local Arctic in search of seals, walrus and bears. There is a tradition that the Starostin family hunted in Svalbard prior to the founding of the Solovetsk monastery (on an island in the White Sea) in 1425, and documents suggesting the Russian Czar had taken possession of 'Grumant' in the mid-16th century. Grumant is Greenland, but it was at first thought that Svalbard was part of Greenland.

Russian scholars believe the anecdotal/documentary evidence is strong proof of Pomore activity in Svalbard prior to the Barents expedition and have even claimed dendrochronological evidence dating from the mid-16th century to support this. Western sources are more sceptical, pointing out that wood could have been carried to Svalbard by currents, or by the hunters themselves. The debate has a political overtone, Norway being consistently nervous about the strength of its sovereignty claim over Svalbard, particularly with a Russian presence on the islands and the oddity of Svalbard's position after the implementation of the Schengen Agreement on 1 January 2001. Since it is certain that the Pomores reached Novaya Zemlya it seems likely that they did indeed reach Svalbard before Barents, though whether this was as early as the 14th or 15th centuries is questionable. The Pomores used the *koch*, a superbly adapted vessel for exploring Arctic waters. The koch was small with curved sides and a rounded bottom so that it would ride up under ice pressure. It had a single mast and sail, but was light enough to be rowed. This, and its shallow draft, made it highly manoeuvrable in ice, its rounded bottom

Above **The ruins of a Russian cross on Kvitøya, one of the islands of the Svalbard archipelago. Although the cross is almost certainly later than the Pomores, it is indicative of the long Russian history of this area of the Arctic.**
Per Michelsen

allowing it to be readily freed if pack ice threatened to trap it. The koch looked somewhat like *Gjøa*, Amundsen's North-West Passage ship. The same design, now known as a *karbas*, is still in use today in the White Sea, a wooden ship usually still held together in the traditional way with nails of juniper. Juniper does not rust or split the wood if ice pressure moves the timbers, as metal nails would.

The Pomores could survive for several weeks in the boats and almost indefinitely off the land. In 1743 four men were accidentally marooned on Edgeøya (off Spitsbergen's eastern coast) when the ice-bound ship they had left for a night ashore had disappeared by the next morning. For six years they survived by hunting, drinking blood to ward off scurvy (the one man who objected to drinking blood died) and were in good health when rescued in 1749. Though this was at least 200 years after the supposed first Svalbard journeys survival technology had altered little over that time, implying an integration with the environment almost to Inuit standards.

Over the years that followed the Russian expansion into Siberia, Pomore skills at navigating rivers and the icy seas off the northern Siberian shore were critical. The term 'cossack' derives from the Chinese for 'a man who has no king', men who lived beyond the emperor's rule. In Russia cossacks were those who avoided or bought their way out of serfdom when it was instigated at the time of Ivan III. Cossacks lived on the edge of society: they were frontiersman, a tough breed who were Russia's first line of defence against Mongol and Tartar incursions, and who led the settlement of Siberia. Ermak was a cossack, and it was cossacks who led the groups of *promyshlenniki* (hunters and trappers) that pushed ever eastwards. By 1620 they had reached Taimyr, rounding Cape Chelyuskin, the northernmost point of the Eurasian mainland. By 1630 they had reached the Lena River. In 1633 the cossack Ivan Rebrov sailed down the Lena to the sea, turned east and reached the Yana River and, later, the Indigirka. In 1642 Mikhail Stadukhin reached the Kolyma River, though by then another cossack, Dimitri Kopylov, had already seen the Pacific. In 1639 Kopylov had led a band of promyshlenniki along the Okhota (hunter) River to a foggy bay crammed with driftwood. The sea that brought the wood ashore was called Okhotsk after the trapping party.

Dezhnev sails east

One of the most significant of all expeditions to the Arctic took place in the north in 1648. Despite the vast wealth of Siberia, new sources of sable and other fur-bearing animals were always being sought. It is estimated that during the last half of the 17th century over 100,000 sable were trapped annually. By 1648 rumours were spreading that the country of the Anadyr River, which reached the Sea of Okhotsk in southern Chukotka, was rich in fur. That way, too, lay mammoth and walrus ivory, and an expedition set out to discover a sea route to both treasuries. The nominal leader of the expedition was a trader, Fedot Alekseyev, an agent for a wealthy Moscow merchant. Moscow appointed the cossack Semen Ivanovich Dezhnev to protect Alekseyev and his promyshlenniki. Little is known of Dezhnev. He was probably a Pomore born in about 1605, and had seen service with Stadukhin. The expedition which now bears his name consisted of seven kochs, his own, those of Alekseyev, and others filled with unattached but eager promyshlenniki, 90 men in total.

The expedition left in June 1648. In ice conditions which must have been remarkably favourable, but weather which was not, the expedition had lost four ships before Chukotka was reached, and another was wrecked on the Chukotka coast. The remaining two, commanded by Alekseyev and Dezhnev, rounded Cape Dezhnev, Chukotka's north-eastern tip, and sighted the Diomede Islands. The men landed on the Chukotka shore where there was a skirmish with the native folk: back at sea the two ships were separated in a storm.

Alekseyev and his men were never seen again, though Alekseyev's Yakut mistress did survive. (Alekseyev's mistress was likely to have been a hostage, it being standard practice among the promyshlenniki to take local hostages which were then ransomed, usually for pelts: it is unlikely that the relationship between Alekseyev and the woman was a love match.) Dezhnev's koch was driven south of the Anadyr River and then ashore. The ship had travelled over 3,000km (2,000 miles) in 100 days and passed through the Bering Strait.

Dezhnev still had 25 men with him. They crossed the mountains to reach the Anadyr but discovered that its valley had neither sable nor game animals (it had, possibly, already been exhausted by local hunters). A group of 12 men went upriver looking for food, but found none, nine men disappearing as they trekked back to the river mouth. The survivors overwintered, then built boats of driftwood and went upriver again. They overwintered once more and then, amazingly, met a group of men from a team commanded by Mikhail Stadukhin who, unaware of the sea expedition, had walked to the Anadyr.

Several more men were killed in fights with locals, but Dezhnev, emboldened by the relative ease with which Stadukhin had reached the Anadyr overland, was determined to explore the area. At the river's mouth he found a huge walrus colony, collecting a load of ivory. He also met Alekseyev's mistress. She told him that Alekseyev's koch had been driven ashore, that all but a handful of the men had been killed in a battle with natives, and that the survivors had died. (There was a persistent rumour that they had reached Kamchatka and lived there for several years, but no firm evidence has ever been discovered to substantiate this.) Finally Dezhnev returned home. Over subsequent years he returned to the Anadyr, collecting over 2 tons of walrus ivory. Later he successfully petitioned for a reward for his discoveries and eventually retired to Moscow.

Bering and Russian America

Strangely, despite both its significance and its value as an epic tale of adventure and survival, Dezhnev's journey was forgotten for almost a century. Before its rediscovery Peter the Great had sponsored an expedition which, though achieving much less than Dezhnev's, has become much better known. Czar Peter was an enthusiastic amateur geographer, but his interest in Russia's Arctic coast had to take second place to foreign wars and the feuding of St Petersburg. In late

Above **A koch, as would have been used by Semen Dezhnev.**
This drawing is from Mikhail Belov *Arctic voyages and the design of Russian ships in the 17th century.*
Richard Sale Collection

Above **The lighthouse/memorial to Semen Dezhnev at Cape Dezhnev, the easternmost point of Asia.**
Richard Sale

1724 Peter helped rescue sailors from a capsized boat in the Gulf of Finland. The icy waters chilled him and he developed pneumonia. As he lay dying he finally gave orders for an expedition to see if Asia and America were joined at the Chukotka Peninsula. Interestingly he noted that he had seen a map which indicated 'a passage through the Arctic Sea'. Did a misty knowledge of Dezhnev's journey exist?

On 26 January 1725 Peter signed the papers that finalised the expedition. Two days later he died. The man appointed to lead the expedition was Vitus Jonassen Bering, a 44-year-old Dane recently retired from Russia's Imperial Navy. To make the voyage the Russians decided to take the expedition overland to the Sea of Okhotsk, then to cross it in ships built at the shore. They would then cross Kamchatka and build a ship for the northern journey on the peninsula's eastern shore. This epic journey took three-and-a-half years. On the journey across Siberia one section of the expedition, separated from the forward party, had to eat their horses, then their leather harnesses, and finally their clothing and boots to fend off starvation. Ill-clad and bootless they survived the winter in holes dug in the snow, a curiously amateur scenario given the abundance of food Siberia offered any man with a gun. At the Sea of Okhotsk the expedition discovered that the local timber was so poor nails were useless and built a craft (the *Fortuna*, probably named in hope rather than expectation) that was held together with leather straps, more raft than ship. In this they successfully crossed to Kamchatka twice (a crossing of 1000km/600 miles each way, a remarkable achievement), ferrying all their supplies and men.

On Kamchatka, Bering had to cross the rugged mountain chain that runs down the spine of the peninsula, an epic journey through blizzards that 'rolled like a dark smoke over moors' with nights spent in snow holes. Living off the land now, his supplies having dwindled away, Bering built his ship, the *Svyatoy Gavriil* (St Gabriel). On 14 July 1728 the ship sailed from the Kamchatka River. Bering had spent three-and-a-half years getting to this point: his ship was stacked with food for another year. His voyage lasted just 51 days. Sailing north-east he hit the southern Chukotka coast, following it east to discover St Lawrence Island (named for the saint's feast day, on which it was first sighted). He then sailed north, bad weather preventing him from seeing the Alaskan coast to the east. During a friendly meeting with some Chukchi natives Bering was told that the Asian coast soon turned west, not east towards America. With this information he discussed options with his two deputy commanders. Alexei Chirikov, a Russian assigned to the expedition as a navigator, felt they should press on to the Kolyma River and so prove the absence of a land bridge. Martin Spanberg, a Dane like Bering, disagreed, believing their mission was accomplished. Bering sided with Spanberg and after a couple of days' sailing, reaching 67°19'N, the ship turned south again.

History has been kind to Bering: James Cook, who surveyed the area 50 years later, named the strait and the sea beyond it (where Bering turned) for him. Cook did not know of Dezhnev's journey; neither did the Russians in St Petersburg, but they were far less impressed by Bering's incautious uninspiring voyage than Cook, despite the leadership he had shown during the crossing of Siberia. He had explored neither the Chukotka nor American shores, he had not proven beyond doubt that no land bridge existed, and he had returned along his outward route when an eastern deviation might (and almost certainly would) have brought new discoveries.

Yet despite official displeasure, when Bering submitted plans for a second expedition they were approved. During this second Kamchatka Expedition (1741/2) Bering discovered some of the Aleutian Islands and Kayak Islands, while his deputy – Alexei Chirikov again – discovered Prince of Wales Island. Chirikov's attempted landing in southern Alaska was disastrous: he sent his first mate, Abraham Dementiev, ashore with ten armed men, but they did not return, forcing Chirikov to depart. A local legend maintains that the native Indians killed the Russians, but some experts believe it is more likely they were drowned when their boats were caught in the now-notorious rip tides of the Lisyansky Strait.

The expedition also included Georg W. Steller, the German naturalist becoming the first European to land on Alaska when, sensing history in the moment, he leapt ashore first at Kayak Island. Steller's name is associated with several Alaskan species, most notably Steller's (or Northern) sea lion and Steller's sea cow. These animals kept some of the members of the expedition alive when Bering's ship (the *St Peter*) was wrecked on one of the Commander Islands. Bering and many other members of his crew died of scurvy on the island, now called Bering Island in his honour. Steller's sea cow was a huge manatee, up to 8m (26ft) long and weighing 6 tons. Its size, slowness, docility and taste were a lethal combination and it was hunted mercilessly by early travellers. It was discovered in 1741: by 1768 it was extinct.

Part of the cargo which the survivors of Bering's second expedition brought back to Russia were sea-otter pelts. The pelts generated a new rush of exploration, the sea otter being pursued eastwards, along the Aleutian chain and through southern Alaska as numbers in each of its strongholds were drastically reduced. It is estimated that in the first 20 years of the 19th century Russia took over 70,000 sea otters, as well

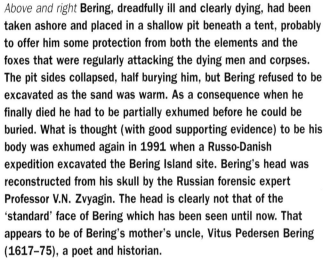

Above and right **Bering, dreadfully ill and clearly dying, had been taken ashore and placed in a shallow pit beneath a tent, probably to offer him some protection from both the elements and the foxes that were regularly attacking the dying men and corpses. The pit sides collapsed, half burying him, but Bering refused to be excavated as the sand was warm. As a consequence when he finally died he had to be partially exhumed before he could be buried. What is thought (with good supporting evidence) to be his body was exhumed again in 1991 when a Russo-Danish expedition excavated the Bering Island site. Bering's head was reconstructed from his skull by the Russian forensic expert Professor V.N. Zvyagin. The head is clearly not that of the 'standard' face of Bering which has been seen until now. That appears to be of Bering's mother's uncle, Vitus Pedersen Bering (1617–75), a poet and historian.**
Institute of Forensic Medicine, Moscow, Russia/Svend Albrethsen

Above **The Russian settlement of New Arkhangelsk as seen during the Litke expedition of 1822/9. The site is now occupied by the town of Sitka. The engraving is by Frederich Heinrich von Kittlitz.**
Anchorage Museum of History and Art, Alaska, USA

as 1,250,000 fur seals, 60,000 beaver and other fur-bearing animals. By the middle of the century the animals were all but extinct and the Arctic fox colonies set up on the Aleutian Islands had almost exterminated many local species. Russia was also economically crippled by the Crimean War and nervous about the vulnerability of its American colonies to the British who were active in the Yukon and whose navy patrolled the Pacific: James Cook had already sought the entrance to the North-West Passage and explored Russian America. Nikolai Muraviev, governor-general of Irkutsk, noted that as the USA was 'bound to spread over the whole of North America' (a view which later concerned both Britain and Canada) Russia must come to terms with the

'surrender of our North American possession'. Russia also hoped that the USA might provide protection from the British for Siberia's vulnerable east coast. What followed is usually termed 'the sale' of Alaska to the USA (for $7.2millon, the Russians having beaten the Americans up from $5,000,000). Despite the price being less than 2 cents per acre, there were many in the US who thought it high, and it took a long while for Russia to extract any cash. But the 'sale' was not all it seemed. It was, rather, a 100-year lease agreement, explaining why it was not until 1969 that Alaska became a State of the Union. There were also oddities over the lease payments which were suspended in 1917 after the Russian revolution, and may have been the basis of the US arms deal with Stalin during the 1939–45 war. The whole subject is shrouded in mystery and even now is largely classified information.

The Great Northern Expedition
Bering's Second Kamchatka Expedition was one detachment of what became known as the Great Northern Expedition, an enterprise which, building on Bering's suggestion, surveyed the entire north coast of Russia from the White Sea to Chukotka (and also the east coast as far as Japan), a monumental exercise. In part the work was carried out to explore the feasibility of a

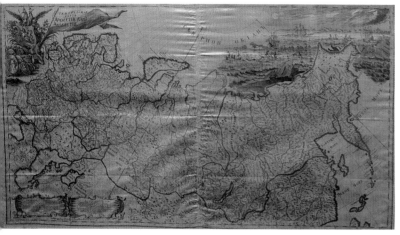

Top **An aerial view of Cape Chelyuskin, the most northerly point of Eurasia. It was first reached on 9 May 1742 by Semen Chelyuskin of the Great Northern Expedition who built a cairn.**
Susan Barr

Above **In 1745 this silk map of Russia was sewn for the Czar. The achievement of the Great Northern Expedition which charted the northern shore was monumental: it was another hundred years before the British had achieved a comparable survey of the Canadian shore.**
Richard Sale

sea route to China – another search for the North-East Passage that had eluded the British and Dutch. The Arctic coast work was completed by five separate teams, their timescales indicating the capricious nature of the Arctic ice. The team charged with surveying from the White Sea to the Ob River failed to complete the task in 1735, driven back by ice and scurvy. The team leaders were court-martialled for failing to carry out their orders, the harshness of that official view being shown when the new leaders did no better in 1736, being forced to overwinter and finally reaching the Ob

Gulf in 1737. The return journey proved no easier, the team finally arriving back in Arkhangelsk in 1739. It had taken six summers to complete the survey.

The team surveying from the Ob to the Yenisey River fared even worse. In the three years 1734–6 they failed to exit the Ob Gulf. Only in 1737 after a sledge party (using reindeer rather than dogs) had been sent out in desperation to complete the task, were ships finally able to make the journey. The teams that were surveying from the Yenisey to the Khatanga River had by far the hardest task, having to round the vast Taimyr Peninsula, Siberia's northernmost landmass. Consequently two teams were used, travelling east from the Yenisey and west from the Lena. The Yenisey team used a ship (the *Ob Pochtalyon* – Ob Postman!) which had reached the Yenisey in 1737. Its commander was Fedor Minin: in five summers he failed to travel more than 450km (280 miles), was court-martialled and reduced in rank to the lowest grade of seaman. Minin did, however, send out a sledge team in 1740. Battling atrocious weather this team managed little more than Minin himself. Heading westward was a team under the cartographer Vasily Pronchishchev which included his wife, who could not bear to be separated from him, and Semen Chelyuskin. In 1736 the team, in the Yakutsk, reached Cape Chelyuskin (then North-East Cape, but subsequently renamed) but were forced to turn back by ice and scurvy. Pronchishchev died of the disease, and within a week his heartbroken wife had died too. Not until 1739 did the Yakutsk, now under Khariton Laptev, try again. Laptev reached Cape Faddeya but was forced to overwinter. In 1740, trying again to reach Cape Chelyuskin, the ship became trapped in the ice and sank; the crew, riddled with scurvy, only just reached safety in time. Laptev gave up the idea of a sea survey, sending out sledging teams which explored all but the most northern Taimyr in 1741. In 1742 Semen Chelyuskin completed the survey, journeying 4,000km (2,500 miles) by sledge, mostly on sea ice.

The final section of coast, from the Lena to Chukotka and on to Kamchatka, occupied the years 1735–41. In 1735 Peter Lasinius in the *Irkutsk* managed no more than ten days sailing from the Lena before the ice trapped him. During the subsequent winter Lasinius and many of his crew died of scurvy. In 1736 Dimitri Laptuv, a cousin of Khariton Laptev, took the Irkutsk as far as Cape Svyatoy Nos. Not until 1740 was the Indigirka River reached. From there a sledge party set out for the Anadyr River, leaving one small part of the Chukotka coast unsurveyed.

The passage completed

Following the success of the Great Northern Expedition in mapping the Russian Arctic coast the idea of a North-East Passage was revived by Mikhail Lomonosov (a Russian academician: Lomonsov was a Pomore and, rumour had it, an illegitimate son of Peter the Great) who suggested that while a coastal passage had been found to be impracticable, a more northerly route might exist. Lomonosov died just before his expedition to explore this possibility set out, Vasili Chichagov taking command. The expedition travelled beyond 80°N between Svalbard and Greenland, aiming for the Bering Strait, but were then stopped by ice. Exploration stalled too, and it was 100 years before another effort was made.

Adolf Erik Nordenskiöld was born in Finland of Swedish parents and studied geology at university. Moving to Sweden at the age of 25 he took part in a number of Arctic expeditions, primarily to Spitsbergen – in 1868 he was on the *Sofia* which reached 81°42′N, then a northing record – but also to the Russian Arctic, particularly to the Kara Sea and as far east as the Yenisey River. These latter journeys taught him a great deal about the area and its ice conditions, and by 1878 he was convinced that with appropriate timing a transit of the North-East Passage was possible. In 1878 Nordenskiöld acquired the *Vega*, a 300-ton, three-masted whaler with a steam engine and, with a crew totalling 30 (including Louis Palander, the ship's captain), set out from Karlskrona in southern Sweden on 22 June. Though Nordenskiöld's journey is often portrayed as a private venture it is worth remembering that it was commissioned and financed by the Russian Czar.

On the first stage of the journey the *Vega* was accompanied by the *Lena*, a much smaller ship with a crew of nine. By early August the ships had reached the Kara Sea, finding it ice-free – Nordenskiöld's earlier voyages had shown him that in late summer the sea had much less ice, though it was frequently ice-filled in early summer.

Nordenskiöld crossed the Kara Sea without incident, reaching Dickson Island (named for Baron Oscar Dickson, patron of many early Arctic voyages) at the northern end of the Yenisey estuary on 6 August. The *Vega* and *Lena* took on fuel from the *Express* and the *Fraser*, two supply ships which had accompanied them, then headed east again, the *Lena* often leading as she drew less water and the coastal waters off Taimyr are shallow. On 19 August the two ships reached Cape Chelyuskin, Nordenskiöld noting that 'the landscape was the dullest

Above **Adolf Erik Nordenskiöld by Georg von Rosem. In the background of the painting the *Vega* is trapped in ice.**
The National Museum of Art, Stockholm, Sweden

Above **Two Chukchi sealskin boats approaching the *Vega*.**
From A.E. Nordenskiöld *Vegas färd kring Asien och Europa*.
Courtesy of the Swedish Polar Research Secretariat

Above **The *Vega* and *Lena* at Cape Chelyuskin.**
From A.E. Nordenskiöld *Vegas färd kring Asien och Europa*.
Courtesy of the Swedish Polar Research Secretariat

and most desolate I have seen in the high north', a sad picture for Eurasia's most northerly point.

Nordenskiöld now attempted to head directly for the New Siberian Islands, but ice forced him south, back to the coast. The Lena delta was reached on 27 August, the *Lena* then leaving to follow the river to Yakutsk. The *Vega* continued through open water, detouring to the southernmost of the New Siberian Islands but being unable to land because of shallow water. By 5 September Nordenskiöld had reached the huge bay of Chaunskaya Guba. The next day they met their first Chukchis. Interestingly, the Chukchis could speak no Russian, but did have a smattering of English, presumably picked up from American whalers. Continuing along the coast Nordenskiöld met the first serious ice of the voyage at Cape Schmidta. This held the ship up for four days: it was to prove a crucial delay as they were stopped again on 28 September, just two days' sailing from Cape Dezhnev. This time the ice did not disperse: winter had arrived and it held the ship until the summer of 1879.

The winter was spent comfortably, a credit to Nordenskiöld's thorough preparations. Scurvy was eliminated by stocks of cloudberries and cranberry juice, and good clothing kept the crew warm in temperatures down to −46°C. The ship's food was good and plentiful, and often traded with the Chukchis for fresh meat. A hole was kept open in the ice in case water was needed to douse a fire (the *Vega* being heated by four cast-iron stoves) and to measure the tides, one of a series of scientific studies which included the building out of snow-blocks a geomagnetic observatory.

On 18 July 1879 the *Vega* became free. Two days later she passed Cape Dezhnev and reached the Bering Strait. The completion of the North-East Passage had been a masterpiece of good organisation and seamanship, and is one of the greatest of all polar voyages. But Nordenskiöld had not yet finished. The *Vega* sailed on to Japan, then around China to the Indian Ocean and across it to reach the Suez Canal. She sailed across the Mediterranean to the Straits of Gibraltar, then around Portugal, Spain and France to the English Channel and the North Sea, finally reaching Sweden in April 1880. At every stop on the way Nordenskiöld was fêted. On 24 April (still Vega Day in Sweden) the ship reached Stockholm. As the ship sailed into the city the sun broke through the clouds and a double rainbow formed above her, entrancing the thousands who had turned out to see the travellers return. Nordenskiöld was made a baron and he continued his travels to the Arctic, making important journeys to the Greenland ice cap. He died in 1901 aged 68.

Above **An aerial view of the remnants of *Baymaud* in Cambridge Bay.**
Susan Barr

Above **By 1920 Amundsen was newsworthy in the USA as this newspaper cutting shows.**
Richard Sale Collection

Amundsen and the *Maud*

The second west-to-east transit, and the third overall, was made by Roald Amundsen in the *Maud*. Amundsen's plan was to repeat Nansen's drift in *Fram*, but the ship was in too poor a condition. Amundsen therefore had *Maud* (named for the Norwegian queen) built, modelling her on *Fram*. At her launch Amundsen smashed a block of ice rather than the customary bottle of champagne across her bow, saying 'You are for ice. You shall spend your best years in ice and you shall do your work in ice'. *Maud* left Oslo in June 1918 with a crew that included Helmer Hanssen, veteran of *Gjøa* and the South Pole, and Oscar Wisting who had also been to the pole.

Amundsen went north, passing Cape Chelyuskin the first summer, but being forced to overwinter soon after. During the winter he fell, breaking his shoulder, was mauled by a polar bear and almost died of carbon-monoxide poisoning. Two sailors (Tessem and Knutsen) also left the ship and headed for Dickson on skis. Both died on the way. Later authors have suggested that Amundsen's known lack of sympathy for sick crew members was the reason behind Tessem leaving the ship, and that Amundsen must therefore bear responsibility for his death. The evidence is less persuasive: Tessem was certainly suffering from headaches (migraine attacks?) but there does not seem to have been undue pressure on him to go. Knutsen volunteered to accompany him: although the journey to Dickson was straightforward it was obviously foolhardy to go alone. What exactly happened is a mystery, but Russian historians believe Knutsen died, probably in an accident, though his

body has never been discovered. A body, believed to be that of Tessem, was found: it is thought that as he was crossing a frozen river close to Dickson he slipped, hit his head and died. A memorial to him has been raised above his grave at Dickson.

Maud was not released from the ice until September 1919, but could only sail for 11 days before being frozen in again near Ayon Island. In 1920 *Maud* was released in early July and rounded Cape Dezhnev. By now Amundsen had given up the idea of immediately repeating the *Fram* drift and headed for Nome, Alaska where he arrived on 27 July. After resupplying the ship he sailed north again. Only three of the original crew were willing to sail this time – one was Oscar Wisting, but this time Helmer Hanssen did not go – and Amundsen intended to recruit Chukchis for the voyage. *Maud* was forced to overwinter at Cape Sverdzekamen (Cape Stoneheart). During the winter her propeller was damaged, and in July 1921 she sailed back to Nome and then on to Seattle. By now Amundsen had lost interest in the expedition, his enthusiasm fired by the thought of flying to the pole. Oscar Wisting tried to take *Maud* north once more, but failed to reach 77° at the New Siberian Islands. *Maud* returned to Seattle where she was seized by Amundsen's creditors. She was bought by the Hudson's Bay Company, renamed *Baymaud* and intended for use as a supply vessel. She was unsuitable, drawing too much water, and was abandoned at Cambridge Bay where she sank at her mooring in August 1930. Today the sad remnants of the ship, just breaking the surface, are a visitor curio.

Развертываются и укрепляются на льду первые палатки

The *Chelyuskin* rescue

Despite the obvious difficulties involved in transits of the North-East Passage Russian (by now Soviet) enthusiasm for a northern sea route was undiminished. In July 1932 Vladimir Voronin took the sealer *Aledsandr Sibiryakov* eastwards, going around the northern tip of Severnaya Zemlya, the first vessel to make that trip. Heavy ice off Chukotka smashed the ship's propeller, but using a makeshift sail the *Sibiryakov* reached the Bering Strait, the first one-season transit. Encouraged, the Soviets sent a fleet of 11 ships eastwards in 1933. One was the 4,000-ton *Chelyuskin*, not an ice-breaker, but sufficiently large to nose through significant ice. Entering a narrow lead off Chukotka the *Chelyuskin* became ice-bound, drifting into Bering Strait, then north-west towards Wrangel Island. After wintering in the ice, on 13 February 1934 the ship was crushed and sank. The quartermaster, who had stayed on board until the end, was knocked over by a shifting barrel as he attempted to jump to safety and was drowned. The 104 survivors – including a baby girl born in 31 August 1932 in the Kara Sea and named, of course, Karina – set up a camp on the ice, the expedition leader Professor Otto Schmidt citing Albanov's journey as the reason for not attempting a crossing of the ice to Chukotka or Wrangel.

Ample supplies were removed from the *Chelyuskin* before she sank and the campers had a reasonably comfortable time awaiting rescue by air, their stay enlivened (or perhaps not!) by a non-stop series of lectures by Schmidt, a devout Communist. Starting on 5 March and continuing until 13 April, seven pilots made repeated flights to a makeshift ice runway and safely rescued all the survivors. The pilots (Lyapidevski, Levanevski, Molokov, Kamanin, Slepnev, Vodopyanov and Doronin) were the first people to be awarded the Hero of the Soviet Union, Anatoli Lyapidevski being the very first recipient.

Following the loss of the *Chelyuskin* there were further transits of the passage in the 1930s, but it has never become a regular route either for Soviet/Russian or other shipping. The passage has also had commercial tourist transits by ex-Soviet Academy ice-breakers, though these too have been limited in number. It is likely that even if global warming reduced the ice cover north of Siberia, Russian nervousness about foreign vessels near its northern shore will mean that the passage will not become a popular route.

Explorers in the west

Canada: *Fram* II

In 1880 the British ceded their rights to the islands discovered by its North-West Passage expeditions to Canada. The move formally ended British interest in the passage and would also, it was hoped, encourage the recently established Canadian Confederation to take control of the area which was by then being seen as 'open land' to whalers and explorers. But the young Canada had more pressing problems – expanding and consolidating its confederacy south of the treeline.

In 1902 Otto Sverdrup, captain of the *Fram* on Nansen's expedition, led his own expedition, the second in *Fram*. This was a masterpiece of organisation and execution. During 1898–1902 Sverdrup and his 15-man crew (one of whom was Sverre Hassel, later to go with Amundsen to the South Pole) charted over 250,000 sq km (100,000 sq miles) of the Arctic using *Fram* and sledges. Ellesmere Island's west coast was explored, Axel Heiberg and the Ringnes Islands discovered. The 'new' lands were named for the expedition's sponsors (Heiberg was a Norwegian consul, the Ringnes brothers owned an Oslo brewery) and at first claimed for Norway. This claim eventually awakened concerns in Canada over the ownership of all the Arctic islands off the mainland coast. With the US making noises that were interpreted as suggesting it might be willing to dispute ownership with both Canada and Norway, Canada eventually claimed all lands north to the pole and compensated Sverdrup for taking possession of his charts as a means of substantiating the claim. The amount to be paid was argued over and eventually settled at $67,000, paid on

Below **Memorial cross on Ellesmere Island. Beyond is the frozen sea of Slidre Fjord and Axel Heiberg Island. Was this cross set up by Sverdrup's crew? Two men died on the trip but both were apparently buried at sea. One of those who died was the ship's doctor who committed suicide. The history of Arctic exploration is littered with the suicides of doctors, probably because of their easy access to drugs. Close to the cross scurvy grass grows. The** site seems too small to be a grave site, which might explain the grass as having sprung from the stomach or pocket of the interred corpse. Did it fall from the pocket of one of the men erecting the cross? If so, that is evidence for it having been erected by Sverdrup as later explorers would not have carried such a basic antiscorbutant.

Richard Sale

11 November 1930. Sverdrup died on 26 November aged 76. He had worked until he was 72 when the Norwegian government belatedly awarded him a pension: he was grateful for the Canadian cash as it offered his wife security.

Canada: the *Karluk* disaster

In the wake of the Sverdrup voyage, and following disturbing news that whalers who had established a base on Herschel Island were 'debauching' the local Inuit, the Canadian government finally acted on the Arctic islands. In 1904 the government bought the *Gauss* (which had taken Drygalski's German expedition to Antarctica), renamed it *Arctic* and placed it under the command of the Quebecois Joseph-Elzéar Bernier. In a series of expeditions from 1904 to 1911 Bernier visited many of the islands of Arctic Canada, retrieving historically important documents left by the British, rebuilding cairns and adding his own cairns and plaques to establish Canadian sovereignty. He also made several unsuccessful attempts to navigate the North-West Passage.

Following Bernier's expeditions Canada underwrote the Canadian Arctic Expedition of Vilhjalmur Stefansson, which sailed in 1913. The voyage, in the *Karluk*, was an Arctic contemporary of Shackleton's *Endurance* and followed the same pattern: ship beset in the ice, ship sinks, crew faces difficult journey to land. However, there was to be no joyful ending; the *Karluk* crew's retreat was a harrowing tale of death and misery. Nor was their journey behind the guiding light of a great leader, the tale – largely ignored for decades, but recently revived – adding another chapter to the story of a controversial explorer.

Stefansson was Canadian-born of Icelandic parents and attracted early attention with his claims that British failure in the Arctic had been the result of a mindset that it was a hostile, barren wasteland where man could not survive unless he took his civilisation with him. In reality, Stefansson claimed, the Arctic was a friendly place, its tundra a vegetation-rich prairie, its sea a wildlife paradise, its abundance able to support any party willing to exploit it. His argument was compelling, but failed to acknowledge that the Inuit rarely travelled in groups of more than ten or so and, despite his description of them as 'fat and healthy', were frequently the victims of hunger. His view that Franklin's men had died through ignorance also made the valid point (condoned by others) that had they split into smaller groups and gone in different directions they

might have survived. Stefansson's pseudo-science convinced the Canadian government and the Hudson's Bay Company who funded the introduction of reindeer (for herding) to south Baffin. Despite Stefansson's 'Arctic Prairie' the project failed. Stefansson had some training as an ethnologist and, based on very flimsy evidence, also suggested that there was a race of blond Inuit on Victoria Island who were the descendants of the Norse Greenland settlers. The tribe proved to be a myth.

Knud Rasmussen savaged Stefansson for his poor ethnography, while Roald Amundsen criticised his claims as an explorer, though some have suggested that Amundsen's criticisms derived as much from self-interest as fact. But despite the criticisms, Stefansson's gift for self-publicity and the apparent plausibility of his arguments to a government willing to be convinced led to his appointment as leader of the Canadian Arctic Expedition. Stefansson's aim was to search for new land in the Beaufort Sea. Some scientists claimed that currents and ice-drift rates meant that there must be land there, perhaps even a vast amount, and Stefansson relished being its discoverer. He had talked several organisations into funding a search, but when the Canadian government offered to provide more money he immediately changed allegiances.

To captain the *Karluk* Stefansson employed Bob Bartlett, the captain of Peary's North Pole ship and arguably the finest ice captain on the planet. Bartlett had serious reservations about the ship and the lack of organisation of the expedition, but nevertheless took *Karluk* northwards from British Columbia in June 1913, heading for the Bering Strait, Point Barrow and Herschel Island, the expedition's winter base.

Karluk's limited speed made for a long trip. Stefansson told Bartlett to hug the Alaska/Yukon coast so that the expedition could go ashore and continue by sledge if need be, but as they neared Herschel Bartlett chose to head north, following open water leads which, he hoped, would eventually allow him to travel east again. But by September the ship was stuck in the ice. The *Karluk* was carrying a curious band of travellers. There were, as would be expected, scientists and sailors, but there were also Inuit hunters Stefansson had recruited in Alaska, one of whom had brought his wife and two children, girls aged eight and three. On 19 September Stefansson announced that he was heading for the shore to hunt caribou and would be gone for ten days. It was a surprising decision as he had already told the party that caribou were virtually extinct on this section of coast. The team he took – his personal

assistant, the expedition photographer (Hubert, later Sir Hubert, Wilkins, the pioneering polar aviator), the anthropologist and two Inuit hunters – looked more suited to finding blond Inuit or new lands than game animals. Stefansson also took the best dogs.

Soon after Stefansson's departure a violent storm battered the area. Stefansson claimed to have seen the ship, stuck fast in its ice floe, being driven westwards by the wind and that open water between his team and the ship prevented him from returning to her. It is probable that he did – he can hardly have fortuitously invented the correct story. He claims to have headed west to see if *Karluk* had reached shore. What is certain is that he linked up with two ships which had also headed for Herschel carrying other scientists and supplies for the expedition. He reported the situation to Ottawa, noting that the ship might, or might not, sink and that those on board would probably survive. Then he headed north to seek his continent.

The *Karluk* and its 25 passengers and crew drifted west to the Bering Strait, then on towards Siberia. Bartlett knew that the ship's design meant she would likely suffer the fate of the *Jeanette* rather than that of the *Fram* and organised his inexperienced team – Alastair Mackay had been the doctor on Shackleton's *Nimrod* expedition (indeed, he had reached the South Magnetic Pole with Mawson and David) and James Murray had also been on *Nimrod*, but the remainder were mostly polar newcomers – to build igloos on, and transfer supplies onto, the ice. He also built sledges for

the evacuation he knew would be necessary. On 10 January 1914 the ice pressure that had often threatened the ship finally succeeded in rupturing the hull. Bartlett was the last to leave, hoisting the ship's flag and putting Chopin's *Funeral March* on his gramophone. It was still playing when the ship sank.

Bartlett now organised the setting up of supply dumps southwards along a route to Wrangel Island. He also sent a party of six to try to reach Herald Island, a small island north-east of Wrangel. Two of this team returned, reporting that the other four had reached open water short of the island and were searching for a route to it. Mackay and Murray, together with Henri Beauchat, an anthropologist, and sailor Stanley Morris, now decided to strike out on their own. Bartlett tried to dissuade them, but when he failed he gave them the supplies they asked for in exchange for a letter absolving him of responsibility for their future welfare, and wished them well. Several days later a returning supply party told Bartlett that there was no sign of the men sent to Herald Island, or any apparent hope of reaching it, and that Mackay's party had been spotted, utterly exhausted. Bartlett swore them to secrecy so as to avoid alarming the rest: so well did they obey that, writing years later, one survivor was still unaware of the conversation.

Finally Bartlett felt ready to leave 'Shipwreck Camp'. Harnessing all of the dogs and manhauling as well, the survivors moved between supply dumps, at each of which an igloo had been built. The team was

Above **William Laird McKinlay using eiderdown to clean his mug before enjoying a meal of blood soup. The** *Karluk* **survivors on Wrangel survived on a diet of eggs and the roots of the sparse vegetation and the occasional seal they were able to catch. The seals brought abundant food, but not for long, the survivors often facing periods of near starvation when their only meals were soup created from rotting meat scraps and other unappetising morsels.**
Richard Sale Collection

eventually stopped by perpendicular ice ridges almost 20m (66ft) high stretching away in both directions. Here Bartlett proved a brilliant leader by encouraging his team to carve through the ridges, using the debris then created to fill in the troughs between them, rather than trying to find a way around and, perhaps, failing. Ignoring Herald Island, Bartlett pushed for Wrangel which was finally reached on 12 March after a gruelling 20-day trek.

But land brought only relative safety. Wrangel was (and is) uninhabited and barren, a home to walrus and polar bear. It was still 320km (200 miles) to the

Siberian coast. With spring fast approaching the sea-ice bridge to the mainland would soon be gone, so on 18 March Bartlett and one of the Inuit crossed Wrangel and headed south. Their journey took 45 days through some of the most dangerous ice Bartlett could remember. Finally they reached Siberia and a Chukchi village. From it, with replenished supplies they travelled 650km (400 miles) to the shore of the Bering Strait and found a ship bound for Alaska. On 28 May they landed and raised the alarm.

Back on Wrangel three of the remaining members of the *Karluk* team tried to reach Herald Island and the four-man team that had headed there. Slowed by breaking ice they failed, then in a blizzard on the return route they became lost and were stopped by open water. They used a small ice floe as a raft but it capsized, dumping the three into the water. Sodden and freezing they camped, but the ice broke up, again separating them. One man, Chafe, frost-bitten and exhausted, but still with the last of the dogs, tied himself to one and released the rest. He reasoned the loose dogs would find the Wrangel camp and that his would follow them, dragging his stumbling body. He was right and, to his joy, he discovered the other two men had also made it. Chafe had six minor operations to stop the spread of gangrene, carried out with a pocket knife: one of the other two had a frost-bitten toe amputated with a hacksaw blade.

To comply with Bartlett's instructions the three men walked to Rodger's Harbour on Wrangel's southern shore, Bartlett believing it was the easiest place a relief ship could reach. Two of them died there, possibly from protein poisoning as a result of their diet, exacerbated by frostbite and exhaustion. Later another member of the team, back at the main camp, died of a bullet wound to the head. It is still debated whether the death was murder, suicide or an accident as the man was cleaning a gun.

In Alaska Bartlett hired the *Bear* to rescue his team. On 20 August 1914, five months after he had left, he brought the ship to within 30km (20 miles) of Wrangel, but was stopped by heavy ice. Forced to return to Alaska for more coal he returned in September to discover that a schooner, the *King and Winge*, alerted by a Russian trader he had met in Siberia, had rescued the survivors on 7 September.

Three men had died on Wrangel. Mackay's team of four were never seen again and in September 1924 an American ship intending to claim Herald Island for the USA found a tent and the bodies of four men: the team

Bartlett had sent had reached the island after all, and had died there. The survivors included all four members of the Inuit family.

While war raged in Europe nothing was heard of Stefansson and it was assumed that he, too, had died. Then in 1918, after five years out of contact, living off the land as he claimed man could, he returned. He had found the last three islands of Canada's Arctic archipelago – Borden, Brock and Mackenzie – but had not discovered the continent he craved. By then *Karluk* had faded from men's minds and Stefansson was greeted as a hero. He wrote a book called *The Friendly Arctic* – an ironic title in view of the death toll on his expedition – in which he gave a biased account of the disaster, blaming Bob Bartlett. Bartlett, who along with other members of *Karluk* believed Stefansson had abandoned the ship rather than going hunting and had already published his own book on the trip, maintained a dignified silence. In 1921 Stefansson organised an expedition to colonise Wrangel Island, an astonishing decision, but not as astonishing as the decision of one of the *Karluk* survivors, Fred Maurer, to join it: perhaps Maurer was trying to exorcise ghosts. Strangely, or perhaps not, Stefansson did not accompany his team of four men and an Inuk woman: one man died and Maurer and the other two men tried to escape by following Bob Bartlett's route to Siberia: they were never seen again. The Inuk was the lone survivor.

William Laird McKinlay, a 25-year-old Scot, survived the *Karluk* disaster then, after a period in hospital, went to war, adding the horrors of the Western Front to those of Wrangel Island. McKinley was wounded and discharged in 1917. For decades he brooded over the injustice of Stefansson's claims about Bartlett. Finally, after 60 years, he published his own account because, he said, he wanted 'to destroy the Stefansson myth, for the man was a consummate liar and cheat'. He also wanted people to understand that despite Stefansson's claims it was Bob Bartlett who was the true hero. The latter wish was granted, Bartlett now being seen as a great explorer in the Shackleton mould. The book was probably too late to secure the first wish. Stefansson was long dead, his latter years spent in honour, though the Canadian government turned down all his subsequent requests for the funding of another expedition.

It has been suggested that Canada's refusal of Stefansson's request was not entirely due to disapproval of his leadership of the 1913 expedition but because he had moved to the USA and it was feared he might betray their flimsy case for sovereignty of the Arctic islands. Following their purchase of the Sverdrup charts the Canadian government sent officers of the Royal Canadian Mounted Police to the Arctic, the presence of a police force underwriting their territorial claims. Larsen's voyages in the *St Roch* can be seen as a further sovereignty statement, though the outrage over the *Manhattan*'s voyage – undertaken without prior consent from Canada – suggests that even in the latter half of the 20th century the Canadians were still nervous about their ownership claims for the archipelago.

Greenland: Egede seeks the Norse settlers

After the failure of the Norse settlements in Greenland there was no contact between Europeans and the Greenlandic Inuit for several centuries. Englishman John Davis met Inuit in 1585 during his voyage in search of the North-West Passage, and there was spasmodic contact and bartered trade during the 17th century. Then in 1703 the Danish king was approached by an Icelander who suggested a more formal trading arrangement and a re-establishment of contact between the Danish Crown (whose territories then included both Iceland and Norway) and Greenland. A few years later the king was petitioned again, this time by Hans Povelsen Egede, a young pastor who wished to find the Norse settlements.

The king accepted both proposals. Egede's search for Norsemen was unsuccessful, but he was charmed by the Inuit and stayed for almost 15 years converting them to Christianity. His attempt to create a new Danish colony failed, however, the settlers abandoning Greenland in the face of their inability to grow sufficient food. During Egede's stay an Inuit child who had been taken to Copenhagen returned carrying smallpox. Around 25 per cent of the Inuit population of Greenland died of the disease, Egede distinguishing himself by his work with the sick and with orphaned children.

But there is a disturbing undercurrent in Egede's evangelism, an inability to comprehend how the Inuit could be so (relatively) good and peaceful, an apparent belief that Christian behaviour in a pagan community was itself shameful. Later scholars (for instance Nansen) have questioned Egede's replacement of shamanism with Christianity and the consequent loss of social cohesion. It is also ironic that the Dane's work during the smallpox epidemic was in relieving the victims of a disease imported from Denmark.

Egede travelled the south-western coast of Greenland from Godthåb – now Nuuk (the settlement he established), searching for a mythical channel said to give access to the east coast. Greenland's west coast was always the more accessible of its vast coastlines: it had the larger number of Inuit settlements and remained (relatively) ice-free so that North-West Passage seekers and Franklin searchers had sailed almost its entire length by the 1880s. The east coast was more forbidding, and settlements there were not only fewer in number but much poorer than those on the west coast, their inhabitants constantly on the verge of starvation. Whalers who headed north along the deeply indented east-coast shore risked confrontation with ice that seemed almost malevolent in its relentless pursuit of their ships. In 1777 a dozen ships were trapped there, then smashed and sunk in turn, their crews transferring to those that remained beset but above water. When the last went down, over 300 men were lost. Later the Scoresbys, father and son, mapped sections of the east coast while carrying out one of the most successful of whaling operations. William Scoresby Snr explored Scoresby Sound, which he believed, wrongly, was the elusive channel that Egede had sought which cut across Greenland, while William Jnr sailed to 72°N, noting the reduction in ice that led him to call for renewed attempts to find the North-West Passage.

Following Scoresby Jnr's voyage the British naval officers Clavering and Sabine went even further north along the coast. South of the Scoresby-mapped coast the German Ludwig Giesecke (reputedly the librettist of Mozart's *The Magic Flute*) and Danish naval officer Wilhelm Graah filled in the gaps to Cape Farewell (Kapp Farvel), though it was not until 1883 that other Danish naval officers, Holm and Garde, discovered Ammassalik, the main Inuit settlement on the east coast. Also active was the German Polar Expedition of 1869/70 under Karl Koldeway and Julius von Payer (later the co-discoverer

Above '**Dangers of the Whale Fishery**' from William Scoresby's *An Account of the Arctic Regions.* **This somewhat fanciful illustration was supposed to convey the dangers of whaling to the book's readers. Though hunting whales, particularly sperm whales, was indeed dangerous for the whalers it was, as noted earlier, lethal for the whale.**
Richard Sale Collection

of Franz Josef Land). The expedition comprised two ships, the steam-driven *Germania* and the sailing ship *Hansa* and was intended to reach the North Pole by way of Greenland's east coast, an ambitious, and foolhardy, idea even with the limited knowledge of the day. When the pack ice threatened, the *Germania* steamed away, an apparently misunderstood message not warning her that the *Hansa* was trapped. The *Hansa*'s 14-man crew built a house of coal on the ice and watched the ship sink, 'groups of feeble rats struggling with death and trembling with cold' and the weather batter their floe almost out of existence. With death apparently inevitable the crew finally escaped the ice and reached southern Greenland. Meanwhile the *Germania*, all hopes of the pole gone, surveyed the east coast.

Greenland: Nordenskiöld, Peary and Nansen

With those sections of the Greenlandic coast amenable to exploration by ship surveyed, attention naturally turned to the vast inland icefield covering more than 1.8 million sq km (around 750,000 sq miles). The first steps on this ice sheet were made in 1751 when the Danish trader Lars Dalager and five Inuit penetrated about 15km (10 miles) from near Paamiut (Frederikshåb). Dalager did as well as other early attempts and rather better than the English mountaineer Edward Whymper, conqueror of the Matterhorn, who in two attempts in the 1860s barely got out of

Above **An illustration of ice travel from Robert Peary's *Northward over the Great Ice* which deals with his Greenland trips of 1886 and the 1890s. The illustration is captioned 'coasting' and shows that Peary had already absorbed some good ideas on polar travel: skis (though he is using the 'old-fashioned' long, single stick), lightweight sledges and Inuit clothing. He also seems to have decided that conservation of energy was no bad thing either.**
Richard Sale Collection

sight of the ice edge near Ilulissat (Jakobshavn). The next journeys on to the inland ice were made by the three giants of polar exploration in the late 19th century – Nordenskiöld, Peary and Nansen.

First was Nordenskiöld. In 1870 he made a tentative exploration with a Swedish colleague and two Inuit from a base camp in Auleitsivik Fjord, south of Disco Bay, reaching about 57km (just over 35 miles). He did not return until 1883. By then Nordenskiöld was over 50 and his great journeys were behind him. Starting from the same place as in 1870 his team penetrated about 116km (72$^{1}/_{2}$ miles). From a camp there the expedition's two Saami members Pava Lars Tuorda and Anders Rossa skied on, returning two-and-a-half days later. They claimed to have reached 42°51'W, a distance of 230km (almost 144 miles), though as they had no means of measuring distances modern opinion favours a turning point of 46°W (about 100km/60 miles from Nordenskiöld's camp). The two men reported seeing no exposed land during their whole journey, which surprised Nordenskiöld who believed that Greenland had an ice-free, perhaps even wooded, heart.

The next of the great three to visit the inland ice was Robert Edwin Peary. Peary was born on 6 May 1856 at Cresson, Pennsylvania. When he was three his father died and his mother moved back to Maine, her own state. Peary grew up as an only child, a strangely preoccupied boy made more silent by a lisp that bothered him throughout his life. By 1886 Peary was an engineer in the US navy. That year he requested, and was granted, three months leave and with the Dane Christian Maigaard (assistant governor of the now-defunct settlement of Ritenbank) set off for the inland ice, pushing 160km (100 miles) inland and bivouacking on the ice.

Two years after Peary's first expedition, Nansen arrived on Greenland's east coast. Fridtjof Nansen was born on 10 October 1861 at Christiania (now Oslo) to middle-aged parents whose previous marriages had already provided them with six children. He was very bright and also a good sportsman, excelling at skiing (where he was brave enough to compete in ski jumping, then an infant, and dangerous, sport). He spent a season on a sealer in Arctic waters while at university, then took the curatorship of the zoology department at Bergen Museum. His work on zoology earned him a doctorate; his later work as a Norwegian statesman and with the League of Nations gained him the Nobel Peace Prize in 1922. As a man Nansen was handsome, and very attractive to women; one of his many lovers was Kathleen Scott, Robert Scott's wife. They had conducted the affair while Scott was returning from the pole (and dying in the process). When news came of Amundsen's success he wrote to Kathleen telling her how much he wished her husband had been first. At the same time he wrote to tell another, Norwegian, that he was glad that Amundsen had succeeded. As a man Nansen was vain and arrogant, and by contrast to his success with women, made few male friends. As a scientist and statesman he was a man of immense accomplishments, and as an Arctic explorer a near genius in his imagination of what might be achieved, his arrogance being transformed into a single-mindedness that carried all before it.

Nansen had dreamed of crossing Greenland by ski since the early 1880s, Peary's 1886 trip giving him the incentive to try immediately. Peary's plan was to return and complete the crossing in 1887, but his navy work took him to Nicaragua where after a survey expedition he advocated a canal across that country rather than across Panama: many thought his idea had the greater merit, but Panama was the eventual choice. Peary's absence gave Nansen his chance. His preparations were meticulous. Many of the Franklin searchers had used dogs, particularly the Americans Kane and Hall, but Nansen had no experience with them. The Saami used reindeer, but they eat only lichen and there might be none on Greenland. Nansen therefore decided to use skis and to manhaul his sledges, though he did take a pony.

Until Nansen's journey no one considered manhauling practical: the sledges were either too heavy, or the runners too thin, and so sank into the snow. But Nansen constructed sledges based on the wide-runnered type favoured by Norwegian farmers. He made the first skis to have metal edges, and created sleeping bags and clothing of new designs. He went to Sweden and questioned Nordenskiöld, then the world's foremost polar expert, who was amazed that the Norwegian was planning to ski east-to-west, the opposite way to all previous expeditions. The logical reason for Nansen's choice might have been that Greenland's west coast had more settlements and so it would be easier to reach a satisfactory end point. But that was not Nansen's stated view – he saw a start from the east as a cutting off of the possibility of retreat. It would be, as he later sensationally remarked, 'Death or the west coast'.

For his trip Nansen chose five companions, all of them expert skiers. They were Otto Sverdrup (later captain of the *Fram*), Olaf Dietrichsen, a surgeon, Kristian Kristiansen Trana, and two Saami, Ole Nielsen Ravna and Samuel Johannesen Balto. Nansen had arranged for the sealer *Jason* to take the men to Greenland's east coast, but the deal was that their drop-off should not interfere with sealing. So despite sailing from Iceland in mid-May it was not until 17 July that the ship was close enough to the coast – off Sermilik Fjord – 'for Nansen to feel able to leave her. The team still had 20km (12$\frac{1}{2}$ miles) to go – the *Jason* dare not risk the coastal ice – and this proved to be a very long way. Soon the scattered pack coalesced, and the two boats were trapped. They were now at the mercy of the drifting ice, attempts to reach the shore being defeated by violent storms. With pony feed dwindling and their own rations being depleted, the pony took its place on the menu. That improved the food supply, but not the spirit of the party: all the men feared a possible drift into the Atlantic, but the Saami, no seafarers, feared it most. Then a visiting bear so terrified Balto that he swore that if he survived he would never drink again. When questioned about this strange remark he confessed that he had only volunteered for the trip because he had been drunk at the time.

The team finally reached the coast on 29 July, but were by then almost 400km (250 miles) south of Sermilik. Determined to approach (if not to regain) the fjord Nansen rowed north, keeping the boats close to the shore. On the journey they met an Inuit group which acted as a guide, and by 10 August the team had reached Umivik, an excellent harbour. Here Nansen decided that, though still 160km (100 miles) short of Sermilik, it would have to do as a start point. For five days the weather kept them in camp, then, on 15 August, after safeguarding the boats and leaving some supplies (in case 'death or the west coast' proved a questionable slogan) they started. The steep climb on to the ice cap was hard going – on the first day they managed just 5km (3 miles) and a climb of 200m (660ft), all of it in *finnesko* (reindeer-skin boats) as the gradient was too much for skis. Two more days of hard labour were followed by a storm that kept them pinned in their tents, in which they slept three to a reindeer-skin sleeping bag to share warmth.

The relentlessly hard climb caused Trana to ask, 'How can people wish so much suffering on themselves that they do this?' but still they continued. By 27 August they were over 2,000m (6,600ft) above sea level, but progress was so slow Nansen was forced to change objectives. He had planned to cross from Sermilik to Qasigiannquit (Christianshåb). The change of start point had been forced by the ice drift; the time lost now forcing a change to the finish point. The team would, he decided, head for Nuuk (Godthåb) which was 150km (about 95 miles) closer. On 29 August they reached ice which sloped gently upwards and so they could walk in showshoes, but not until 2 September at over 2,500m (8,200ft) above sea level were they finally able to use skis.

Even with skis the effort was considerable, and almost every day the men were hungry and thirsty. They were also skiing across a polar desert, with nothing to break the white monotony: as the first men to do this the psychological burden must have been considerable. The weather was also trying, with temperatures falling to –40°C and occasional gale-force winds creating whiteouts and forcing snow through every tiny opening in the tents. On the move the chill factor of the wind was appalling. On 4 September Nansen noticed that first his nose hardened and had to be massaged, then his throat went numb and stiff and he had to wrap 'some mittens and other things' around it. Then, worst of all, 'the wind found its way in through my clothes to the region of my stomach and gave rise to horrid pains'. That is from his book. His diary is more explicit, noting 'p [penis] was in the process of freezing'. He solved the problem by stuffing a felt hat down his trousers.

On 19 September the wind blew from behind the team and they rigged sails on their sledges. After several unsuccessful attempts, a steering system was evolved and soon they were speeding along. So much ground was being covered – 70km (about 44 miles) during the day – that Nansen decided to keep going as night fell: it was an almost fatal decision as a huge crevasse was only spotted at the last second. During the day they also saw land ahead: the next day they found pools of water on the glacier and for the first time in weeks could drink their fill. As the ice dropped sharply Nansen was able to identify that below them was a fjord which ran inland from Nuuk. By 24 September they were off the ice, the first time for 40 days: they had crossed 560km (350 miles) of ice.

By 26 September they had almost reached the head of the fjord. The men built a boat, stretching tarpaulin over a scrub-wood frame. In this Nansen and Sverdrup, after a trying time following a river to the fjord, set off for Nuuk. They arrived on 3 October, though it was the 12th before the rest of the team were brought in.

Though Nansen managed to get mail on to the last ship leaving for Denmark that summer he and his men spent the winter in Nuuk. When the team returned to Norway an estimated one-third of the population of

Above **Resting on the inland ice. These engraved illustrations are from Nansen's book on the crossing.**
Richard Sale Collection

Above **Though it was common in Norway to cross-country ski with a single stick Nansen's men invariably used two on the Greenland crossing. However, the sticks were still very long and had no basket to spread the thrust.**
Richard Sale Collection

Above **During the crossing Nansen also realised the value of harnessing the wind. Sails were used by most later explorers, and are a feature of almost all modern expeditions.**
Richard Sale Collection

Oslo was there to welcome them, and they were fêted for ten days. Nansen, in particular, was greeted as a hero, not only in Norway but all over Europe. His reputation as a polar traveller was made: the *Fram* expedition would further it and it would never diminish. In that respect, the difference between Nansen and Amundsen, whose polar achievements were greater, deserves a book in itself.

Nansen's crossing was a bitter blow to Peary whose desire for fame became the chief purpose of his life. He believed that his reconnaissance of 1886 gave him proprietorial rights over the ice cap (much as he later felt over the pole) and resented Nansen's intrusion which he saw as cheating. But he determined to make his own journey, choosing a part of Greenland that was still unexplored: his would be not only a journey of danger, but also of discovery – altogether a better effort. Peary's team was a curious one, comprising his wife, Jo; Matthew Henson, his valet from Nicaragua; the Norwegian Eivind Astrup, an expert skier; Langdon Gibson, a hunter; meteorologist John Verhoeff; and Dr Frederick Cook 'surgeon and ethnologist'. Cook was ten years younger than Peary and had no previous experience of exploration. Later Peary was to note that he felt 'much confidence' in Cook. Later still he was to fear and despise him as a rival, and to loathe him as the attempted usurper of a prize he felt was rightfully (if not, perhaps, actually) his own.

The expedition also included nine fare-paying passengers sent by the Philadelphia Academy of Natural Sciences who were to conduct experiments while the ship was in Greenland. The team sailed from New York in June 1891 in the *Kite*. On 11 July in the pack ice of Melville Bay, north-west Greenland, the ship's rudder struck ice: the tiller swung violently and broke both of Peary's lower leg bones just above the ankle. He had Cook to thank for not only setting the leg so expertly his recovery time was minimised and the leg healed completely, but also for placating the paying passengers when it looked as though the expedition might be called off.

The team established a winter camp in Red Cliff House, McCormick Bay. There Peary and Cook took the first of the series of photographs, some of which appear in Peary's books, more of which appear in their respective collections. Some of those of naked Inuit women would grace the pages of *Playboy*, but most are formal poses – and include men as well. That Peary's interest was not entirely anthropological is supported by his fathering children by an Inuit woman, as did Matthew

Above **Peary's team for his 1891/2 expedition. The very young-looking Henson was to stay with Peary throughout his Arctic career, but Cook became an implacable opponent, in part because of the death of Verhoeff and, later, that of Astrup.**
Richard Sale Collection

Henson. Their half-Inuit grandchildren still live in north-west Greenland.

On 3 May 1892 Peary, with Astrup, Cook and Gibson, each with a four-dog team, set off for the 'White March' on the inland ice. In using dogs Peary logically extended Nansen's advances in polar equipment, adding Inuit lore – he also built snow igloos for camps – to Nansen's Saami-based ideas. The route to the ice was difficult and Peary's leg was hurting. Once on the ice two dogs died and another escaped. Peary now sent Cook and Gibson, with two dogs, back, continuing with Astrup and 14 dogs (one of which soon died). Both men and dogs ate pemmican; later in the trip the dogs' diet was supplemented by being fed their weakest remaining member after it had been killed and cut up.

On 5 June Peary and Astrup crossed the high point of the ice (at 1,740m/5,700ft) and sledged on, the days merging in monotonous similarity until finally on 1 July they reached land again. In bright, warm sunshine they found purple, white and yellow flowers, and twittering snow buntings instead of ice. There were also musk-oxen, which supplemented Peary's wholly inadequate food rations: without the meat from the oxen the two men would probably have died.

What Peary believed he saw to the east was the Arctic Ocean running through a channel – Peary Channel – separating Greenland from a neighbouring island. To the south he saw only frozen ocean. Seeing land where there was only ocean, and (more rarely) ocean where there was land, were mistakes others had and would continue to make, but this one by Peary would have serious implications for others later.

After three idyllic days – warm and sunny, with bees buzzing, butterflies flitting between the flowers, delightful birdlife (including a gyr falcon) and musk-ox steaks – the two men set off for Red Cliff House. Taking a more southerly route which rose to 2,440m (8,000ft) they arrived on 6 August. It had been a remarkable journey even if its successful outcome had owed more to the good fortune of finding muskoxen than meticulous planning similar to Nansen's.

In the little time they had before the *Kite* sailed the team now explored Inglefield Gulf. Verhoeff and Peary had developed a mutual dislike early in the expedition – one reason why Verhoeff did not go on the inland ice trip. This may be why he decided that he would prefer a walk back to Red Cliff House rather than a return by boat. He did not arrive, and despite searches no trace of him was ever found.

Back in the US, Peary's journey – he had sledged some 2,200km (1,400 miles) – was well received. He even had a congratulatory letter from Nansen signed 'Your Admirer'. He lectured extensively, Matthew Henson bringing the five dogs that had survived the inland ice trip on stage at the start of the talk: the dogs lay at Peary's feet as he spoke and, so it is said, stood and howled, in unison and on cue, when he finished. The lecture usually brought the house down. Peary enjoyed the adulation, but knew that he must keep travelling to ensure a constant supply. In 1893, with the approval of the US president (but most definitely not of his overruled navy superiors) he went north again. Astrup and Henson ('my coloured man') were with him, but Cook was not. Cook had asked permission to publish a short report in a medical journal and had been refused: Peary would tolerate no competition. Annoyed, Cook resigned from the expedition.

A new winter hut – Anniversary Lodge – was built and there on 12 September Jo Peary gave birth to a daughter, the Pearys first child: despite her genteel upbringing, Jo was a formidable, courageous woman. Apart from the birth the expedition achieved little, an attempt on the inland ice failing in bad weather. Eivind Astrup surveyed Melville Bay while Peary was away on the attempt – a significant survey, much to Peary's great annoyance – and most of the team went home in 1894. Peary, Henson and Hugh Lee stayed on, and in 1895 Peary repeated his sledge journey to the northeast coast. He took a different route, but again survived only because of the muskoxen there. He then found three meteorites, two of which he transported back to the US. The meteorites – the source of Inuit iron – were very well received and turned the indifferent expedition into an apparent success. His powerful Washington friends persuaded a reluctant navy to allow Peary to return in 1896 for the third, and largest, meteorite. He failed to reach it.

In 1897 the navy, exasperated with his trips, posted him to the west coast, far away from the Arctic, but Peary's friends again intervened and, against official desires, he was granted five years' leave of absence. That year he brought home the largest meteorite and six live Inuit. The acquisition of both meteorites and Inuit is now viewed suspiciously. Peary often spoke of 'my Eskimo' seemingly believing he owned the Inuit around his Greenland bases, just as he later felt that he owned the pole. He once asked of the Inuit 'of what use are they?' and answered himself that they existed only to help him discover the pole. Peary felt that taking the meteorites was acceptable; the Inuit no longer needed a source of iron as he gave them all the iron goods they required (true, though is that the only point?), and he felt justified in surrendering six of their number to the cause of science as he was their saviour. In reality the Inuit did not feel any unreserved adoration of Peary such as many (including Peary) have claimed. They were impressed by the size of his ships and by his gifts, but much less so by him.

It is doubtful whether the six Inuit he brought back to the US thought very highly of him. They were displayed as circus freaks and five died quickly in an unfamiliar New York climate among unfamiliar

Above left **Peary handing out gifts to the Inuit.**
USA Library of Congress

Above right **Inuit obtaining iron from a meteorite. The drawing is by Albert Operti who accompanied Peary on the 1896 trip.**
Richard Sale Collection

The photograph, *above left,* **(taken by Peary's wife) and drawing,** *above,* **show controversial aspects of Peary's dealings with the Inuit which further fuelled Dr Frederick Cook's animosity towards him. Peary's consistent use of the expression 'my Eskimo' and his insistence that he knew what was best for them (even better than they did themselves) have become an embarrassment even to his supporters.**

American illnesses. The only survivor, Minik, an eight-year-old boy, lived on for another 20 years. It was hardly a happy life – as a boy he had not only watched his father and relatives die, but attended a fake burial for his father, only later discovering that his skeleton was exhibited in a museum glass case. The story of the six Inuit is an unpleasant tale of racist abuse and Peary's involvement in it, and his silence during it, does him no credit.

Peary returned to Greenland in 1898, intending both to explore further north and to reach the pole. Henson was with him again but not Astrup who died in January 1896. Frederick Cook later accused Peary of responsibility for the death, claiming his rage at Astrup over the Melville Bay survey had unhinged the young Norwegian and that he had committed suicide as a result. Cook extended the argument to include Verhoeff, whom he also maintained had committed suicide because of Peary's dreadful behaviour. The true cause of Astrup's death is still debated, while Verhoeff's death also remains a mystery.

Consistently paranoic, Peary was now concerned

that Otto Sverdrup, leading the second *Fram* expedition, would steal his ideas, just as Nansen had, and decided to push to Adolphus Greely's Fort Conger base on Ellesmere Island with Henson, the Inuk Ahngmalokto, 16 dogs and three sledges in midwinter and so ensure that Sverdrup could not use it the following spring. Peary and Sverdrup actually met – Sverdrup invited Peary for a coffee, but Peary snootily declined: Henson claims that it was this meeting which made Peary decide on the winter trip to Fort Conger, so convinced was he that Sverdrup had designs on the pole. In fact Sverdrup had no interest in either the pole or Fort Conger and the hasty decision was to cost Peary his toes. Though his report of the incident to Morris K. Jesup, president of the American Museum of Natural History and sponsor of the trip, is laconic and dispassionate ('I found, to my annoyance, that both feet were frosted', '...it was evident I should lose parts or all of several toes' and '...the final amputation was performed') the reality was horrific. When Peary removed his boots, frost-bitten skin fell from his toes, leaving bones emerging from festering flesh. Yet after losing

Above **Peary's ships *Windward* and *Erik* at Nuuk. This fascinating shot is one of a pair of stereo images taken to add to the enjoyment of the US public. The exploits of Peary and other Arctic explorers were hot news in the USA (and in Europe) even before the Cook–Peary controversy gripped nations.**
US Navy Historical Centre

Greenland: the Danes complete the coastal map

Peary's exploration left only the north-eastern coast of Greenland unexplored. The 1906 Danish expedition led by Ludvig Mylius-Erichsen was intended to fill that gap. The expedition sailed in the *Denmark* in 1906, establishing a base at Danmarkshavn at about 75°N. After overwintering, a series of supply depots was established northwards, including one in a cave near Lambert Land (which already lay north of Peary's supposed coastline). Eventually two teams set off northward. At North-East Foreland (well to the east of Peary's supposed coastline) the teams separated. Mylius-Erichsen, with Höeg Hagen and the Greenlander Jorgen Brönlund, headed west to find the Peary Channel. Johan Peter Koch, Tobias Gabrielson and Aage Bertelsen headed north to find the cairn Peary had erected at Cape Bridgman. Koch was successful and had, during his journey, peered into Independence Fjord. On his return he met Mylius-Erichsen whose team had spent a wearying time exploring Danmark Fjord: Peary's Channel had not been found. Koch was convinced it did not exist at the end of Independence Fjord either, but Mylius-Erichsen felt duty-bound to check. The two teams parted. Koch reached the ship after 84 days' sledging: his team had covered almost 2,000km (1,200 miles).

When Mylius-Erichsen had not arrived by September search parties went out, but found nothing. The search was resumed in spring 1908. At the cave on Lambert Land they found the huddled body of Brönlund and a note he had written explaining that Hagen had died on 15 November, and Mylius-Erichsen on the 25th after they had tried to return to the ship over the inland ice. In an act of selfless bravery Brönlund had struggled on, with frost-bitten feet, carrying the notes of the trip to where he knew his body would be found. His own poignant last message began, 'Succumbed at 79 Fjord after attempting return across inland ice in November. I arrived here in fading moonlight and could go no further because of frost-bitten feet and the dark...' The three had followed Independence Fjord to Peary's viewpoint. Forced on to the inland ice by open water as the sea ice melted in late summer their dogs had died and, as winter folded its cold, dark arms around them, so had they.

Koch's search for the bodies of Mylius-Erichsen and Hagen failed. In 1910 the Danes tried again to find them, sending Ejnar Mikkelsen (who had been on the Ziegler-Baldwin expedition) and six others in the 40-ton *Alabama*. One of the crew was Iver Iversen, a mechanic

his toes by 15 March 1899, he was back on the ice by 19 April. Whatever the merits of his North Pole claim and no matter how dubious his treatment of his team members (particularly in this instance, of Henson who undoubtedly saved his life at Conger) and the Inuit, Peary could be eye-wideningly brave.

In 1900, after a winter on north-west Greenland, Peary followed Lockwood's route along the north coast, then pushed on, reaching, and naming, Cape Morris Jesup (Greenland's most northerly point at 83°39'N). The team continued past Cape Bridgman until their supplies finally ran out at Cape Wyckoff on Clarence Wyckoff Island, off the eastern tip of Peary Land, the island that lay beyond the 'Peary Channel'. This trip was the most significant of all Peary's expeditions on Greenland, though he spent two more winters in Greenland. In both 1901 and 1902 he tentatively pushed towards the pole from Ellesmere Island, reaching 84°17'N in April 1902.

Above **Mylius-Erichsen's expedition unloading from the *Danmark*. The performance of the motor car was not much more impressive than it had been for Shackleton.**
Richard Sale Collection

Above **Brönlund's grave site in north-east Greenland.**
Leif Vangaard, Danish Polar Centre, Copenhagen

collected in Iceland from another ship when the *Alabama*'s mechanic turned out to be incompetent. Landing near Cape Bismarck, Mikkelsen relocated Brönlund's body that year and erected a cairn over it. But the autumn journey was at the cost of five toes from one man's foot, amputated without a doctor or antiseptic, and with half a bottle of whisky as anaesthetic.

After wintering on the ship two teams set out in the spring of 1911. Mikkelsen and Iversen went north hoping to find the bodies of Mylius-Erichsen and Hagen, and then to follow the Peary Channel to the west coast. There should have been three men, but Jørgenson, who had survived the amputation of his toes, was not fit to travel. A second team of three men went inland to explore a *nunatak* (rock 'islands' which project above the surrounding 'sea' of ice) discovered by Alfred Wegener during the *Danmark* expedition.

Two men were left at the ship. When the sea ice near the *Alabama* melted she sank, but the two men escaped in time and, together with the returned nunatak team built a hut and then erected a series of cairns to the north as a warning to Mikkelsen should he be forced to return that way. One of these cairns was found by a sealer who sailed to their rescue. To the north and, of course, unaware of the *Alabama*'s fate, Mikkelsen and Iversen had crossed the inland ice and descended, with difficulty, to the head of Danmark Fjord. They found no bodies, but did locate a note in a cairn raised by Mylius-Erichsen. It said that the Peary Channel did not exist, that Peary Land was not an island but part of the mainland. A second note detailed the desperate journey in the heavy snow of late summer with the dogs dying of exhaustion, a prelude to the terrible journey across the inland ice and Brönlund's heroic struggle.

That struggle was about to be repeated by Mikkelsen and Iversen. By the time the two men had reached Lambert Land, battling through the same wet snow, and unable to find any wildlife, all but two of their dogs had died of exhaustion and starvation, and Mikkelsen was so debilitated by scurvy he could no longer walk. Had they not found depots laid down by Koch for Mylius-Erichsen the two would have died. As it was their journey was a fight against appalling weather and starvation punctuated by short periods of eating at the depots. They also ate their last two dogs, even consuming the livers though they knew they were poisonous. At one point Iversen was so desperate for food that he asked Mikkelsen to carry their rifle as he feared he might shoot and eat him. Interestingly, during a discussion on cannibalism (and whether one could eat the other if he died) Iversen said that first he would have to cut off the hands as they are what make a person human: several of the skeletons found by the Franklin search teams had had their hands removed.

Eventually, 30km (20 miles) from Danmarkshavn and its hut, they had to leave everything behind as they no longer had the strength to carry anything except their own weight – and barely that. As they approached the hut they had to rest less than 50m from it as they were too exhausted to go on. After resting at the hut they tried to go back to recover their records, but could make no progress through vile weather. In desperation they turned towards the *Alabama*. Utterly exhausted they reached the site: the ship was gone and a note in the hut they found there said their colleagues had gone too.

The two men survived the winter by hunting and eating the supplies left at the hut. During one hunting trip Iversen claims that he saw his grandfather sitting on a rock wearing his familiar red cap: when he returned to Denmark he found that the old man had died at precisely the time he had the vision. In the spring the two returned for their records, recovering everything except Mikkelsen's diary which had been eaten by a bear. Too weak to attempt the journey south to the Inuit settlement at Scoresbysund they waited all summer for rescue. It did not come. After another winter things were looking grim: they were short of food, suffering from scurvy and Mikkelsen had a threatening

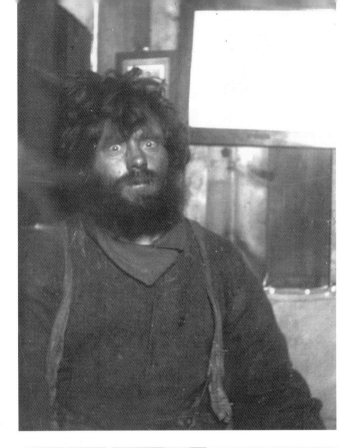

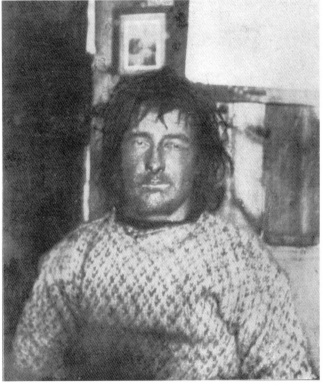

Top and above **Ejnar Mikkelsen and Iver Iversen after their two-year ordeal. The suffering they endured is etched into their faces, while their staring eyes reflect the isolation of their stay in northeast Greenland.**
Danish Polar Centre, Copenhagen

Left **Knud Rasmussen and Peter Freuchen, who led most of the Thule Expeditions which added enormously to an understanding of Inuit culture, chiefly in Greenland.**
Richard Sale Collection

Above **In 1912 Koch and Wegener used horses to cross Greenland's ice cap. Though at odds with Antarctic experience the Danes found the horses worked reasonably well on the relatively firm ice-cap surface and had the advantage of being fresh meat on the hoof. The disadvantage was the need to cut subterranean stables to shelter the horses during storms.**
Richard Sale Collection

boil-like tumour on his neck. Using the knife with which he ate and skinned carcasses, suitably sharpened, and a pool of water as a mirror as Iversen could not bear to do it, Mikkelsen lanced the tumour, the pain causing him to faint. Soon after this operation the two fell out for the first time in the more than two years they had spent together – a mutual silence over an ill-chosen song by Iversen. They had just made up when a rescue ship arrived.

Mikkelsen and Iversen's survival against almost overwhelming odds is arguably the greatest in polar history. Others have endured similar, perhaps worse, conditions, but never for as long. And the pair had also found the records which completed the mapping of Greenland.

Mylius-Erichsen's discovery of Peary's errors was confirmed in 1912 by the first expedition in a series which was to become legendary, the Thule Expeditions. It was led by the Greenland-born, part-Inuit/part-Dane Knud Rasmussen who was accompanied by Peter Freuchen (who had been on the *Danmark* expedition). In part the journey was a search for Mikkelsen, but as it started from the west coast it linked the journeys of Peary and Mylius-Erichsen. Rasmussen, a brilliant anthropologist, went on to lead most of the seven Thule expeditions which did much to bring the culture of the Inuit to the western world. On the Fifth Expedition Rasmussen sledged all the way to the Bering

Strait, becoming the first man to traverse the North-West Passage by land (ie ice). During the traverse, in 1923/4, Rasmussen heard Inuit stories about British sailors as far back as John Ross, showing that the oral tradition of the Inuit was almost as good as the written word. Their tales confirmed some of the more surprising (and disbelieved) stories that 19th-century Western travellers had been told about expeditions dating back to the time of Frobisher. Rasmussen also discovered further relics of Franklin's last expedition.

After the delineation of Greenland's coast the island became a scientific study area. In 1912 J.P. Koch and Alfred Wegener (both of whom had been on the *Danmark*) and two others crossed the inland ice westwards from Danmarkshavn to Laxefjord, a distance of 1,100km (700 miles), about twice as far as Nansen's transit and 300km (186 miles) more than Peary and Rasmussen. They overwintered on the ice before starting out, the first men to do so. The team used horses rather than dogs, eating them in turn as they became exhausted: they had taken 16 animals, but six died in a stampede when they first went ashore.

Wegener was later to die in another overwintering (1930/1) on the ice, exhaustion overtaking him as he struggled to get off the plateau. At the same time the British Arctic Air-Route Expedition set up a base on the inland ice to study weather conditions and so determine if trans-Atlantic flights across Greenland were feasible. The expedition, led by the 23-year-old Henry George (Gino) Watkins, established their base in August 1930. On 3 December Augustine Courtauld was left alone there when it was realised there were insufficient supplies for the planned two-man team. Not until 5 May 1931 was he relieved, a total of 153 days of solitude, far more than Byrd experienced in the Antarctica. A search party on 18 April failed to find the buried station and Courtauld was feared dead, but he survived, with none of the mental scars that might have been expected given that he had lived in fear of his tent collapsing under the weight of snow or his air becoming exhausted. He had not changed his clothes for five months; had run out of lighting oil and so lived in darkness; had taken no exercise; had little food, and been forced to suck snow for water to conserve fuel. His pressure cooker failed the morning of his rescue.

Below **Pelts of Arctic fox and Arctic wolf drying at a trapper's hut in Muskoxhavn, north-east Greenland.**
Richard Sale Collection

share of Greenland until 1933. In that year four men raised the Norwegian flag at the Myggbukta trapping station on east Greenland, and Norway claimed Eirik Raudes (Eirik the Red's) Land, encompassing east Greenland north of the Inuit settlement of Illoqqortoormiut (Scoresbysund). That settlement was established only in 1924/5 when the Danes moved – some would claim, with justification, though deported would be a better word – a number of Inuit from Ammassalik. The ownership of Eirik Raudes Land went to the International Court at The Hague. The Danish claim was supported by Greenland (a campaign led by Knud Rasmussen) and by the USA whose foreign policy was still dominated by the Monroe doctrine: the US had no wish to add a third country to Canada and Denmark in the American Arctic sector. The court found in favour of Denmark. Today, although Greenland has been granted home rule, the Danes still maintain a military presence at Daneborg on the north-east coast and annually patrol the east and north coasts by dog sledge (the Sirius patrol) in order to reinforce its sovereignty.

Greenland: adventurer's paradise

In 1978 the Japanese Naomi Uemura, the first from his country to have climbed Everest, used a dog-sledge to travel to the North Pole (5 March–28 April), the first solo journey there. Evacuated by aircraft because of poor weather, Uemura began a second journey on 10 May from Cape Morris Jesup. Resupplied during his trip he sledged the length of the inland ice, completing his journey on 22 August, the first 'long axis' crossing of the ice cap.

Today, crossings of the inland ice are virtually a rite of passage for polar explorers and mountaineers, east–west or west–east traverses being completed regularly. Special mention must, however, be made of two journeys. In 1996 two 25-year-old Norwegians, Rune Gjeldnes and Torry Larsen, parachuted on to the south-

Greenland: Eirik Raudes Land

About the same time as these first winterings on the inland ice Greenland was the centre of an international court case. Norwegian fur trappers had been overwintering on Greenland's east coast since the early years of the 20th century, their presence fuelling a dispute that had rumbled on since Norway had transferred from the Danish to the Swedish crown in 1814. Since Eirik the Red had been Norwegian, Norway had protested about the continuing Danish possession of West Greenland. Norway gained its independence in 1905, but the upheavals in Europe during the next two decades meant that it did not make moves to acquire a

Svalbard

With a few relatively minor exceptions the coastline of the Svalbard archipelago had been delineated by the early 18th century, the discoveries of whalers being allied to the more scientific work of such expeditions as that of the Russians in the 1760s and the British navy under John Phipps in 1773. Later, Swedish expeditions in particular carried scientific studies inland as well as along the coast. Otto Torell in the *Magdalena* visited the fjord now named for his ship, while Nordenskiöld sailed to 81°42'N in 1868. Soon after, scientific parties were overwintering on Spitsbergen (Nordenskiöld leading the first party to do so in 1872/3: that expedition also sledged across and around Nordaustlandet – North-East Land). In 1896 and 1897 the British explorer Sir Martin Conway surveyed a large area of central Spitsbergen and climbed many of the main peaks.

Though Conway's expedition was an exploration/adventure, the scientific studies had a purpose: to see if Svalbard had exploitable resources.

It had. It is known that early sealers and whalers had exploited Svalbard's readily accessible coal, but the first commercial mining venture was in 1899 when Soren Zachariassen hauled coal from Isfjorden to Norway. By the first decade of the 20th century several companies had been formed with money not only from Norway, but Britain, Holland, Russia and the USA. The major name was that of the American capitalist John Munroe Longyear. He first visited Svalbard as a tourist in 1901 (a 'hotel' was set up in Adventfjorden in 1898: it was to this that Zachariassen sold some of the first coal he mined), then bought one of the original mining companies to form, with Frederick Ayer, the Arctic Coal Company. The company mined in Adventfjorden, finding a seam so rich that 200 miners were employed. The village built to accommodate them was called Longyear City. As Longyearbyen it is now Svalbard's administrative centre. Other major mining centres were Sveagruva and Pyramiden (Swedish companies, though the

latter was sold to the Russians), Barentsburg (Dutch, but sold to the Russians) and King's Bay (Norwegian: now the site of the Ny Ålesund research centre).

After gaining its independence Norway was granted sovereignty over Svalbard in 1920 at a conference to which, significantly, the Russians were not invited. Signatories of the Svalbard Treaty recognise Norway's position, but are granted equal rights regarding mineral exploitation. During the 1939–45 war the Germans set up a base near Longyearbyen, Svalbard being important as a meteorological station because of the Arctic convoys to Russia. The Norwegians landed troops and the Germans retreated. Later *Tirpitz* and *Scharnhorst* bombarded the Norwegian bases. Following the war the Russians sought to modify the Svalbard Treaty, fearing NATO occupation of the archipelago. Their attempt was rejected, though Svalbard became, and remains, demilitarised. Russian suspicions meant that they continued to mine coal at Barentsburg and Pyramiden even though it was uneconomic to do so. The Norwegians did the same at Longyearbyen, the faintly ridiculous situation being reached of the two nations spending money for no better reason than that the other one was. The rise of tourism has, however, compensated Norway for its decision to stay at Longyearbyen. The airport there allows tourists to arrive in just a couple of hours from Tromsø (itself easily reached from anywhere in the world). From Longyearbyen tourist ships explore the historically interesting sites and scenically magnificent fjords of Spitsbergen, though lately new regulations have taken certain sites off-limits as tourists were

looting them, even to the extent of digging in old whaler graveyards for bones.

As the polar bear is totally protected and Kong Karls Land and Edgeøya off the east Spitsbergen coast – both off-limits to tourists – are important bear denning areas, such tourist ships offer excellent chances of seeing bears in their natural habitat. Again, though, there has been a need to restrict tourist traffic, though this time by winter visitors using snow scooters. Incidents in which bears and Svalbard reindeer were harassed – potentially lethal for the animals, the bears overheating if forced to run long distances, the reindeer using energy which may not be replaceable in the harsh Svalbard winter – have led to the introduction of specific routes from which visitors are not allowed to deviate.

Left **Longyearbyen today.**
Richard Sale

Above **Longyeardalen before the city was built.**
From Fries and Nystrom *Svenska polarexpeditionen 1868 med kronoångfartyget Sofia.*
Courtesy of the Swedish Polar Research Secretariat

Right **Barents named Spitsbergen for the pointed mountains he saw there. It is not clear which ones he first spotted as there are many examples on the island. These peaks are at Haitanna, Hornsund, at the southern end of the island.**
Per Michelsen

Left top **Lonnie Dupre, in front, and John Hoeschler kayaking in Melville Bay, north-west Greenland.**
Lonnie Dupre/John Hoeschler

Left below **Sledging in northern Greenland during the Dupre/Hoeschler circuit of the island.**
Lonnie Dupre/John Hoeschler

Above **Dupre and Hoeschler's camp at Cape Raven in east Greenland. In the foreground is a lake, the sea ice of the fjord being visible beyond the ridge.**
Lonnie Dupre/John Hoeschler

ern inland ice on 19 March determined to make the first complete north–south traverse of Greenland. Abseiling down the ice front they used kayaks in an attempt to paddle to, and around, Kapp Farvel (Cape Farewell), Greenland's southernmost point. This attempt was defeated by weather which made the crossing dangerous, though the two did come within sight of the cape. Having paddled back to the mainland they regained the ice cap and, using sails (wings) to aid the towing of 175kg (386lb) pulks, they skied north, reaching Cape Morris Jesup where they were collected

by air on 13 June. Their trek of 2,928km (1,830 miles) was the longest unsupported ski journey at that time, but has lately been bettered by others in Antarctica.

Then in 1997, American Lonnie Dupre (who in 1991 had completed the first west-to-east dog-sledge transit of the North-West Passage) and Australian John Hoelscher planned an 18-month clockwise circumnavigation of Greenland by kayak and dog-sledge. Their plan called for a 2,400km (1,500-mile) kayak trip along the west coast from Paamiut to Qaanaaq during the summer of 1997, then a 4,160km (2,600-mile) dog-sledge trip from Qaanaaq around the northern tip of the island and along the east coast to Ammassalik during the spring of 1998. Finally there would be a 1,488km (930-mile) kayak journey around Greenland's southern tip to complete the 15-month venture. The men's kayaks could be tied together to form a catamaran, a safer option on the open sea, and one which also allowed the possibility of a sail to aid progress. The trip did not go according to plan. Fierce headwinds made the first leg much more difficult than had been imagined and it was not completed before the men had to move to Qaanaaq in late August. After training runs during the winter Dupre and Hoelscher set out on 14 February, but were forced to abandon the trek in late

Jan Mayen

One of the most spectacular of Arctic islands is Jan Mayen. Only 54km (34 miles) long and 2.5km (1½ miles) wide at its narrowest point it is dominated by Beerenburg, an active volcano which rises to 2,277m (7,470ft). Fumaroles add a sense of other-worldliness when viewed against the glaciers which flow down the peak into the sea. The island is composed of black lava sand and jagged red-brown lava cliffs, the sombre colours a complete contrast to the vivid green of mosses and lichens. After the whalers had deserted the island, it was for decades rarely visited. In the First International Polar Year (1882–3) it was the base for the Austro-Hungarian expedition: later it was visited by fur trappers who exterminated the Arctic fox population. In 1922 the Norwegians (who have sovereignty) set up a meteorological station. In 1960 a LORAN (radar) station was added for both civilian and military trans-Atlantic aircraft. Both stations are still in operation. Today the island is occasionally on the itinerary of tourist ships, landings by air being largely restricted to station personnel.

Right **The volcano of Beerenberg, which dominates the remote island of Jan Mayen, is rarely seen, its height and position attracting clouds.**
Richard Sale

March by relentless cold, bad weather and appalling ice conditions. They had reached Cape Jefferson at the northern end of the Kane Basin. The pair then transferred to Ammassalik and kayaked 1,200km (750 miles) to Qaqortoq. They were forced to stop there by the fast approaching winter. Since that first attempt, Dupre and Hoelscher have completed the circumnavigation.

From February to May 2000 they sledged 2,900km (1,800 miles) between Constable Point, near Scoresbysund and Qaanaaq. The trip, rivalling Uemura's as one of the longest ever accomplished by dog-sledge, involved both pressure-ridged sea ice and glacier travelling, the latter at one point requiring the belaying of the dog-sledges because of crevasse danger. Their camp was also invaded one night by a pack of hungry wolves. The weather was unkind too, the team at one stage being tent-bound during a five-day storm. During the trek Dupre and Hoelscher rediscovered the world's northernmost piece of land, Oodaaq Island which lies just 379.5 nautical miles from the North Pole. The island, which measures only 28m by 14m (92 by 46ft) and is 1m (3¼ft) high, is a gravel bar consisting of quartz and slate and has proved elusive in the past as it is frequently hidden by the pack ice and its position was not accurately fixed. Dupre and Hoelscher give its position (by GPS) as 83°40.5'N, 30°39.5'W.

Returning in 2001 the pair kayaked the short sections of the west coast that they had not been able to complete in 1997 (Paamiut to Qaqortoq and a section south of Savissivik), then completed the journey from Constable Point to Ammassalik, a distance of 1,100km (690 miles) between late July and early September. This section of the east Greenland coast is among the most inhospitable on the island, with mountains falling directly into the sea, the kayak trip being extremely hazardous, involving long sections of open sea.

In all, Dupre and Hoelscher travelled over 8,000km (more than 5,000 miles) around Greenland and an additional 2,300km (1,450 miles) of 'cultural' journeys around the Kane Basin, Nares Strait and Inuit villages, a truly remarkable feat and one unlikely to be repeated in the foreseeable future.

Right **'Nie zurück' (No Return) by Julius Payer. Payer was a gifted artist as well as a fine Arctic explorer and painted this picture of the heartbreaking incident where the crew of the *Tegetthoff* had to be persuaded that though the ship offered an apparent end to their misery they had no choice but to ignore it, heading for Novaya Zemlya instead.** Heeresgeschichtliche Museum, Wien, Austria

Explorers in the east

Russia's Arctic islands

The Czar's silk map (see page 70) shows Novaya Zemlya (which had been discovered as early as 1032), but none of the other four archipelagos of the Russian Arctic. Novosibirskiye Ostrova (the New Siberian Islands) were first recorded in 1770 when Ivan Lyakhov, who was trapping furs near Cape Svyatoy Nos, noticed a herd of reindeer heading south towards him across the sea ice. Following their tracks northwards he discovered two islands, and tracks coming from further north. In 1773 Lyakhov took a boat north and discovered a larger island. On it he found a copper kettle, indicating that more discreet trappers had come this way before: the island is still called Kettle Island.

In 1848 Henry Kellett, captain of the *Herald*, sailed through the Bering Strait as part of a Franklin search expedition and discovered Herald Island, naming it for his ship. He climbed to the top and saw land to the west. This was called Kellett's Land on early British maps. Though it is likely that this was the first time Wrangel Island had been seen, it may have been spotted previously by whalers. The American Thomas Roys in the *Superior* made the first whaling trip through the Bering Strait in the same year (1848), and was rapidly followed by others. By 1852 there were over 200 whalers working the waters near the strait. The whalers were by then already searching for new grounds so decimated was the bowhead population. By 1858 the strait was fished out and the whalers transferred to the sea of Okhotsk, exhausting that by 1860. The whalers then turned to hunting walrus and also to the Chukotka Sea. In 1867 Thomas Long in the *Nile* saw Wrangel, naming it for Baron Ferdinand von Wrangel, who had explored the Siberian coast by land in the 1820s (writing a superb description of the Chukchi tribes) and may have sighted the island. It is Wrangel – Long's name – rather than Kellett's which is now the accepted name for the island. Wrangel had never been inhabited and was rarely visited, and was largely ignored. Finally, Vilhjalmur Stefansson's abortive attempt at settlement in 1921 seems to have stirred the Soviets into action and in 1924 the armed ice-breaker *Krasny Oktyobr* (Red October) landed a party who formally claimed sovereignty for the USSR. A two-man wintering party (Ushakov and Urvantsev: see below) was left on the island.

Franz Josef Land was the next island group to be discovered, though the formal discovery of 1873 was almost certainly preceded by a sighting in 1865 by Nils Fredrik Rønnbeck in the sealer *Spidsbergen*. Rønnbeck sighted what he modestly called Rønnbeck Land while sailing north-eastwards from Svalbard, and there are no candidates other than Franz Josef. The now-official name of the islands derives from the undisputed discovery by an Austro-Hungarian expedition. The 24-man expedition left Bremerhaven in June 1872 in the *Tegetthoff* (named for Admiral Wilhelm Tegetthoff) under the command of Karl Weyprecht and Julius van Payer. Weyprecht, a naval lieutenant, commanded at sea, while Payer, an army lieutenant, was in charge on land. The object of the expedition was to reach Asia, but to do so by way of the open polar sea rather than the North-East Passage, belief in the existence of the sea having not finally died. The *Tegetthoff* met the *Isbjørn*,

which had made a preparatory journey the previous year on 12 August, the two celebrating the birthday of Emperor Franz Josef on the 18th, then going separate ways. In 1871 the *Isbjørn* had reached 79°N.

On 21 August, at 76°22'N, the *Tegetthoff* was trapped in the ice (see below). All winter the ship drifted, but the hoped-for release in 1873 failed to materialise. By 30 August 1873, now fogbound as well as trapped, the ship had drifted to 79°43'N. When the fog lifted the crew were astonished to see land; Cape Tegetthoff on Hall Island. Not until November had the ice around the ship consolidated sufficiently for the Austrians to cross the 40km (25 miles) or so and set foot on the new land for the first time. They headed east, reaching an island named Wilczek (after the *Isbjørn's* commander) where they formally claimed all

Left **Nikolai Urvantsev.**
Arctic and Antarctic Institute, St Petersburg, Russia

Below left **George Ushakov.**
Arctic and Antarctic Institute, St Petersburg, Russia

the land of the archipelago for Austro-Hungary, naming it Franz Josef Land for their emperor.

With the ship sealed in for another winter, and it becoming clear that she might not survive a second period of intense ice pressure, the decision was made to abandon her in the summer of 1874. Payer therefore decided to explore Franz Josef. He made three trips, on the second of which, lasting 28 days, he sledged north to Cape Fligely on Rudolf Island (named for the emperor's son), the most northerly point of the archipelago. There Payer erected a cairn and left a note (which was found in 1899 by the Duke of the Abruzzi). With summer now approaching Payer's team made a nervous journey back to Wilczek Island wondering if the *Tegetthoff* would still be there. She was, and the entire crew – now 23 as one man had died of tuberculosis – abandoned her, hauling everything they could carry in the ship's boats. Their journey southward started on 20 May and rapidly became a fight for survival against cold, hunger and scurvy. Then on 15 July the men were appalled to see the *Tegetthoff* in the distance. Despite eight weeks of body- and mind-shattering effort the northward drift of the ice had returned them to within 14km (9 miles) of the ship. Many wanted to re-board, but Weyprecht and Payer persuaded them that the ship was doomed and that their only chance of survival lay in heading south again. With the wind shifting in their favour they now made real progress and in mid-August finally reached open water. They had hauled their boats over 550km (340 miles), but were only 240km (150 miles) from the *Tegetthoff*.

But the men's ordeal was not yet over. They were running very short of food and when they finally reached Novaya Zemlya were unable to land near supply depots that the *Isbjørn* had laid down because of rough seas. With the boats being driven away from the coast and things looking distinctly bleak the men were fortunately spotted by the Russian ship *Nikolai*. They were rescued, fed and given the news that peace had descended on Europe and that Napoleon had died.

The final Russian Arctic archipelago, Severnaya Zemlya, was not discovered until the Arctic Ocean Hydrographic Expedition of 1910–15. Anxious to establish an easily navigated North-East Passage in the wake of its defeat by Japan in the war of 1904–5 Russia built two ice-breakers, *Taymyr* and *Vaygach*, to more thoroughly explore the Siberian coast. The series of voyages by the two ships culminated in the first transit of the passage from east to west. The leaders of this historically important expedition were Boris Viltiski and Alexander Kolchak, both of whom were anti-Communist. Viltiski escaped to London after the transit, but Kolchak led the White Russian forces in Siberia. He was captured and executed by firing squad in 1920. During the 1913 voyage of the two ice-breakers the southern island of Severnaya Zemlya – initially called Nicholas II Land, but changed to Northern Land after the Revolution – was discovered. The archipelago was thoroughly explored by George Ushakov, one of the greatest of all Russian Arctic travellers. Ushakov had lived on Wrangel for three years (1926–9) to bolster Russia's sovereignty claim and was made leader of the Northern Land Expedition in 1930. Accompanied by Sergei Zhuravlev, a hunter/trapper, and Nikolai Urvantsev, Ushakov set out by dog-sledge on a journey of 3,000km (almost 2,000 miles) that took two years. Ushakov was proudly Communist – his names on the archipelago include Cape Hammer and Sickle and October Revolution Island – but Urvantsev was not. Following the expedition Ushakov was awarded the Order of Lenin. Urvantsev, an Arctic explorer with a pedigree almost the equal of Ushakov's, vanished in Stalin's purges, but not before he had established Irkutsk University. Urvantsev was written out of the official book on the expedition but today, thankfully, his name has been reinstated, his contribution recognised.

In 1947 the skeletal remains of a human, together with traces of a camp, were discovered on Severnaya Zemlya. Though never formally identified they are believed to be of a member of a team lead by Russian geologist V.A. Rusanov. Rusanov, accompanied by his French fiancée Juliette Jean and a small crew, disappeared in 1912 during an attempt to take a ship west–east through the North-East Passage. This sad discovery implies that Rusanov had perhaps made it to the archipelago before the official discovery, but the evidence is by no means conclusive. Other items obviously from Rusanov's trip were found hundreds of miles to the west and these imply that the expedition failed to escape the Kara Sea. The skeletal remains are, therefore, another enduring Arctic mystery.

Above **Ermak, the world's first ice-breaker, named for the cossack who led the Russian annexation of Siberia. Though the ship's concept was Soviet she was actually built in Newcastle-upon-Tyne, England, in 1898.**
Arctic and Antarctic Institute, St Petersburg, Russia

Voyages in the eastern Arctic

Russian interest in northern sea routes was rekindled by Nordenskiöld's voyage. In the 1890s Vice-Admiral Makarov had the *Ermak* built, the world's first ice-breaker, and attempted to reach the North Pole with her in 1899. He failed, reaching 81°28'N close to Svalbard, but he had laid the groundwork for the voyages of the *Taimyr* and *Vaygach* which, as noted earlier, completed the second transit of the North-East

Passage. Russia's continuing enthusiasm for a northern sea route led to a near disaster in 1933, but before that, in 1914, a Russian ship was involved in a trip every bit as harrowing as the more famous voyages of the *Jeanette* and the *Karluk*.

The *Saint Anna*, with Georgi Brusilov commanding, left Arkhangelsk on 4 September 1912, much too late in the year for Arctic travel. Brusilov had been delayed in Alexandrovsk (now Murmansk) and had also failed to sign on the crew he needed. His second-in-command had not arrived and he could find only five experienced sailors. As he left the White Sea Brusilov had an unknown deputy, Valerian Albanov, and his crew of 23 included a woman, Yerminiya Zhdenko, who was to act as nurse. The objective of the trip was to discover new whaling and sealing grounds, though there was also a vague suggestion of making the second transit of the North-East Passage.

Brusilov may have been seduced by Nordenskiöld's (correct) suggestion that the Kara Sea was ice-free in the late summer – if so he was abruptly brought back to reality when, after traversing the Yugorski Strait, the *Saint Anna* became ice-bound close to the Yamal Peninsula on 15 October. The crew walked to the peninsula and saw the tracks of local reindeer herders. These locals offered salvation, but the crew decided to stay with the ship: it was an understandable, but incorrect decision – during the next 17 months the *Saint Anna* drifted slowly north, finally reaching 82°58'N off the northern tip of Franz Josef Land. There a simmering conflict between Brusilov and Albanov finally boiled over. The problem seems to have been Albanov's exasperation with Brusilov's incompetent leadership; Albanov demanded to be relieved of his duties and requested permission to leave the ship. Food and fuel were running low (the samovar, that ubiquitous Russian feature, was by now fuelled only by bear fat and seal blubber) but Brusilov had no plan other than to hope the ship would break free. Brusilov gave his permission for Albanov to leave. To his surprise, but also to his delight, 13 men decided to go as well.

Albanov supervised the construction of sledges and kayaks and loaded them with supplies which Brusilov itemised and made him sign for, increasing Albanov's antagonism. For a map Albanov had only the one in his copy of Nansen's book *Furthest North*. Using this he hoped to reach the base camp of the Russian Georgi Sedov who was using Franz Josef as the starting point for his expedition to the North Pole (though he did not know which island Sedov had decided to use) or Frederick Jackson's Elmwood Camp.

Albanov seems glad to have been away from the ship. It was only 120km (75 miles) to land and the second winter had been appalling, the bear-grease lamps creating an evil smoke and condensation which caused mildew to form on all surfaces: everyone on board was soon covered in a layer of greasy smoke residue. Yet the ice turned out to be little better. The 14 men left on 10 April and dragged their sledges just 5km (3 miles). They were then kept in their tents for three days by a blizzard, an inauspicious start. In the absence of sleeping bags the men slept in *malitsas* – smocks of reindeer hide, fur on the inside – two men huddling together, their legs inside one malitsa, their head and torso in another. After the blizzard Albanov sent one clearly ailing man back to the ship: another man volunteered to take his place, a remarkably brave offer given that these on the *Saint Anna* thought the ice party were, at least, misguided.

Albanov calculated their position as the weather improved: they had walked 5 km (3 miles) south but had drifted 35km (22 miles) north. Despite this discouraging news the men pressed on. By 16 April daily visits from their shipmates stopped as they had travelled too far from, and also now lost sight of, the ship. By day 11 of the trek their fuel was exhausted and they were forced to suck icicles or to drink small quantities of seawater to survive. On that day three men gave up and returned to the ship.

The trek of the remaining 11 men became a nightmare. If they arrived at a *polynya* (an area of open water: such pools are often found in the frozen ocean, kept open by currents or consistent winds) they could shoot seals and so obtain blubber to heat water, but if they did not hunger, cold and thirst were almost overwhelming. On 3 May one man went off in search of flat ice he claimed to have seen – was he brave or had he gone mad? – and disappeared. The rate of progress was about 3km (2 miles) daily despite the use of the kayaks in leads and the slow progress and monotony began to sap the men's mental strength. To Albanov's horror they became listless and childlike; one fell into the sea when he attempted to climb an iceberg from his kayak, just for the fun of it. To add to Albanov's worries the symptoms of scurvy began to appear and the southwesterly drift of the ice (the wind had changed) meant he became unsure as to the direction in which Franz Josef Land lay. Even when they shot a polar bear the men's health did not improve as they ate the liver and so overdosed on vitamin A. Albanov realised that the liver was the cause of their illness and forbade its future appearance on the menu, probably saving them from the fate of Andrée's team.

Albanov was increasingly frustrated by the men's attitude. Some had become fed up with hauling the kayaks and wanted to abandon them despite the fact that when the pack ice broke up they would be crucial to their survival. Their failure to realise this, coupled with their lack of interest in where they were, a problem which exercised their leader constantly, exasperated Albanov. He was aware that they had drifted west, but that they were now drifting south – would they miss Franz Josef altogether and reach the Barents Sea? It meant almost certain death if they did. Finally on 9 June he spotted land to the east, though it took another 17 days of exhausting trekking over unruly ice to reach it. During that time two men made off with the best of the equipment, clearly intent on saving themselves at the expense of their comrades. Albanov swore that if he ever saw them again he would kill them. Ironically he did see them when they finally made landfall at Cape Mary Harmsworth on Alexandra Land. Mellowed by the flowers blooming on the island, by the thought of feasting on gull eggs and by their remorse, Albanov relented.

Albanov fixed his position when he found a note left by Frederick Jackson, and decided to push east for Cape Flora. Again he was frustrated by his men who seemed willing only to sleep. One man declined to move at all and was left behind. When, overcome by conscience, the men returned for him, he was dead. The apathy is strange given the imperative of reaching Cape Flora; one suggested explanation is that the periods of malnutrition had led to vitamin deficiencies which can create such a condition. Whatever the cause another man soon died, leaving eight to struggle on. During the crossing of Prince George Land four men, including Albanov, had used the remaining two kayaks, the others having been abandoned at various times when exhaustion was overwhelming, to take all the equipment by sea while four men skied cross-country. The expected rendezvous failed, the four kayakers pushing on alone. These survivors reached Bell Island, a base used by Englishman Benjamin Leigh Smith during his expeditions on 1880–2. Leigh Smith's trips were for exploration, scientific study and hunting and he built a substantial hut at what he named Eira Harbour after his ship: it is still there and in remarkably good condition. The *Eira* suffered the same fate as her predecessor the *Tegetthoff*, being holed and sunk by ice pressure. As a result Leigh Smith and his crew were marooned on Cape Flora, unable to reach the Eira Harbour hut. The misery of their enforced winter was doubtless relieved by the fact that they managed to offload 320 litres (70 gallons) of rum and a huge quantity of champagne, whisky, gin, sherry and beer before the ship went down.

Had Albanov found Leigh Smith's hut he might have been able to rest and eat well, and to make use of a rowing boat Leigh Smith had left. But despite, as he later discovered, walking within 100m of it, he missed it and so decided to press on for Cape Flora. On the sea crossing between Bell and Northbrook Islands a violent storm forced Albanov and his companion Alexander Konrad on to an ice floe. To escape the savagery of the weather the two got into their malitsas. When the floe broke up in the violent seas they fell into the sea 'like two unwanted kittens thrown together in a sack to be drowned'. But they survived, and managed to reach Cape Flora on 9 July, 90 days after leaving the *Saint Anna*. Of the second kayak there was no sign. At Cape Flora Albanov and Konrad found huts and supplies in plenty, remnants not only of Jackson's expedition, but those of Abruzzi, Ziegler and Sedov. Exhausted, filthy and dressed in lice-infested rags the two men were finally able to relax. They expected to overwinter, but were discovered just 11 days later by the *Saint Foka*, a supply ship looking for Sedov.

Albanov and Konrad were the only survivors of the *Saint Anna*. Of the four skiers, the other two kayakers, the Saint Anna and those who remained with her, no trace was ever found.

Striving for the pole

The first attempts

It is an arguable point which expedition has the right to be termed the first to attempt to reach the North Pole as many of the early travellers, for instance Henry Hudson, assumed that to reach Cathay it was necessary merely to sail north over the pole, the pole itself being an incidental along the way. Arguably the first to sail north with the specific intent of reaching the pole was the Englishman Constantine Phipps who, in 1773, sailed the *Racehorse* and the *Carcass* (the latter commanded by Skeffington Lutwidge) past Svalbard. He failed of course, but the trip was a valuable experience for a 14-year-old midshipman called Horatio Nelson. It was also almost Nelson's last trip as he only narrowly avoided being killed by a polar bear. It is said that only the firing of a gun from the ship, which frightened the bear away, saved Nelson's life. The young man's excuse

for the encounter was that he wished to take a bear skin back for his father.

After Buchan and Franklin came William Edward Parry, hero of attempts at the North-West Passage. In 1827 Parry took the *Hecla* (and his new wife's pet dog Fido) to Spitsbergen's north coast. Having pocketed the £5,000 prize for reaching 110°W he was now intent, at the very least, on collecting another £1,000 for reaching 83°N. It was not to be: Parry had realised that his best hope lay in dragging sledges across the ice, but hedged his bet on finding open water by fixing steel runners to the two boats he took on the trek. This allowed his men to use the boats to cross leads, but the boats were heavy and exhausting to drag. With Parry in charge of one boat and James Clark Ross the other the expedition set out. The weather was awful, almost constant rain making the snow soft, so increasing the friction on the runners. The men were soaked, often falling into pools on the ice surface to add to their misery, and so perpetually cold. Parry also discovered,

Above **Walruses attack a boat from the *Trent (top)*; the expedition driven into the ice (below). Both illustrations are taken from Frederick Beechey's book *A Voyage of Discovery towards the North Pole*, which detailed the Buchan/Franklin expedition of 1818. Beechey was one of Franklin's officers.**
USA Library of Congress

Left **The *Racehorse* and the *Carcass* on 31 July 1773. It is not clear that the clergy would approve of the game being played on the ice: leap-frog has always had a curious reputation. The next to try for the North Pole after the Phipps expedition were David Buchan, in the *Dorothea*, and John Franklin, in the *Trent*. They followed the same route along Spitsbergen's western shore, but after a violent storm had threatened to crush their ships and another storm had freed them from the ice, the expedition was abandoned.**
Richard Sale Collection

as others were to find later, some with disastrous consequences, that as his team went north – painfully, and painfully slowly, often reduced to a speed of only 250m (273yd) per hour – the ice was drifting south at almost the same speed. Finally he was forced to admit defeat. He had established a record (82°45'N) but not won the prize: he was 220km (170 miles) north of the *Hecla*, but had walked several times that distance.

Above **The boats hauled up for the night. The apparent domesticity of this illustration from Parry's book *Narrative of an Attempt to reach the North Pole* is at odds with the realities of the trip.**
Richard Sale Collection

After Parry's attempt British naval expeditions returned to the quest for the North-West Passage, but during the search for Franklin further voyages were made northward. The graves on Beechey Island opened up the possibility that Franklin had headed north and in 1852 Edward Belcher had explored Wellington Channel, his men sledging across northern Cornwallis, Bathurst and Melville Islands. In the same year Lady Jane Franklin provided a ship, the *Isabel*, and the Admiralty a crew under Edward Inglefield, to try another route northward. Inglefield followed Baffin's route, passing Cape Isabella and naming Cape Sabine (soon to become infamous) as he traversed Smith Sound and looked into what he thought was the polar sea. Inglefield also named Ellesmere Island which forms the west side of Kane Basin and Smith Sound.

The Americans head north

Inglefield's route north attracted the attention of Americans who were keen not only to help find Franklin but also to pursue their own ambitions of reaching the North Pole. Exploration of the route was to prove that the British did not have a monopoly on disaster in the Canadian Arctic. The first American to follow Inglefield was Elisha Kent Kane, a man whose courage and perseverance outweighed poor health: he suffered from rheumatism and a bad heart, and died of a stroke when only 37. Kane had already been on one search expedition, the first to have been sponsored by the New York businessman Henry Grinnell in response to Lady

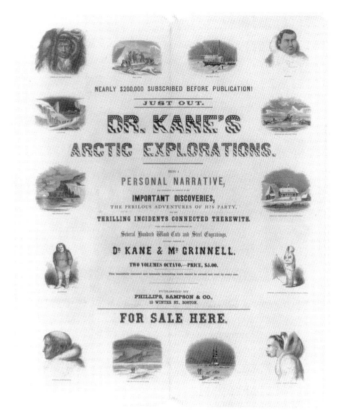

Top **The Second Grinnell Expedition to the Arctic. The image has a convoluted ancestry, being an engraving by John Sartain from a painting by Jas Hamilton which was itself based on an Elisha Kent Kane sketch.**
USA Library of Congress

Above **Kane's two books on the Grinnell expeditions sold phenomenally well: over 60,000 copies in the first year of publication and reviewed, almost always favourably, over 1,000 times. It was said that only the Bible was seen on more American tables. The books remain classics of Arctic literature, both well written and beautifully illustrated.**
USA Library of Congress

Top **Isaac Hayes' team rounding Cape Alexander.**
Richard Sale Collection

Above **A lithograph of Charles Francis Hall from the only known photograph of him.**
Permission of Chauncey Loomis

Franklin's request to the US. Kane had been surgeon on the First Grinnell Expedition (two ships, the *Advance* and the *Rescue*, commanded by Edwin De Haven) which had been one of the several at Beechey Island when the first traces of Franklin's men had been found. Now, three years later, Kane was commanding his own expedition. In the *Advance* – which was little bigger than Frobisher's ship – with a crew of 17, Kane sailed beyond Inglefield's northernmost point, reaching the Kane Basin. His hope that this was the open polar sea – which was still claimed to exist by some scientists and whalers – were now dashed: the ice advanced and Kane was forced to overwinter at Rensselaer Harbour on the Greenland coast. He had come equipped with dogs and sledges to pursue the journey north, but the dogs died of a mysterious illness.

Despite this setback much was achieved. Isaac Israel Hayes, Kane's surgeon, sledged along Ellesmere Island as far as Cape Frazer, and another team reached the Humboldt Glacier on Greenland ('a plastic, moving, semi-solid mess, obliterating life, swallowing rocks and islands and ploughing its way with irresistible march [to] … the sea', as Kane noted in his book of the expedition). The *Advance* failed to escape the ice when summer came, forcing a second overwintering. With little fuel or fresh food, and scurvy beginning to take its toll, Hayes took half the men and headed south, hoping to reach a Danish settlement. They managed 480km (300 miles) but were forced to retreat after spending three months held captive by a savage winter. The return trip was an epic involving the rounding of Cape Alexander on a ledge which narrowed to 40cm (15in) above a drop into the sea and certain death. On the *Advance* Kane and the others survived only because local Inuit gave them food. Finally in the summer of 1855, with the *Advance* still locked into the ice, all the men headed south. Using sledges and boats they made it to Upernavik in August.

Kane's surgeon Isaac Hayes returned with his own expedition in 1860. Sailing in the *United States* with a young astronomer, August Sonntag, Hayes overwintered near the entrance to Smith Sound. He and Sonntag made trips on to glaciers flowing from Greenland's inland ice, but on one Sonntag fell through the sea ice. Though he was quickly dragged clear he died during the night and Hayes abandoned the trip.

As he neared the US on his return journey Hayes passed the *Rescue* which was taking Charles Francis Hall north for the first time. Hall was on another Franklin search expedition, one which was to form the basis of

most subsequent attempts to piece together Franklin's fate from Inuit testimony. Hall's was the last American expedition for a decade, the Civil War calling a halt to such frivolous adventures. When peace returned, so did Hall, heading north again in 1871, this time in the *Polaris* and intent on reaching the North Pole.

Hall believed that he 'was born to discover the North Pole. That is my purpose. Once I have set my right foot on the Pole, I shall be perfectly willing to die.' It was a partially prophetic comment. With him were Sidney Budington as captain, the German Emil Bessels – a surgeon with previous Arctic experience – and two Inuit families (including several children). One of these families Hall had befriended on his Franklin searches, the other was that of Suersaq, also known as Hans Hendrik, who had already proved invaluable to Kane and Hayes and would later accompany Nares. The *Polaris* sailed to 82°11'N, the furthest north reached so far in the Kane Basin, then overwintered on Greenland's coast at 81°37'N, the furthest north anyone had done so to date. Though Hall called the winter base Thank God Harbour it was not really a harbour, the ship lying in the lee of a vast iceberg called Providence Berg, clearly a heartfelt name. At the harbour, on 8 November 1871, Hall died.

The expedition now broke up in confusion. Budington and Bessels were the senior expedition members, but Budington thought Bessels arrogant, and Bessels thought Budington an ignoramus. When summer came Budington tried to take the ship south, but it was soon beset again. The ice was now drifting south and had soon cleared Smith Sound. There might have been optimism among the crew, but it was soon shattered when on 15 October gale-driven ice threatened to sink the ship. Anxious to save what they could the team began to unload boats and stores on to an ice floe. This job had not been completed before the gale separated the floe and the ship, and to the horror of those on each the two drifted apart and were soon lost to each other's view. As the ship drifted away, above the screaming wind a voice could be heard calling forlornly from the ice floe, 'Goodbye *Polaris*'.

Those on the ship were driven north to the Greenland coast near the Inuit settlement of Etah whose hunters had earlier kept Kane's team alive. The crew, now numbering 14, built a house with wood from the *Polaris*, survived a reasonably comfortable winter and then, in boats made from more *Polaris* timber, went south in June 1873, soon being picked up by a whaler.

On the ice floe the other members of Hall's team –

Above **Emile Bessel's sketch of Hall's funeral. In the background can be seen the observatory built for the expedition's scientists. It had a coal-burning stove to warm them as they studied astronomy and local geology, meteorology, and so on.**
Permission of Chauncey Loomis

one was a baby born on 12 August 1872 to Hans Hendrik and his wife, an addition to the three children they already had – had a more dramatic winter. The Inuit were all on the floe. Though they included a nursing baby, they could also build snow igloos and hunt seals from the kayaks that had been offloaded. That kept the party alive when the stores from the ship had run out. The 19 men, women and children spent the winter on the ice floe, which was roughly 150m (165yd) square. They were often hungry and, when the sun returned, also fearful that the ice floe would suddenly break up and hurl them into the sea. Eventually, on 1 April 1873, they crowded into the two salvaged boats – built to accommodate a maximum of 12 men – and prayed for a ship to spot them as they had to abandon a lot of food and clothing. Two ships passed without seeing them but on 30 April, close to the Labrador coast after having drifted about 2,400km (1,500 miles), they were taken on board the *Tigress*. Two days after their rescue there was a violent storm: it would almost certainly have overwhelmed the two boats.

Hall's expedition had been an official US venture, sanctioned by President Grant and underwritten by the navy, so there was a board of inquiry into its conduct and the death of the leader. It heard that the expedition had been far from happy. Budington had been a secret – and not-so-secret drinker – which brought him into conflict with the god-fearing Hall; Hall and Bessels had disagreed repeatedly, Bessels once threatening to leave the ship and to take the German crewmen, of whom there were several, with him; some members of the crew were upset with Hall's strange and occasionally autocratic methods, and fearful of continuing the northern journey. It also learned that Hall had experienced strange symptoms for two weeks before his death, bouts of violent sickness interspersed with periods of recovery. The problems had started with what Dr Bessels called an 'apoplectical insult' – a stroke – which he verified by noting paralysis, testing it with a needle. The board decided that Hall had indeed, died of apoplexy. Suspicious of the board's finding, in 1968 Chauncey Loomis, a Dartmouth professor who was writing a biography of Hall, persuaded the Danes to allow an autopsy. This proved difficult as Hall's internal organs had fused with, and become indistinguishable from, his flesh. But hair and fingernail samples showed large amounts of arsenic, almost certainly administered during the last two weeks of his life. Hall had exhibited classic symptoms of arsenic poisoning and had also been convinced he was being poisoned by Budington or Bessels, but, as Loomis rightly notes, at this remove from the event nothing definite could be determined. Perhaps Hall did indeed have a stroke – he noted on one sledge trip that he could no longer run in front of the dogs: clearly he was unwell – and, perhaps fearful of Bessels, had self-administered patent medicines. In the 1860s many of these contained arsenic. Yet Bessels' treatment of Hall – when it was allowed – was curious. He declined, when requested, to administer an emetic which would have cleared Hall's stomach of any poison and continued to inject him – nominally with quinine, but quinine crystals and arsenic powder would have been indistinguishable to those crew members who saw the injections prepared – long after the 'fever' he said he was treating had subsided. When Bessels was not allowed to treat Hall his condition improved. Yet what, if he was guilty, was Bessels' motive for murder? He was clearly at odds with Hall, but could that really have led a civilised man to murder? Of course, the harshness of, and fear induced by, the Arctic has done strange things to men's minds. Hall's death was obviously suspicious, but must remain a mystery.

The British try one last time

Having stayed away from the Arctic since Belcher's near-farcical expedition, the British navy, inspired by Hall's voyage, decided to try again for the North Pole. In 1875, with the blessing of Queen Victoria and Prime Minister Disraeli (just as Hall had received a blessing from President Grant) George Nares set out with the *Alert* and the *Discovery*. Despite the lessons of the Franklin disaster and the myriad search expeditions, the British Admiralty had learned nothing. Both ships were huge rather than small and manoeuvrable, the crew numbered 120, too many to live off the land; the sledges which had already proved too heavy and cumbersome were again taken; the food was much the same as that which had probably contributed to Franklin's downfall.

Yet despite their size Nares brilliantly took his ships through the Kane Basin ice. The *Discovery* wintered in Lady Franklin Bay, the *Alert* continuing to winter near Cape Sheridan where the Alert meteorologist station is now placed. It was a new record northing, both for a ship and for a wintering station. In 1876 Albert Markham took a sledge team north from the *Alert* establishing a new furthest north record of 83°20'26"N on 12 May. By then all hope of the pole was gone and survival was in the balance. The men were exhausted by boat-hauling – they had reached a point only 117km (73 miles) from the ship but had walked over 800km (500 miles) as they had to return for the second of two boats each time as they were so heavy – boats had been taken in case open water was reached. The men were also crippled by scurvy. Finally the one reasonably fit man was sent alone to cover the last 50km (30 miles) to get help. Nares, concerned by the state of Markham's men – one of whom died – immediately sent a rescue party out for his second land party. This team had traced Ellesmere Island's north coast as far as Alert Point, but would all have died of scurvy without the rescue team.

Two sledge parties also set out from the *Discovery*. That ship's crew had enjoyed better health due largely to Hans Hendrik (Suersaq) supplying them with fresh meat. One sledge party surveyed the Ellesmere coast south of the ship and returned in reasonable health, but the other, under Lewis Beaumont, which had surveyed Greenland's north coast, found itself returning in deep, soft snow. Exhausted and with two men dead from scurvy Beaumont found open water between him and the *Discovery*. At that stage a rescue party arrived and the remaining men were saved.

Nares now had less than one-fifth of his men free of scurvy and wisely decided to abandon a second over-

Above **The exhumation of Charles Francis Hall. Hall lay in a plain pine coffin in a shallow grave. When the lid was removed the body was found to be wrapped in the US flag, its colours staining his flesh. In a morbidly humorous touch, Hall's last resting place had been made by the *Polaris* carpenter – Nathaniel Coffin.**
Permission of Chauncey Loomis

wintering and to head for home. In the inquiry which followed the expedition the evidence of two doctors that the sledge party's scurvy had been caused by a lack of lime juice was rejected. John Rae's view that fresh meat, fish and vegetables were effective anti-scorbutants, and evidence that lime juice itself aged significantly and so became less effective with time, were quietly ignored. One of the committee who decided that everything possible had been done and nothing could be improved, either on the matter of anti-scorbutants or equipment, was Clements Markham, cousin of Albert Markham who had almost died returning from the furthest north, and the man instrumental in appointing Robert Falcon Scott to lead the expeditions to Antarctica.

Above **A sledge party from the *Alert* making a push for the pole.**
UK National Maritime Museum

The Americans try again: Greely and the *Jeanette*

In 1875 Karl Weyprecht, co-leader of the expedition that discovered Franz Josef Land, proposed that rather than the piecemeal approach to Arctic exploration that had, up to that time, been the norm, a co-ordinated international effort should be made to carry out scientific studies in the area. This was agreed, and during the International Polar Year of 1882/3 a dozen stations were set up and manned through the winter. A Dutch expedition in the *Varna* was trapped by ice in the Kara Sea before reaching the proposed station, but the crew and scientists escaped to the mainland unharmed. All except one of the other stations were manned successfully and uneventfully. The exception was the US expedition under the command of Adolphus Washington Greely: its story is one of the most horrific for which there are the first-hand accounts of survivors.

Greely took his expedition of 25 men (including himself and two Inuit hunters) north in the *Proteus* in the early summer of 1881, eventually reaching the point where Nares's *Discovery* had overwintered. Here a base – Fort Conger, named for a US senator who had been a principal supporter of the expedition – was built, and the scientific studies of the Polar Year began. But Greely's trip had a dual purpose: he had also been told to try to reach the pole or, at least, to better Nares' record. To that end James Lockwood, one of Greely's two officers, laid down depots along a route towards the north Greenland coast.

The summer of 1882 seems to have been idyllic. Insects and butterflies flitted among the flowers, and muskoxen provided a ready source of fresh meat. There was internal dissension within the team – Greely had alienated his other officer, Frederick Kislingsbury, the team doctor Octave Parry and some of his men with his stubbornness and poor decision-making – but they were not to have an instrumental effect on the course of the expedition. In early April Lockwood headed north with one dog-sledge and three manhauled sledges. After four weeks of travelling most of the party was sent back, Lockwood continuing with Sgt David Brainard, the Inuk Frederick (Thorlip Frederick Christiansen) and the dog-sledge. Finding and using depots left by Beaumont's party from the Nares expedition Lockwood pushed on, eventually reaching the northern end of Lockwood Island at 83°24'N. They had extended Beaumont's survey by 240km (150 miles) and Markham's furthest north by 6.5km (4 miles). After 60 days they were back at Fort Conger. It had not, strictly, been an attempt at the pole, but it was a notable achievement and established a new northing record.

During the same summer Greely explored Ellesmere Island, surveying a good deal of country and discovering Lake Hazen (named for General William Hazen, chief signal officer of the US, Greely's commanding officer). The expected supply ship did not arrive, but with supplies and game still (relatively) abundant there was no need for concern. Another winter passed and in the summer of 1883 Lockwood tried to go north from Ellesmere. Unfortunately open water stopped him (though it is doubtful if he would have managed to break his own record by more than 1° or so). Instead Lockwood headed west, discovering and tracing Greely Fjord.

Back at Fort Conger the length of separation from civilisation and continuing uncertainty over the absence of a relief ship was taking its toll. As Greely's dispute with Parry intensified the commander tried to have the doctor arrested for insubordination. Eventually, with the situation at Fort Conger deteriorating, Greely decided to head south to where supply dumps should have been laid down even if the relief ships had been unable to reach the expedition. Of two possibilities, Cape Sabine on Ellesmere or Littleton Island on the Greenland coast, he chose the former.

Greely's choices have been debated ever since. Should he have stayed at Fort Conger where game was plentiful? He did not know he had been abandoned, and without a relief ship Conger meant starving slowly rather than starving quickly. Should he have gone to the

Greenland side where the Inuit of Etah had a history of helping expeditions? Again, how was he to know that the Cape Sabine cupboard was bare?

The team loaded everything including all the scientific data into two boats, and headed south through difficult ice and bad weather. It took 16 days to cover the 320km (200 miles) to Cape Sabine but just as they approached it the wind dropped, the pack ice came together and the boats were trapped. It took a further 19 days for the men to cross the last 21km (13 miles) of ice to Ellesmere, most of that time being buffeted by blizzards. They reached land on Pym Island off Cape Sabine. It took two men a further eight days to reach the cape and return with a note that told Greely he and his men were in for a long, hungry winter.

General Hazen had attempted to get a relief ship north in the first summer, but had at first been thwarted by Robert Lincoln, son of Abraham Lincoln and now US secretary of war. Lincoln responded to requests for a ship with queries on the spending related to the expedition. Eventually a ship, the *Neptune*, sailed. Despite several attempts to get through the ice it got no further than the mouth of Kane Basin. Minimal supplies were left at Cape Sabine and Littleton Island and the ship retreated. The next year the command of the relief operation was given to Ernest Garlington. He was a cavalry officer, promoted when many of the officers on his unit, the 7th cavalry, were killed with Custer at the battle of Little Big Horn. As an army man he was an odd choice for a naval expedition, but Hazen was army too, as was Greely and his expedition.

The relief party had two ships, the *Proteus* (which had taken Greely north) and the *Yantic*, a much slower ship which soon lost contact with the faster vessel. The *Proteus* reached Cape Sabine on 22 July, but Garlington did not unload any supplies, preferring to head north. The ship's captain, Richard Pike, favoured waiting one or two days as there was considerable ice in Kane Basin, but eventually agreed to steam north again. Soon, in sight of clear water, the *Proteus* was caught by ice floes and very quickly began to sink. Garlington threw as much material overboard as possible, but the majority of the supplies for Greely were lost, and much of what he did salvage drifted away on the ice. Garlington now left enough at Cape Sabine to last Greely three weeks then took the rest and headed south. He left a note on Littleton Island which was picked up by the *Yantic* when she arrived. Faced with deciding whether to go north towards Greely or south after Garlington, Frank Wildes, the

Top 'The Farthest North of All Time', engraving by Albert Operti (who later accompanied Peary to Greenland), of Lt Lockwood, Sgt Brainard and the Inuk Frederick at 83°24'N on 13 May 1882.
USA National Archives and Records Administration

Above Hauling ice at Fort Conger. Left to right are the Inuk Jens, Greely, Cross and Kislingbury.
USA Library of Congress

Above **The *Proteus* sinking.**
USA National Archives and Records Administration

Yantic's captain, headed south, leaving no supplies at Littleton. The *Yantic* and Garlington's men were eventually united at Upernavik. There it was decided that it was too late in the year to go north again and the *Yantic* sailed back to St John's on Newfoundland. A flurry of telegrams now sought advice. But though pressed by General Hazen and, especially, by Greely's wife, Robert Lincoln vetoed a further attempt to go north. Greely had been abandoned.

On Pym Island Greely's men built a rough hut of stone around an upturned boat. They collected what Garlington had left at Cape Sabine and, as there was little meat, Greely sent a team of four, including two Inuit, to collect such supplies as Nares had left at Cape Isabella, 65km (40 miles) away. It took five days to get there, but the cache contained only about 65kg (140lb) of meat. On the way back with this one man, Joseph Elison, became so cold that two others had to stay with him, attempting to warm him in a four-man sleeping bag, while the last man went for help. All four were saved, but only for a greater nightmare. The two Inuit hunters tried desperately to find game but apart from the odd seal there was nothing: Cape Sabine was no Fort Conger. Eventually one Inuk died of scurvy aggra-

vated by exhaustion, the other drowning when his kayak was ripped by ice.

The death of the Inuit and the coming of winter meant an end to fresh food. With supplies dwindling Greely cut the food ration – mouldy bread and soup heated by burning rope and bootsoles – to about 160g (6oz) daily. Eventually even the buffalo-hide or sheepskin sleeping bags were being boiled and eaten, and by May men were dying daily. One day Charles Henry was discovered to be stealing food. Greely convened a court martial and Henry was sentenced to death in his absence. Too weak to carry out the sentence himself Greely allowed three NCOs to organise it. The facts of the death were never published, but it seems that fearful of Henry's strength – he was bigger than most in the crew, and now better fed – the men lured him away on a pretext and shot him in the head without warning. On the day of the execution the doctor died, his end perhaps aided by self-administered drugs.

When spring came the diet of old leather and tallow was supplemented by seaweed, lichen, flowers, sand fleas and shrimps. These 'supplements' became the only 'food' when everything else edible ran out on 12 May. It took all the survivors' energy to bury their dead comrades in the shallow graves of a makeshift cemetery. Then they were forced to move from the hut to a tent on a drier site because meltwater was making it unbearable. Many of the men could now hardly stand, and death seemed to be both inevitable and welcome. Greely wrote what he thought might be his last note, a curious mixture of pathos and bathos that prefigured Scott: 'Seven of us left – here we are – dying, like men. Did what I came to do – beat the old record.'

In Washington the government had finally realised that Greely might be in trouble, though funding was stalled while a relief bill was debated (at length) and passed. Finally the *Thetis* and *Bear* sailed north. To his considerable aggravation Garlington was not given command, that going to Winfield Schley. On 22 June after following notes left by Greely's men at Cape Sabine and Cape Isabella the ships arrived at Pym Island and discovered the horrors of the camp. Only seven of the 25 men were alive, and of those Joseph Elison was in a pitiful state. Frost-bitten on the trip to Cape Isabella he had seen all the flesh rot from one foot leaving the bones exposed. The skin had sloughed from his hands and his comrades had tied his spoon to his stump so he could eat what little was still available. Dr Parry had amputated both feet and some of his fingers: on the *Thetis* he lost his remaining fingers, then half his legs. His condition worsened and his leg stumps were amputated: it was all to no avail, Elison dying two weeks after rescue.

Schley not only brought back the survivors but also those bodies he could retrieve. The cemetery was a gruesome sight, with heads and feet sticking out of the earth, a testimony to the exhaustion of the burial parties. The exhumed bodies displayed unmistakable signs of cannibalism, much of the flesh having been cut from the bones. The survivors denied all knowledge of this, and an official inquiry decided that any flesh which had been removed had been 'with a view no doubt to use as shrimp bait'.

The aftermath of the expedition was sordid. Some of the survivors exhibited themselves in a freak show for $1,000 per week until ordered to desist. Hazen accused Garlington and Wildes of cowardice, and Lincoln of incompetence. The government closed ranks to defend Lincoln, and Hazen was tried for 'conduct prejudicial to good order'. He was found guilty, but merely censured and allowed to retire quietly: he died two years later. Garlington's career suffered, but having been party to one infamous act he was later involved in another, the massacre of native Americans at Wounded Knee. For that he received the Congressional Medal of Honour, the United States of America's highest award. Greely did well on the lecture circuit and

Above **Greely's camp, photographed by the expedition's rescuers.**
US Navy Historical Centre

Below **The remains of Greely's hut on Pym Island.**
Robert Wallace

following spring (March 1882) Melville again set out. After a two-week search the bodies of the first to die were uncovered from the snow. As he walked nearby Melville tripped over something – it was the frozen hand of De Long protruding from the snow.

Twenty men had died, eight in the lost boat, 12 in De Long's party, with little to show for the loss except the discovery of two small islands. Of the survivors, Danenhower later shot himself, another went insane. Melville, who took the brunt of the criticism for his delay in reaching Bulun, was in the *Thetis* when the remnants of Greely's expedition were found at Cape Sabine.

Nansen and the *Fram*

Two years after the discovery of De Long's body the 23-year-old Fridtjof Nansen read an article about relics of the *Jeanette* being found on an ice floe off Qaqortoq (Julienhåb) on the south-west coast of Greenland. The author of the article, Professor Henrik Mohn, conjectured that the discovery implied a current flowing across the Arctic Ocean from Siberia: Nansen realised that such a current might take a ship over, or very close to, the North Pole. If the ship could survive being trapped in the ice it would be released near the coast of Greenland. What was needed was a vessel strong enough to resist ice pressure and a team of men willing to spend perhaps five years on board her.

For the ship Nansen turned to Colin Archer, son of a Scottish immigrant to Norway and a boat-design genius. The ship Nansen and Archer built was the *Fram* – Forward – her cost borne by the Norwegian government as an expression of national pride: later Nansen was influential in the gaining of Norwegian independence. *Fram*'s hull was a half-egg in cross-section with a minimal keel (on some ships the keel had been gripped by ice and then pulled downwards) and a removable rudder (for a similar reason). The crossbeams and stern were huge and of well-seasoned oak to withstand ice pressure. The ship had both a steam engine and sail capability. She also had a windmill which generated electricity for lighting. *Fram* was large, 34.5m (183ft) lay on the waterline and grossing over 400 tons. Visitors to Oslo who take a trip to the Fram Museum at Bygdøy, across the harbour from the city, can compare *Fram* and *Gjøa* which are both preserved there. The latter is tiny by comparison, but *Fram* did not need the manoeuvrability of *Gjøa*: her task was merely to be imprisoned in, resist the pressure of, and drift with, the ice.

Besides Nansen *Fram* had a crew of 12, including Otto Sverdrup, who had crossed Greenland with Nansen, as captain, and Hjalmar Johansen, the son of a townhall caretaker. Johansen had gained a place at university to study law but had to leave when his father died as he could no longer afford to stay. So keen was he to go with Nansen that he not only applied in writing but visited Nansen unannounced. Johansen agreed to do any job and was taken on as a stoker.

When the ship arrived in Vardø, the final Norwegian port before departing for Siberia, the crew celebrated their last night ashore in the time-honoured way – by getting drunk. To their shock Nansen berated them, telling them that if it were not for the fact they were leaving that day he would dismiss them all. It was the first hint of the occasionally difficult times to come. Nansen was a strange leader: he was domineering and arrogant, his undoubted intelligence producing, as one man noted 'a mania for interfering in everything'. Nansen believed he was an authority on all subjects and could do everyone's allotted job better than they could. Yet he was also, and often, cheerful, humorous and good company.

The *Fram* sailed through the Kara Sea, around Cape Chelyuskin and north along the New Siberian Islands to enter the pack. On 5 October 1893 the rudder was raised: *Fram* was frozen in. At first, to Nansen's confusion, the ship drifted south, but soon began his expected steady drift north. Though the ship was cramped, life was tolerable. By luck Nansen had loaded food – canned vegetables and preserved cloudberries, a Norwegian delicacy – which kept the crew free of scurvy. The winter was brutally cold at first as Nansen, fearful of fire and wishing to preserve fuel, refused to allow any heating: he was persuaded to relent when the inside temperature dropped to –30°C. There were excursions on the ice enlivened by occasional polar-bear visits, and regular feast days. And the *Fram* behaved just as Nansen and Archer thought she would: on the open sea she rolled and pitched dreadfully, but when the ice closed around her she rose on it and drifted serenely.

Fram drifted through the winter, the summer of 1894 and into a second winter. But it was clear that her direction was north-west rather than north. On 12 December 1894 she passed the record northing for a ship (set by Nares' *Alert*), but by then Nansen had realised she would never reach the pole and announced his intention of heading north with one companion and all the dogs. His chosen partner was Hjalmar Johansen. During the winter sledges and kayaks were built ready for the trip. On 6

January 1895 *Fram* broke the record for furthest north (held by Lockwood), but almost succumbed to ice pressure, the most frightening time of the whole journey. But neither the new record nor the careful preparations for the voyage stopped Nansen's mood swings. When he and Johansen finally departed on 26 February 1895 almost everyone left on the *Fram* was glad to see the back of him. But those who cheered did so too soon: only 500m from the ship a sledge broke. It had to be repaired and Nansen did not finally depart until 28 February: that day the *Fram* was at 83°50'N and still heading north.

With them Nansen and Johansen had six sledges, 28 dogs and 1,100kg (2,426lb) of equipment. Accompanied by other members of the crew the procession made just 6km (3½ miles) despite shedding some load. After two further days of agonising progress Nansen had to admit that they had started too early (the sun only reappeared on 3 March) and with too much weight. He returned to *Fram*, leaving Johansen on the ice (though two men skied out to join him). *Fram* was now beyond 84°N. The loads were reorganised and on 14 March they set off again, with just three sledges and 760kg (1,676lb) of equipment.

Nansen had secretly thought that with just 6° of latitude to cross the pole would be easily reached. But the pressure ridges of the ice soon proved him wrong. Progress was slow and it was also bitingly cold, with daytime temperatures down to −40°C and reaching −47°C at night. For days neither man had any respite; even at night in their double reindeer-skin sleeping bag they were cold. Fixing latitude from the sun Nansen found that they were travelling much more slowly than he had anticipated; at their rate of progress they would not reach the pole until at least two weeks after his calculated date. Unless things improved they would have to turn back before reaching it.

Progress did not improve. Their clothes, the sweat of effort freezing them into suits of armour, chafed their bodies causing sores; Johansen fell through the ice and almost froze; and the dogs had to be killed one by one. On 4 April Nansen calculated they were at 86°2.8'N when he had hoped they were much further. They continued for three more days then Nansen went ahead on skis. Before him lay a sea of hummocky ice. Later he wrote of his thoughts: 'There seems little sense in carrying on any longer; we are sacrificing valuable time and doing little.' And so, at 86°14'N, a new record by almost 3°, they turned for Franz Josef Land.

At first the going was comparatively easy, a fact which led them to travel too long without camping.

Above **Nansen and Johansen about to set off from the *Fram*. Nansen is second from the left, Johansen fourth from the right.**
From Fridtjof Nansen *Furthest North*.
Richard Sale Collection

That in turn led them to forget to wind their watches. The watches stopped, but as they had little idea how long they had stopped they could no longer be sure of their longitude. To compensate they steered an easterly course as, like Albanov before them, the pair could not afford to miss Franz Josef on its west side and finish in open ocean. The weather continued to hold, though the routine killing of dogs darkened their mood, and latitude checks showed they were still a long way from Franz Josef.

Then the weather changed: the wind shifted bringing blizzards and, worse, altering the ice drift unfavourably. Johansen was becoming tired, the strain of managing two sledges to Nansen's one wearing him down. When the third sledge was finally abandoned on 13 May Johansen was joyful. Summer having arrived the temperature rose, but this also meant more open water slowing their progress. Nansen was also increasingly concerned about their position. Julius von Payer had claimed to have seen Petermann Land lying north of Cape Fligely: he had been fooled by ice and atmospherics, but Nansen did not know that Petermann was a myth.

As May progressed the melting ice proved more difficult and food was also running low and had to be rationed. June brought the first sight of seals and gulls: Nansen shot two gulls, giving the men their first fresh meat for months. But the temperature also rose above freezing making the going, through slush, even worse.

Despite the gulls both dogs and men were now starving. Slaughtered dogs provided blood soup for Nansen and Johansen, but meagre meat for the remaining dogs. When the slush would no longer support a man on skis the two kayaks were bound into a catamaran and paddled. It was almost as hard as walking. On 21 June, 100 days from the *Fram*, Johansen shot a seal, the first of several. It was the first sign that things were getting better, and they improved still further when a polar bear and her two cubs were shot.

No longer hungry, Nansen and Johansen waited in the camp they had established on 21 June until 19 July. By then rain and high temperatures meant that kayaking was easy. Four days later they recognised that the cloud bank they had been staring at for a month was actually a glacier. Currents and wind made sure that reaching land was not easy, and Johansen was lucky to survive an attack by a polar bear (he shouted for Nansen to get the gun and then told him 'you must look sharp', remembering to use the formal Norwegian form of 'you'; the two men maintained that formality, despite four months together on the ice: not until New Year's Day 1896 did they agree to exchange the formal 'de' for the familiar 'du'). On 7 August they reached the ice edge. It was a joyous moment but meant the end for the last two of the 28 dogs that started out from *Fram*.

What the two men had seen was Eva-Liv Island (named later by Nansen for his wife and daughter) in north-eastern Franz Josef. What they first landed on was Adelaide's Island, a little way south, on 10 August. Thinking he was on the west side of the archipelago Nansen decided to kayak west to Gilles Land and then on to Svalbard. Gilles Land had been seen by Dutchman Cornelis Gilles in 1707, but it was not where he claimed it was: he had actually seen Kvitøya. Had Nansen been where he thought he was and headed west he and Johansen would have found 400km (250 miles) of open sea. It is doubtful whether the men would have survived.

As it was, when they headed west, the two kayaks strapped together as a catamaran again, the two men had to endure a walrus attack before finally landing at Helland's Point on north-west Jackson Island (as Nansen later named it). Now, in late August, it was clear winter was coming. Desperate to avoid another winter, but trapped by ice and weather, the pair eventually landed on the southern coast of Jackson Island.

There they built a hut of low walls of stones and turf, digging out the floor and draping walrus skins over a huge log laid between the end walls. Inside it was remarkably snug. With plenty of fresh bear and walrus meat cooked over a blubber fire, a comfortable enough winter was passed. Nansen actually gained weight, though he also had a bout of chronic lumbago and had to be nursed by Johansen.

On 19 May 1896 they refloated their catamaran and headed west again, still unsure of their exact whereabouts. Disaster almost struck in June when the poorly moored catamaran floated away. Nansen took off his top clothes, and dived into the chilling water to retrieve it. With his limbs becoming numb he barely reached the shore again. A few days later a walrus almost sank them. They beat the walrus off, but one kayak was holed and by the time they got ashore much of their equipment was wet. For two days they stayed in their camp to dry things out. On the second day Nansen thought he heard a dog barking and, leaving Johansen behind, set out on skis to investigate.

At his Elmwood base Frederick Jackson was told that there was a man approaching and wandered out to meet him. Jackson recalls in his book on his own trip, 'I saw a tall man on skis with roughly made clothes and an old felt hat on his head. He was covered with oil and grease, and black from head to foot... His hair was very long and dirty, his complexion appeared to be fair, but dirt prevented me from being sure on this point, and his beard was straggly and dirty also... I inquired if he had a ship? "No," he replied "my ship is not here" – rather sadly I thought.'

Jackson thought he recognised a man he had met when he lectured in London in 1892. After discovering he was right he said, 'I am damned glad to see you.' The relief Nansen and Johansen must have felt can only be imagined, yet within days Johansen was noting that his once sociable, agreeable companion had returned to his normal arrogant self. The two sailed in Jackson's ship *Windward* on 7 August and were in Vardø on the 13th. On the 20th they heard that *Fram* was also safely home. The ship had reached 85°56'N in November 1895, but had then drifted south again. She was released from the ice in August 1896. After calling at Svalbard to see if there was any news, Sverdrup took the ship on to Norway, arriving on 20 August just a week after Nansen and Johansen.

Nansen returned to Oslo a hero, the raptures his courageous trek had engendered echoing not only across the country but the world. The dissenting

voices – those who thought that for a leader to abandon his expedition was a monstrous and unjustifiable act; those who felt the trek had been foolhardy; Peary's acerbic comment that Nansen should at least have tried to return to *Fram* – were drowned out by the cheering. *Fram* was the second and last great expedition of Nansen's life, but such was the success of it and his Greenland crossing, and the manner of the accomplishment of both, that they were to maintain his reputation as an explorer throughout his life.

Andrée and the *Eagle*

Otto Sverdrup had two reasons for stopping at Svalbard on his way home with *Fram*. The prime reason was, of course, to hear of any news of Nansen and Johansen. The other was to check on the progress of the Swede Salomon August Andrée who was planning a balloon flight to the North Pole. Andrée had become interested in balloons in 1876 at the age of 22, but it was not until 1893 that the interest had developed into a passion with practical results. From 1893 to 1895 he undertook nine flights in his balloon *Svea*,

Top left **Nansen's photograph of the winter hut on Jackson island.**
Richard Sale Collection

Above left **The remains of the winter hut. In this recent photograph of the camp site on Jackson Island the same rocky profile dominates the background to the shot.**
Susan Barr

Top right **The two kayaks strapped together to form a catamaran. This shot, as with several others in Nansen's book *Furthest North*, had to be staged after Nansen and Johansen had returned to civilisation.**
Richard Sale Collection

Above right **Jackson greets Nansen at Elmwood. There was no camera present when the actual meeting took place so it was recreated the following day. Nansen dressed as he had been the previous day, but by then he had washed, and trimmed his beard and hair. A lock of his hair is still preserved in the Fram Museum, Oslo. Jackson was overwhelmed by meeting Nansen: of Johansen he said only that he 'seems a splendid little fellow'.**
Richard Sale Collection

including one of 400km (250 miles) which took 16½ hours, and one of 284km (177 miles) that crossed the Baltic Sea from Stockholm to Eskörn Island. The latter was particularly interesting as Andrée used a guide rope trailing on the sea to slow the balloon, and sails on it to alter the direction of travel. He found he could vary the direction by up to 27° from the wind. By 1894 Andrée was considering the use of a balloon in the Arctic. He believed that he had a balloon which was gas-tight for 30 days, more than enough time judging from his earlier flights, and thought he had solved the potential problem of icing on the fabric – the guide ropes, three of them, each 350m (382yd) long and made of coconut fibre, would not only allow manoeuvrability, but would keep the balloon low enough for ice not to form. The endpoint of the flight could not, of course, be fixed: Andrée assumed that given enough time in the air the balloon was bound to reach somewhere.

In June 1896 the *Virgo* took Andrée's balloon, the *Örnen* (Eagle), to Danskøya, an island off Spitsbergen's north-western corner. The site is now called Virgohamna, Virgo Harbour. The crew of three – Andrée, Nils Ekholm and Nils Strindberg – waited until 21 August (Sverdrup visiting them on the 14th) but the wind was consistently wrong. On that day the *Virgo* had to leave for Sweden and the three men went with her. In 1897 Andrée returned. Nils Ekholm, concerned

Above **A superb cartoon published in Sweden during the 'race' for the North Pole between the Salomon Andrée and the Norwegian Fridtjof Nansen. Nansen in his boat is left behind as Andrée is reeled into the pole by a smiling Inuk. The people of Sweden applaud while the Norwegians can barely conceal their sorrow and fury. Quite how the Inuk – or anyone or anything – was actually supposed to haul Andrée down to the pole is another matter.**
Richard Sale Collection

Right **Just before the launch of the *Eagle* the three crewmen compose themselves in the gondola.**
Richard Sale Collection

Below right **The launch of the *Eagle*. The guide ropes, whose loss put a risky venture even more in peril, can be seen still dragging on the beach.**
Richard Sale Collection

with the hydrogen leakage rate he had measured in 1896, had pulled out, his place taken by Knut Frœnkel. The *Eagle* was launched on 11 July, but immediately there was a problem. Andrée had changed his guide ropes, attaching the coconut-fibre ropes to hemp ropes with a simple screw, the idea being that if the lower section of the rope hooked firmly on to any projection on the ice the screw could be used to detach it, saving the top section of rope. But the wind rotated the

Above **This shot by Nils Strindberg of the stricken *Eagle* is one of the ghostly images of the expedition which emerged when the discovered film was developed.**

Courtesy of the Swedish Polar Research Secretariat

balloon and the coconut ropes unscrewed themselves. Without their ballast the *Eagle* rose to 600m (2,000ft): within seconds of the launch Andrée had lost not only his steering potential but his perceived protection against icing. The balloon headed north-east and, an hour later, disappeared from view.

In those days before radio Andrée's only available means of communication were carrier pigeons (fast, but not too reliable) and buoys which, rather like messages in bottles, were unpredictable. Five buoys were eventually picked up, but by then all hope for the team was gone. Only one pigeon was recovered when it was shot four days later: its message read 'July 13 at 12.30pm. Lat 82°2'N, Long 15°E, good speed towards east 10° south. All well. This is the third pigeon post. Andrée'. Despite many searches, continued until 1899, nothing

else was heard of, or from, the balloon. The shot pigeon was stuffed and presented to the inconsolable fiancée of Nils Strindberg.

On 6 August 1930 the Norwegian sealer *Bratvaag* anchored off the south-western tip of Kvitøya, the rarely visited island to the north-east of Svalbard's Nordaustlandet. The scientists brought by the ship disembarked and, 200m (218yd) inland, discovered a snow-covered camp and the remains of the three balloonists. A more extensive search in September revealed the diaries of the crew and, most remarkably, about 20 photographic negatives that could still be printed. The images, when developed, must have given the darkroom staff a start, reaching across 30 years to record the sad end to the *Eagle*.

The flight had been uneventful at first, *Eagle* heading north-east to about 82°30'N. Then, at about 2am on 12 July, the wind backed to east. The balloon headed west, then north-east again. Rain now caused the balloon to fall and the gondola struck the ice. It banged across the ice for several hours, then one of the shortened guide ropes became trapped. For 13 hours it stayed trapped, then broke free. Ice began to form on the balloon and soon it was dragging the gondola across the ice again. By 7am on 14 July the flight was over. The balloon had travelled 830km (520 miles) in 65½ hours and had landed at 82°56'N.

The three men were forced to head south across the ice hauling three sledges, on one of which was a boat. At first they decided to head for Cape Flora on Franz Josef Land, but soon revised the plan when they realised how slowly they were moving. By early September they were sick with stomach cramps and severe diarrhoea. They were also exhausted and set up camp on an ice floe, allowing its drift to carry them south. On 5 October they reached Kvitøya but now, inevitably, faced an Arctic winter with little chance of relief and none of escape. The diary entries became shorter, more fragmented and enigmatic, and finally stopped in mid-October.

From the position of the bodies it was clear that Strindberg had died first, as his body was buried beneath rocks in a gap between two boulders, though his death must have occurred after the diaries of Andrée and Frœnkel stopped as it is not mentioned. The cause of death has been the subject of speculation ever since the discovery. From the photos and diaries it is clear that polar bears were shot for food. Analysis of meat samples discovered at the camp showed the presence of trichinae (a parasitic nematode). If the meat had been eaten raw or poorly cooked the men could have developed trichinosis (which would explain the severe diarrhoea) and died. That is still the opinion of many experts, though cold, exhaustion and even suicide, induced by their hopeless position, cannot be ruled out.

The Italians head north from Franz Josef

After Leigh-Smith, Jackson and Nansen had better established the geography of Franz Josef Land, many explorers with designs on the pole believed it would make an ideal starting point for expeditions northward. The first of these was Walter Wellman, an American journalist, who arrived in 1898. Wellman had already tried once from Svalbard, reaching 81°N in 1894. In 1898, accompanied by three other Americans (one of whom was Evelyn Baldwin) and five Norwegians, Wellman (in the *Frithjof*) took one of Jackson's huts and a great deal of supplies from Elmwood and, prevented by ice from heading far north, set up a base at Cape Tegetthoff and a northern camp on Wilczek Island. The main expedition spent a comfortable winter at Cape

Above **Andrée's camp site on Kvitøya, a rarely visited site due to the remoteness of the island and the difficulties of approaching it because of sea ice. The last acts of the Andrée expedition were immensely moving. The bodies were brought home from Kvitøya by a ship accompanied, as it neared port, by a flotilla of smaller craft. There was a state funeral attended by the Swedish king. But most touching of all was the gesture by Gilbert Hawtrey, an English schoolmaster living in New Hampshire. Anna Charlier, Strindberg's fiancée, had married Hawtrey when, after a dozen years, all hope of Nils' return was gone. She had accompanied Hawtrey to the US and taught piano at his school, the stuffed pigeon from Andrée's balloon flying above the instrument. She died before the discovery on Kvitøya, but Hawtrey did not, and on hearing the news had Anna's body exhumed and her heart sent to Sweden to be buried beside her first love.**
Per Michelsen

Tegetthoff, but two Norwegians, Bjørvik and Bentsen, had a rougher time at the northern camp. Bentsen sickened and eventually died, leaving Bjørvik alone and miserable. In February Bjørvik was relieved by Wellman as he moved north. Already disheartened by the death, Wellman and his team of four and 42 dogs were enveloped in a storm which disrupted the ice causing the loss of most of their equipment and eight dogs, and they abandoned the attempt short of 82°N: the expedition sailed for home in the *Capella*, a Norwegian sealer.

The next to try his luck from Franz Josef was Luigi Amedeo, Duke of the Abruzzi, who arrived in 1899 with a large team of Italians and Norwegians. The duke's plan was to sail his ship, the *Stella Polare*, north along the coast, sledging on when ice prevented further progress. On 6 August the Italians were visited by Wellman and the *Capella*'s captain. Captain Støkken's son was part of the duke's team. The *Stella Polare* sailed north of Rudolf Island. The duke hoped that Petermann Island did exist, despite Nansen's claim, but he was disappointed and as wintering in the open sea was a recipe for disaster the ship returned to Teplitz Bay on the west coast of Rudolf. The journey to the pole started in the spring of 1900. In charge was the duke's deputy, Umberto Cagni, who led a team of four (himself, Simone Canepa, Alessio Fenoillet and Giuseppe Petigax) supported by three teams who returned at intervals after carrying supplies. All the teams used dog-sledges. Sadly the second support team failed to reach Teplitz Bay: one of the three lost was Henrik Støkken, son of the captain of the *Capella* – their meeting on the *Stella Polare* was their last. In 1901 Captain Støkken returned, looking for his son: he failed to find any trace of him or his two Italian colleagues and erected a memorial to them at Cape Flora.

Cagni's team spent 104 days on the ice travelling 1,200km (750 miles) and reaching 86°34'N, a new record. On his return, Cagni claimed that the journey over the sea ice was too difficult and that future attempts should be made from Greenland. When Captain Støkken returned in search of his son, another expedition, the first of two financed by New Yorker William Zeigler, also arrived in Franz Josef, intent on disproving Cagni's pessimistic assertion. The first expedition, in 1901/2, was led by Evelyn Baldwin who had been with Wellman in 1898/9, and also with Peary in Greenland in 1893. With 15 Siberian ponies, over 400 dogs and a total of 42 men, the expedition was massive. Its ship, the *America*, was elegantly described by one observer as being like a floating haystack. Baldwin set up base (Camp Ziegler) on Alger Island, well south of what he had hoped, but ice prevented the *America* going further north. In the summer of 1902 Baldwin started laying depots towards the north. His teams worked under a considerable handicap as the leader refused to allow them to take sleeping bags as these took up space which could be better used. Despite the misery this involved, by June a series of depots had been laid to Rudolf Island. At that point, and for no very good reason, Baldwin took the expedition home. It had been, as someone noted, a complete waste of effort.

In 1903 Zeigler financed a new attempt. Not sur-prisingly he did not appoint Baldwin as leader, preferring Anthony Fiala, who had been with, and unimpressed by, Baldwin in 1901/2. Again the expedition was large (though only half the size of Baldwin's). Its base was in Teplitz Bay where supplies from Abruzzi's expedition were found to be usable. The *America*, which again transported the team, was frozen in, but ice pressure in December wrecked her and she disappeared in a storm in January 1904. Fiala's first attempt at the pole was thwarted by bad weather and equipment failures after just two days. Now, faced with a lack of enthusiasm for continuing, Fiala returned to Cape Flora with most of the team. Jackson's Elmwood was occupied and coal was found locally, securing fuel in case of a second winter. A supply ship (Wellman's *Frithjof*) failed to reach the base and a second overwinter was indeed required. In March 1905 Fiala finally attempted the pole again. His team reached 82°N but open water then stopped progress. Again Fiala's men lost heart and a retreat was ordered. This time a relief ship managed to reach Cape Flora. It was the *Terra Nova* which, five years later, took Scott to Antarctica.

As Fiala's team was being evacuated from Franz Josef, Robert Peary was heading north again. His furthest north in 1902 (84°17'N) was still a record in the western Arctic, but over 2° less than Cagni's attempt from Franz Josef Land. Peary's efforts in 1901/2 seem curiously tentative, at odds with his obsession with fame and the pole. Arguably the most experienced polar traveller of the time, with an enviable record of exploration in northern Greenland, he had actually achieved very little in his quest for the pole. His 1901 journey seems lacking in conviction. His backers thought so too and sent Dr Frederick Cook to examine him. Cook suspected pernicious anaemia and recommended eating liver, to which Peary replied, 'I would rather die'. Cook also looked at his feet and told him, 'you are through as a traveller on snow on foot'. Peary was then 46. The news would have been unwelcome, the messenger, a rival and a younger one at that, unpopular. A relationship which had started with mutual respect was turning sour.

During the years after his 1902 furthest north achievement – another journey where the result failed to justify the preparation – Peary had recharged his mental batteries, refitted his expedition coffers and now, in 1905, approaching 50, was ready for another (probably his last) try. He had a new ship (the *Roosevelt*: Peary had not lost his touch in keeping real power on his side) and had taken her to a point just beyond that reached by the *Alert*: it was only 3km (2 miles) beyond, but it satisfied Peary's lust for records. Early the following year supply depots were established ready for the pole attempt. That began on 6 March. The journey was troubled by a huge lead, by ice drift and bad weather, and by early April it was clear the pole was unattainable. Even a new record northing was doubtful. But Peary decided on a last dash and, achieving daily travel rates which were, if true, remarkable, reached 87°6'N on 21 April, bettering Cagni's record by 32'. There are many who doubt Peary's claim (particularly as he was still troubled by his amputated toe stubs and also had a hernia) though most experts believe he probably got very close to Cagni's latitude, perhaps even going a little further. But the doubts generated by his unlikely account of the last dash colour judgements over his later claims.

At his northern point, whatever it was, Peary turned and headed, not for his ship, but for the Greenland coast which, because of ice drift, was now due south. Feeding killed dog to remaining dogs and burning sledges for fuel, the team made it – but only just. Then on the route west to the ship Peary's team overtook one of their supply teams. It was fortunate they did: though Peary was almost out of food and fuel, the supply team was in a far more desperate position and would likely have died had he not arrived.

The last miles to the ship were desperate. Had Peary not known the coast so well and been so experienced it would have ended tragically. As it was he brought 12 men (his eight and the supply team's four) to safety.

Cook and Peary

In September 1909 an astonished world was informed that the North Pole had finally been reached. Not once, but twice. On 2 September Dr Frederick Cook announced via a telegram office in the Shetland Isles (where the Danish supply ship taking him from Greenland to Denmark stopped briefly) that he had stood at the pole on 21 April 1908. Then, on 6 September Robert Peary used a similar office in Indian Harbour, Labrador, to say he had reached the pole on 6 April 1909. Each had friends in high places and within days the *New York Herald*, which had backed Cook, and the *New York Times* and National Geographic Society, behind Peary's, had begun a war. It was a dirty war in which the reputations of both men were tarnished beyond redemption, and one which, 90 years on, shows no signs – nor has much chance – of ending in a truce, honourable or otherwise.

Above **Cagni's Furthest North Camp at 86°18'20". The next day the team marched to 86°31'.**
From Luigi Amedeo di Savoia, Duke of the Abruzzi *On the Polar Star in the Arctic Seas*.
Richard Sale Collection

Below **Peary at his furthest north, 87°6'N, on 21 April 1906.**
From Robert Peary *Nearest the Pole*.
Richard Sale Collection

Returning from his claimed furthest north in 1906 Peary found that his ship, the *Roosevelt*, needed a refit. The work was not completed in time to sail in 1907, so Peary did not head north again until 1908. Now 52, he must have known that if he failed in 1909 he would be unlikely to have another chance. His expedition was huge: in addition to the 22 who started out on the *Roosevelt* there were 49 Inuit from Etah and 246 dogs. The *Roosevelt*'s captain, Bob Bartlett (captain, too, in 1905/6, later captain of the *Karluk* and a great Arctic explorer in his own right) again took the ship to Cape Sheridan on Ellesmere's north coast. From there a wintering base was established at Cape Colombia. On 28 February 1909, 24 men, 19 sledges and 133 dogs set out north.

At one stage they were held up by a huge open lead for six days (of good weather). When the lead closed the caravan moved on. One by one the support teams departed south. Sadly, during the return of one of these support teams Ross Marvin, Peary's 'secretary', drowned in a lead. Finally, on 1 April, Peary sent Bartlett and the last support team back. Bartlett had wanted to go all the

Above **Cook's camp at Svartevoeg on the northern coast of Axel Heiberg Island.**
From Frederek Cook *My Attainment of the Pole.*
Richard Sale Collection

Below **Crossing the ice on Peary's trip to the pole. The original black-and-white print was hand-coloured to add dramatic effect.**
USA Library of Congress

way, and had certainly wanted to reach 88°: he took one last latitude observation – 87°46'49"N. Peary and his team were 246km (154 miles) from the pole. With him Peary now had Matthew Henson, the Inuit Egingwah, Ooqueah, Ootah and Seegloo, five sledges and 40 dogs. This team reached the pole at about 1pm on 6 April. On those last five days they had averaged almost 50km/31 miles per day (straight-line distance). On the first 31 days they had averaged about 17km/10½ miles per day (straight-line distance again). Peary remained at the pole for about 30 hours, then raced back to the *Roosevelt*, arriving on 27 April, just three days after Bartlett, who had travelled at least 490km (310 miles) less. At Etah on 17 August Peary heard that Cook was claiming to have beaten him to the pole, but on Labrador went ahead with his announcement.

Cook's claim was even more remarkable than Peary's as the latter had retraced his own earlier journeys. Cook was sponsored by John R. Bradley, gambling club owner and big game hunter, and sailed, in 1907, in a ship bought by and renamed after him. The *John R. Bradley* was captained by Moses Bartlett, cousin of the *Roosevelt*'s Bob. Cook and Rudolph Francke were dropped off at the Inuit village of Annoatok close to Etah. Francke had been employed by Bradley as a cook and was somewhat taken aback to discover he was now to accompany Cook on a journey towards the pole. After overwintering at Annoatok the two set out in February 1908 with nine Inuit. Instead of going north, the 'normal' (and Peary) route to the pole, they headed west, crossing to Cape Sabine, then traversing Ellesmere Island to reach Cape Thomas Hubbard at the northern tip of Axel Heiberg Island, a journey of over 800km (more than 500 miles). At the cape Cook left a large supply dump, then on 18 March headed north across the sea ice with just two Inuit companions, Ahwelah and Etukishook, two sledges and 26 dogs. He reached the pole on 21 April, having travelled about 800km (500 miles) in 34 days.

On the return ice drift pushed them west and persistent fog and poor weather prevented them from calculating their position. With food running very short they at last had clear weather and were able to pinpoint their position. They were in the Prince Gustav Adolf Sea, with land to the south and west, and Axel Heiberg off to the east. Cook now continued to head south, taking Hassel Sound between the Ringnes Islands and reaching the Grinnell Peninsula on the north-western tip of Devon Island. They had by now run out of ammunition and had to fashion harpoons,

Above **On his journey Cook built igloos as camp sites, so there was no need to carry tents.**
Byrd Polar Research Centre, Ohio State University, USA

bows and arrows from muskox horn and whalebone. The three men headed east along Jones Sound, then overwintered in an old Inuit winter house, continuing towards Greenland in February 1909. Once more low on food they existed for a short time on candles and hot water until a bear was killed. By the time they reached Annoatok they were hungry again, so much so that they were barely able to stand and had eaten all their leather straps. They had been away 14 months, having taken food for just two.

Cook was fêted on his arrival in Copenhagen, but things rapidly turned sour for him. On his journey south Peary spoke with the two Inuit who had accompanied Cook and claimed they told him that they had never been out of sight of land. In the US Peary's vitriolic attacks on Cook, in telegrams and to the press, had the opposite affect to that intended, rapidly drawing sympathy for Cook. In several polls public opinion was 80 per cent in Cook's favour, often higher. Outside the US the less heated atmosphere allowed more sober judgements, and these tended to back Peary. Cook's position was made much worse by an independent, but coincidental, charge that his claim to have climbed Mount McKinley, North America's highest peak, was a fraud. In the end Peary won over the majority, often grudgingly, as Cook was a far more amiable man, a complete contrast to the blustering Peary who lacked Cook's social skills. In the early 1920s Cook became involved with an oil company and was tried, convicted and imprisoned for fraudulently claiming that land owned by his company was oil-bearing. There seems little doubt that the perceived frauds over McKinley and the pole contributed to his downfall. Cook served seven years of a 14-year term: it was during his time in Fort Leavenworth (where he rapidly became the most popular prisoner, both with inmates and staff) that he was visited by Amundsen. In the end it was shown that the land was oil-bearing, just as Cook had claimed. He was released in 1930. On 5 May 1940 he suffered a cerebral haemorrhage; he was given an unconditional pardon by President Roosevelt on 16 May, and died on 5 August. To the end he maintained the validity of his claim to the pole, recording a tape for posterity. Its final words were 'I state emphatically that I, Frederick A. Cook, discovered the North Pole.'

By contrast to Cook, who suffered public humiliation with forbearance and good grace, Robert Peary railed against the injustice of not being given full credit for his discovery for the rest of his life. He had sacrificed his best years to the search for fame and the pursuit of the pole. He had been away for most of his eldest daughter's formative years, and had never seen a second daughter who had died aged seven months. The honours he received could not assuage his bitterness, which, his wife claimed, hastened his death on 20 February 1920. Ironically the stated cause was pernicious anaemia, the illness Cook had diagnosed all those years before. It is of course possible that the bitterness was not solely due to the fact that what he felt was his just reward for his life's work – the pole – had become soured by dispute. If he had not actually reached the pole, and had known he had not, then the bitter taste could have been that of defeat. Peary managed to convince most of the world of the validity of his claim. A dishonest man might convince himself that he deserves a prize, but unless he is especially deluded he will not be able to convince himself that he has actually secured it.

Millions of words have been written on Cook and Peary. At the time the dispute was simple – was it Cook or Peary who first reached the pole? Now the question is different – did either of them? This is not the forum to review the evidence, but certain observations can be made. Peary's claim is based on extraordinary rates of travel. Most of those who have sledged to the pole consider them too high: some ludicrously so. In a carefully considered book Wally Herbert judged that Peary did not reach it, his claim being immediately rebuffed by a 'scientific study' commissioned by the National Geographic Society, still Peary's staunchest supporter.

There is also the fact that Peary took only Henson and Inuit to the pole. Was this because he wanted to be the only white man there, or was it to hedge his bets, as in those non-politically correct days no one would take the word of a black man or a native against that of a white man? Amundsen, a friend of Cook, agreed Peary's claim (indeed, he changed his own plans and headed south as a result) but noted that Peary's word had to be taken as he was alone: 'Of course, the Negro Henson was too ignorant to know whether they reached it or not.' Today that seems a shocking comment, but it was the general opinion of the time. It also accords with Peary's own view of Henson: despite occasional admissions that Henson was his right-hand man and an essential part of the team, Peary also famously upbraided him for not calling him 'sir' at all times – 'You will pay attention when I am talking to you and show that you hear directions I give you by saying "yes, sir", or "all right, sir".'

But much more importantly, and a fact which gave even his staunchest supporters of the time something to think about – particularly those who, like Peary, had experience on ice – was that by his own admission Peary took no measurements of his longitude, nor magnetic variation, and made no allowance for ice drift. His claim to have gone north along the 70°W meridian is at odds with all experience of ice movements and, unsupported by longitude readings, stretches credibility. If he really did travel by dead reckoning as he claims, then at his final camp he had no idea where he was. This would explain his poor humour there when approached by Henson: his sun shot might have told him that he was still some way from the pole. The strange omissions from his diary are certainly consistent with that view.

But if Peary's claim lacks credibility the situation is no less problematic for Cook supporters. There is the curiosity of cropped photographs. There is the contradictory testimony of his Inuit companions: when interviewed by others they at first backed up his claim to have reached the 'Great Navel' as they call the pole (the Inuit name is usually given as Great Nail, the

explanation being that the place the white explorers sought must be something tangible, and iron was the most valuable commodity to an Inuk, but the true translation of the Inuit is navel, now nail), but are later claimed to have stated that they had never been out of sight of land. Cook's supporters make much of the earliest statements, claiming that the later ones were made under duress; the Inuit were often accused of telling the white man what he wanted to hear. The charge was made at the time of Rae's discovery of Franklin's fate, and there was some truth in it, but Cook's two Inuit seem to have told a consistent tale of not reaching the pole throughout the rest of their lives.

There is the issue of whether enough supplies could be carried by the three men to last the described trip, as Cook makes no mention of hunting. But, as noted above, Cook had set out with food for eight weeks and survived 14 months, so his team were clearly capable of looking after themselves well. There is the fact that Hassel Sound, 'narrow' according to Cook, is actually wide. In claiming it to be narrow Cook was following Sverdrup who also stated it was narrow (from observation only). In reality it is 24km (15 miles) wide at its narrowest point. Cook was a remarkably good observer of natural phenomena, yet it has to be said that it is occasionally very difficult to be sure where sea ice ends and a low coast begins, and he did accurately place a small island at the sound's northern end. His supporters note that whether he did or did not traverse Hassel Sound has no bearing on the validity of his pole claim, but it does: if he was not telling the truth about that, relatively trivial, aspect of his trip, why believe his pole claim? All the doubts raised by the sceptical about Cook's journey are rebutted by his supporters, usually by cogent arguments, though occasionally the logic of the rebuttals is clamorous and suspect. But Cook's opponents are often equally hysterical.

One interesting consideration is the fact that Cook, a humane man, was appalled by Peary's treatment of both members of his expeditions and the Inuit. Cook claimed that both Verhoeff and Astrup had been driven to suicide by Peary, and felt that Peary's constant reference to 'my Eskimo', implying ownership, was distasteful. He also disliked Peary's assumed 'ownership' of the pole. Did Cook conspire to teach Peary a lesson for his arrogance?

Finally there is the mystery of the phantom and actual land of Cook's journey. In 1906 Peary claimed to have seen land, Crocker Land, to the north-west of Axel Heiberg. Cook claimed to have seen Bradley Land, as he called it, to the south of Peary's. Many have suggested that Cook's Bradley was based on Peary's Crocker and is evidence of his fraud. When Donald McMillan went to explore Crocker Land in 1913/17 he too saw it from Ellesmere Island. When he reached it had disappeared. Yet when he returned to Ellesmere McMillan saw it clearly again and would have sworn to its existence had he not known with certainty it did not exist: Crocker/Bradley was phantom. But there are those who believe that Cook may have seen ice islands now known to exist at about the same position as he claimed for Bradley Land. And if he did see those ice islands then he must have been in a position to do so.

Meighen Island, to the west of Axel Heiberg, is fact. When Cook had his first clear day after fog on his return from the pole he claimed to have seen land to the west and south, and Axel Heiberg to the east. As has been pointed out, from where he was Meighen Island would have been clearly visible: it rises to about 150m (500ft). Some of the anti-Cook faction claim it would have obscured his view of Axel Heiberg, but that is not so if his position was calculated accurately. However, he claims there was land to the west which is only possible if he was further south than he thought. In that case Meighen would have been even further north. But these are minor issues in comparison to a real mystery. Cook's Inuit companions plotted the journey they said they had actually made on a map based on Sverdrup's discoveries, and they accurately plotted the position and size of an island they claimed to have seen to the north-west of Axel Heiberg. It was clearly Meighen Island, at that time undiscovered (it was not officially discovered until 1916 when Stefansson came this way). Why then, if Cook had discovered Meighen, did he not mention it to lend greater credence to his supposed fraudulent story?

At this remove in time the truth of the two claims can no longer be ascertained. While in general the polar environment does a remarkable job of preserving objects left either deliberately or casually, the nature of the Arctic Ocean precludes such survivals. No new evidence is likely either from the north or from the diaries and logs of the two men and their expeditions. No one will ever know for certain which, if either, was telling the truth. Overall it is probable that Peary got close to the pole, but did not reach it, defeated by his own navigational naïveté and incompetence. The Cook claim is more intriguing. There are seemingly compelling reasons for discounting it, not least the fact that by his own admission Cook was no navigator: how could someone incapable of plotting longitude and having difficulty with latitude possibly know where he was on the shifting ice of the Arctic Ocean? Yet equally compelling ones suggest he did indeed travel a long way out across the ocean towards the pole and so, perhaps, might have reached it. It is also the case that whichever journey Cook actually made – the one he defended or the one told by his companions – it was both more interesting and tougher than Peary's.

The Cook/Peary tale is a manifestation of an age in which mysteries are seen as either evidence of a conspiracy or nuisances which get in the way of a precise interpretation of the world. In another age the tale, which has elements of both, might also be seen as having a 'whodunit' beauty of its own, for while it is likely that neither Cook nor Peary reached the pole, it is possible that one or both of them did.

Balloons and aeroplanes

Andrée's flight had failed, but it had always been a risky venture. Balloon technology was at its limit and Andrée's steering method was, at best, haphazard. Ten years later airships had replaced balloons, offering acceptable steering in all but the worst weather. Gas leakage had also been reduced, and with a higher speed and better steering, flight times were also lower. The first to try the new technology was Walter Wellman, the man who had already tried his luck with a dog-sledge.

This time Wellman chose Spitsbergen for his base. In 1906 he brought the first airship to Danskøya (where Andrée had launched) but abandoned the attempt when it became apparent that his engines were useless. He returned in June of the following year. It took until August to reconstruct the 1907 hanger, but in that month the weather was continuously awful. Only on 2 September could the airship (the *America*) finally be pulled from the hanger. Initially towed by a small steamer, she flew 24km (15 miles) northwards, but was then hit by a storm. As Wellman noted, 'there ensued a hard fight between the storm and the motor. The latter triumphed'. It was just as well, as the storm threatened to crash the *America* into jagged mountains.

Wellman was back on Danskøya in 1909, and the *America* was launched on 15 August. Wellman had this

Top **Cook's Inuit at the North Pole.**
Byrd Polar Research Centre, Ohio State University, USA

Right **Hand-coloured print of Peary's North Pole shot.**
USA Library of Congress

time fitted two guide ropes, just as Andrée had, believing that if the airship was kept close to the ground hydrogen leakage would be minimised. But in a re-run of Andrée's launch one of the guide ropes fell off and the *America* climbed rapidly. Fortunately this incident was observed by the Norwegian coastal steamer *Farm* which, sensing trouble, gave chase, and rescued the *America*'s four-men team.

For a few years, despite the debate over the validity of Cook and Peary's pole claims, interest in reaching the pole died. Then the 1914–18 war intervened and not until the 1920s was another attempt made to reach the North Pole. The development of air travel, in both airships and aeroplanes, had moved on and, as always, man was enthusiastic to apply the latest technology to tackle problems in remote and hostile areas. The main enthusiast was Roald Amundsen whose *Maud* expedition had completed the North-East Passage, but entirely failed to emulate *Fram*'s ice drift. Amundsen left *Maud* in 1921 to buy an aircraft, but his first attempted flight from Alaska to Spitsbergen failed due to bad weather. He tried again in 1923, using a plane with an insufficient fuel capacity; his plan was to carry a sledge and kayak, and to complete the journey with these after he had made a forced landing. He was perhaps fortunate that his plane crashed on its first trial flight.

In 1925 Amundsen renewed his acquaintanceship with Lincoln Ellsworth whom he had declined to take on *Maud*. Ellsworth was the son of a wealthy American financier who agreed, after some soul-searching, to underwrite an expedition of two seaplanes. The two Dornier-Wal planes (N–24 and N–25) were to take off from King's Bay (Ny Ålesund) on Spitsbergen, each carrying three men and enough food for three weeks. The plan was to land at the pole, transferring all fuel and men into one plane for a continuing flight to Alaska. The planes took off on 21 May 1925 and flew for eight hours. Then, assuming they were close to the pole, they landed. Once down they discovered that a headwind had reduced their speed: they were only at 88°N. The N–25, piloted by Hjalmar Riiser-Larsen, with German mechanic Ludwig Feucht and Amundsen on board, had engine trouble on the descent. They were forced on to a narrow lead and come to rest against an iceberg. The N–24, piloted by Leif Dietrichsen, with mechanic Oskar Omsdal and Ellsworth, landed in a large pool, but col-

lided with an ice floe, and the cabin filled up with water. The two crews could not at first see each other, but after 24 hours had made visual contact and exchanged messages by semaphore: they were 5km (3 miles) apart. Over the next few days ice drift took the doomed N–24 crew closer to the N–25. Eventually the entire team was back together again, but only after Omsdal had fallen into the sea, knocking out seven teeth on the ice edge as he did so.

The six men managed to get N–25 safely on to the ice floe. Then Amundsen spelled out the reality of their situation. They could try and build a runway for N–25; going on half rations gave them until 15 June to do so. At that time each man could choose to try to get to Greenland (across several hundred kilometres of sea ice) or to stay with the plane, trying to get it off the ice until food ran out. The stark choice galvanised the men, but several attempts to construct runways failed. Finally, desperately, the N–25 was hauled on to another floe and a channel was cut in a pressure ridge, allowing access to an area of level snow. This was stamped down, the nightly drop in temperature freezing it. On the morning of 15 June Riiser-Larsen fired the engines. The plane lifted off just metres from the runway's end, missed an iceberg by centimetres and flew on. Using dead reckoning they reached Hinloppen Strait, off northern Spitsbergen, where they were forced to land as fuel was running out. The next day a sealing ship was spotted and, using the remaining fuel, the six men drove the N–25 towards it. They had been away 26 days and the sealing captain looked at them as though they were ghosts. Sadly the joy of reaching King's Bay was tempered by the news that Ellsworth's father had died on 2 June.

The following year Amundsen and Ellsworth were back at King's Bay ready to try for the pole again, but this time in an airship, a dirigible designed by the Italian Umberto Nobile who was to accompany the expedition. Despite Amundsen's attempts to reduce his role, Nobile was intent on maximising his share of the glory of the trip and Benito Mussolini, Italy's Fascist dictator, was equally intent on maximising the propaganda benefit for his own ends. Amundsen and Ellsworth arrived on Spitsbergen in early April and were joined on 29 April by Richard Byrd of the US navy, his plane a Fokker tri-motor named the *Josephine Ford*, and his pilot Floyd Bennett. Byrd had asked permission to use King's Bay for a proposed flight to Greenland, but now announced that he intended to fly to the pole. Amundsen, perhaps conscious of his switch from North to South Pole and the

Above **Byrd's plane *Josephine Ford* being taken ashore at King's Bay, Spitsbergen.**
USA Library of Congress

Below **Byrd and Bennett take off from King's Bay, Spitsbergen.**
USA Library of Congress

subsequent furore, did not object. Perhaps, too, Amundsen reasoned that the main prize was already lost: at that time it was assumed the pole had already been reached (by Peary, Cook's claim having been dismissed, Peary's not yet questioned). Amundsen offered Byrd every assistance, including a stack of survival gear none of which, despite his plan, Byrd possessed.

On 7 May 1926 Amundsen's airship, the *Norge* (originally designated the N–1 – Nobile 1 – its name changed by Amundsen) arrived, having been flown from Italy. During the flight Riiser-Larsen had been horrified by Nobile's dismal efforts as pilot. Nobile was now equally aghast at Amundsen's refusal to race Byrd for the privilege of first flight to the pole: the loss of this chance for glory must have been a very hard blow to the Italian. At 00.37 GMT on 10 May Bennett and Byrd took off. At 16.07 the plane was back, and they claimed to have reached the pole. Byrd announced that just as they began their return trip he had dropped and broken his sextant, the flight to King's Bay being by dead reckoning, a fantastic feat. Byrd was welcomed as a hero, his and Bennett's achievement being soon heralded across the world. Then, in 1960, the Swedish meteorologist professor Gösta Liljequist analysed the capabilities of the plane, its flight timings and local weather charts, and concluded that Byrd was unlikely to have flown beyond 88°N. By then Byrd had completed an illustrious naval and polar career and had died. It was assumed that he was unaware of his failure, but more recently it has been noted that many computed positions were added to his charts after the flight. There was also the curiosity that Byrd had taken a huge number of small flags to drop at the pole and not one of them was seen by the *Norge* three days later. It has also emerged that Floyd Bennett confided in a friend that he and Byrd had made no attempt at the pole: the *Josephine Ford* having developed an oil leak, they had merely flown about for the requisite number of hours beyond view of King's Bay and then returned. The idea that Richard Byrd died unaware that he had not reached the pole, and that he had performed a near-miraculous feat of navigation on the return route, must therefore be re-evaluated. There are also persistent rumours that Byrd's South Pole flight was not quite as it seemed.

Blissfully unaware of any problems with Byrd's flight, at 1am on 11 May the crew of 16 – including Amundsen, Ellsworth, Nobile, Riiser-Larsen, the Swede Finn Malmgren and Oscar Wisting, Amundsen's faithful companion – lifted the *Norge* off from Ny Ålesund. At

1.30am on 12 May the *Norge* circled over the pole, flags of the USA, Norway and Italy being dropped on to the ice, attached to sharpened aluminium stakes so they stood upright and flapped in the wind. (Nobile defied Amundsen and Ellsworth by making the Italian flag much bigger than those of Norway and the USA, so large that it fouled on the airship and momentarily threatened a propeller.) Amundsen and Wisting, the first two men to see both poles (and, arguably, in the teams that were first to reach each pole) shook hands.

So far the flight had been uneventful, but beyond the pole the *Norge* ran into fog and began to ice up. Icing on the radio aerials prevented communication, and chunks of ice thrown from the propellers threatened the gas bag. By adjusting altitude the icing was minimised, allowing the airship to continue. At 7.30am on 13 May the Alaskan coast near Point Barrow was seen, but low cloud forced the *Norge* to fly high and to go along the coast to reach the Bering Strait avoiding Alaska's inland mountains. One of the two engines began to fail, and the spare would not start. After a flight of over 50 hours the crew were exhausted (not least because there were only two seats). The intended landing at Nome was abandoned and at 8am on 14 May the *Norge* touched down at Teller 90km (56 miles) to the north-west.

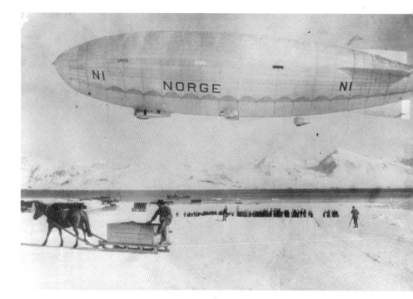

The flight had been a major success, but its aftermath was ugly. To their annoyance Amundsen and Ellsworth discovered that Nobile had, in secret, persuaded the Norwegian backers of the expedition to add his name as co-leader. In Italy Mussolini promoted Nobile to general and ordered him to lecture to the 'Italian colonies' in the US. A large crowd of Italian-Americans were gathered at Seattle when the expedition arrived: Nobile, in military uniform, made the Fascist salute and was fêted while Amundsen and Ellsworth were virtually ignored. Nobile's lecture tour – in which he claimed to have both masterminded the expedition and piloted the airship, neither of which was correct – creamed off much of the available audience (and their entrance

Above right **Amundsen, Byrd, Bennett and Ellsworth after Byrd and Bennett's flight.**
USA Library of Congress

Above centre **The launch of the *Norge*.**
USA Library of Congress

Right **The airship mast at Ny Ålesund, King's Bay, Spitsbergen.**
Per Michelsen

money) leaving both Amundsen and Ellsworth short of cash. Ironically, Nobile eventually believed his own propaganda about being a major explorer, a delusion that led to tragedy.

For his own expedition Nobile decided to use an airship similar to the *Norge* (but called *Italia* to reinforce the nationalistic identity of the expedition) to make a series of three flights, two exploring Severnaya Zemlya and the area north of Greenland, one to the pole. The latter was to include the setting down of a party of six scientists during an extended stay. Despite Nobile's attempts to drum up enthusiasm for the venture even Mussolini seems to have been lukewarm, as nothing very new was being proposed.

After one aborted attempt, a 60-hour flight from King's Bay to Franz Josef Land, Severnaya Zemlya and Novaya Zemlya were made in mid-May 1928. Then, on 23 May, the *Italia* with a crew of 16 (14 Italians, the Swede Finn Malmgren who had been on the *Norge* flight, and a Czech) took off for the pole, flying via Cape Bridgman on Greenland's north coast. On the eastern leg to the pole the wind was favourable, boosting the average speed to 105kmph (66mph). But the same wind slowed the return, while cloud hampered navigation. Although the airship was in radio contact with the *Citta di Milano*, her support ship, the fixing of position by radio was a young science. The cloud caused heavy icing of the *Italia* and at 10.33am on 25 May, after 55 hours flying, she began to descend rapidly. The gondola smashed into the ice, ripping it from the ship which, freed of the load, rose even more rapidly, taking six men to their doom. No sign of the ship or men was found, though the survivors reported seeing a column of smoke later, implying a hydrogen fire.

Of the ten men who lay on the ice, one was dead, Nobile had a broken arm and leg, and Natal Cecioni (who had also been on *Norge*) had a compound leg fracture. The survivors had little equipment and their radio did not, at first, work. With no polar experience there was fear and dissension, and eventually three men, Adalberto Mariano, Filippo Zappi and Finn Malmgren set off in an attempt to reach Spitsbergen and get help. With the gondola on the ice north of Nordaustlandet this was probably a forlorn hope, but with no radio and few supplies, waiting for rescue was none too enticing either.

The radio operator Giuseppe Biagi repaired the radio and began to transmit their position, but all that was heard from *Citta di Milano* was an endless string of telegrams and press statements. In fact a radio operator on the ship had picked up the SOS, but his superior, convinced everyone was dead, dismissed the report. Only when a radio ham near Arkhangelsk heard the SOS and informed Moscow was the position of the survivors fixed.

The loss of the *Italia* was a blow to national pride, especially when of the 18 ships, 22 planes and 1,500 men of six nations deployed to search only one seaplane was Italian. After the position of the survivors' camp – which included a red tent which was to become famous as a symbol of the failed expedition – was fixed it was overflown on 18 June, 23 days after the crash. On 23 June the Swedes Einar Lundborg and Birger Schyberg landed at the camp. The plan was to evacuate one man (as the Swedes' Fokker CVD could accommodate only three), then to return with a single pilot to rescue two men at a time. Nobile wanted Cecioni taken as he was the most seriously injured, but Lundborg thought Nobile himself should go to co-ordinate rescue operations. That was a strange, misguided idea, but Nobile agreed and, accompanied by his dog Titina which was his constant companion (and had been on *Norge*), flew out. The news spread around the world rapidly – a Fascist general had saved himself and his dog before his companions. A furious Mussolini demoted Nobile, and the expedition leader's attempts to influence the rescue were quietly ignored. In his own version of the *Italia* disaster Nobile claims that it took more courage for him to go than to stay as he understood the possible consequences. He did not, perhaps, understand them clearly.

On 24 June Lundborg returned alone, but his plane's skis dug in on landing turning it over, and Lundborg became a member of the Red Tent camp. Further flights were cancelled due to fog until 6 July when Schyberg flew in to pick up Lundborg. Before further flights could be made the Russian ice-breaker *Krassin*, the world's most powerful, developing 10,500hp, crashed through ice up to 3m (10ft) thick and reached the Red Tent on 12 July. Two days earlier a look-out plane from the ice-breaker had spotted men on the ice: Mariano and Zappi. Mariano was exhausted and frost-bitten, but Zappi was in much better shape and told a remarkable story. The three-man team had made slow progress, then Malmgren (who had been in pain since the crash) had collapsed and asked to be left to die. Not only had the Italians done so, but they had taken his food portion. When found Zappi, who claimed not to have eaten for 12 days, was wearing some of Malmgren's clothes. The Russians, appalled by Zappi's demeanour, were also suspicious of his healthy appearance. Later Zappi

contradicted himself and claimed Malmgren had died before they left him, and even admitted cannibalism, though this was later officially denied. The suspicion that Malmgren might have been murdered further tainted the expedition. By contrast to Zappi, Mariano's condition was wretched: he lost a foot to amputation and died a few months later. The crew of three of the only Italian rescue plane also died when they crashed on their way home.

Most tragically of all, the *Italia* disaster also resulted in Amundsen's death. He had been at a celebration dinner for Hubert Wilkins and Carl Eielson, who had flown a Lockheed Vega plane from Point Barrow to Spitsbergen via the pole, when news of the *Italia* came through. He immediately offered his services, claiming past disagreements meant nothing when lives were at stake. Mussolini did not agree and told the Norwegian government their assistance was not required. Realising the stupidity of not helping when Svalbard was Norwegian territory, the government was forced to drop Amundsen, putting Hjalmar Riiser-Larsen in command.

Amundsen was nearing his 56th birthday, but looked much older. He had recently published his autobiography which had stunned everyone, including his friends, with its paranoia and bitterness. In common with most great achievers Amundsen was an almost demonically driven man, perpetually striving to the limit, yet lonely and fearful. One third of his book was taken up with his pursuit of Nobile over the *Norge* aftermath. He was relentless, just as he had been in his pursuit of Hjalmar Johansen. Did he now feel guilt over Johansen's death and Nobile's need to prove himself?

Top **The Red Tent from the air. The photograph has a curiously superimposed look suggesting the image may have been manipulated in some way.**
Richard Sale Collection

Above **Nobile and Titina after their rescue.**
Richard Sale Collection

Left **The wreckage of Lundborg's plane after the crash landing of 24 June 1928. Luckily Lundborg escaped serious injury.** From F. Behounek *Männen på isflaket*, courtesy of the Swedish Polar Research Secretariat

The chapter on the South Pole was short and mentioned the incident at the Royal Geographical Society's dinner in London where Curzon had proposed 'three cheers for the dogs' after Amundsen's speech (making matters worse by urging the Norwegian to stay calm and not respond), and the attitude of the Americans to Frederick Cook. In the US on a lecture tour after the *Norge* expedition Amundsen had visited Cook in Fort Leavenworth jail, a kind gesture for an old friend fallen on hard times, but the American press, egged on by the National Geographic Society, Peary's champion, saw it as support for Cook against Peary. As the press pictured the former as liar, the latter as hero, Amundsen was pilloried. The Curzon incident betrayed a guilt Amundsen felt over Scott's death; the Cook incident merely heightened his bitterness and alienation.

The autobiography clouded his reputation at home. Norway had always been ambivalent about him; the country had loved Nansen, yet for all his accomplishments, the strange, brooding Amundsen had never been taken to their hearts. Nansen had a wife and children, and a reputation as a lady's man. Amundsen was known for pursuing married women by letter with pleadings of overwhelming love which disappeared the moment they left, or were tempted to leave, their husbands. These weird, platonic relationships contrasted with rumours of sordid deeds in seedy brothels. The curious incident of Kakonita and Camilla did not help. These two young girls had been rescued from poverty in Chukotka during the *Maud* expedition – Kakonita motherless, dirty and lice-infested, Camilla an unwanted half-breed. They had been taken to Oslo as foster children, to be given a home, security and an education. It was a laudable act until Amundsen, apparently tiring of them or the responsibility, packed them off to Seattle for return to Chukotka. The two settled in America and lived contented lives there, but it was no thanks to him.

So when Norway declined his offer to help with the *Italia* search Amundsen was embittered once again. But his honour was now at stake: he had said he would go, and he must. So when the French offered him a Latham 47 seaplane for a private mission he accepted immediately. He met pilot René Guilbaud and his crew of three in Bergen, together with his own chosen companion Lief Dietrichson. By the time they reached Tromsø it was clear the Latham was unsuitable. But Amundsen had given his word, and the six men took off on 18 June. When they were overdue in Spitsbergen the rescue effort was so directed towards *Italia* that nothing was done: Amundsen was the great survivor. Searches were made some days later, but not until 31 August was anything found, when fishermen hauled in a float and fuel tank from the plane. It seemed they had been removed in an attempt to construct a raft. It is hard to know if the idea of the indomitable explorer striving to the last and dying a lingering death is more, or less, painful than a tired old man's life ending quickly via a plunge into the sea.

Drift stations and submarines

The general acceptance of Peary's claim to have reached the North Pole not only forestalled Amundsen's attempt, and persuaded him to head south, but also all ground-based attempts for almost 60 years, with the exception of that by the Russian Georgi Sedov who made an attempt from Franz Josef Land in 1912. After two winters and summers largely involving science and survey, Sedov set off with two others. Scurvy had already killed one man; Sedov was sick; it was mid-February, the polar night; and the trio had insufficient equipment and supplies for the proposed six-month trek to the pole and back (or on to Canada). Other expedition members tried to stop the men, but they continued. Sedov died on Rudolf Island in early March: the other two managed to return safely. It was during the retreat of the remainder of Sedov's expedition that Albanov and Konrad (the survivors of the *Saint Anna*) were met. The fact that Sedov did not have a radio also resulted in the first Arctic flight by an aeroplane (as opposed to balloon or dirigible), made in 1914 by the Russian pilot Jan Nagursky. He flew a French-built Maurice Farman seaplane from Krestovaya Bay, Novaya Zemlya. The plane had been shipped there in pieces and assembled by Nagursky and his mechanic Kuznetsov in the open in appalling weather. The two then made a total of five flights across the Barents Sea, but failed to find any trace of Sedov.

In the Soviet Union the *Chelyuskin* affair had demonstrated that camping for long periods on sea ice was feasible, even comfortable if supplies were adequate. It could be argued that Nansen, Cook, Peary and others had already shown this, but *Chelyuskin* showed the viability of a fixed camp and team. The logical extension was a deliberate floe camp, the Arctic drift allowing science to be pursued across the Arctic Ocean. Specifically such drift stations would contribute to an understanding of the drift itself and to the opening of a sea route along Russia's northern coast. The first drift station was set up in June 1937. In charge was Ivan Papanin, accompanied by two scientists, Yevgeni Fedorov and Petr Shirshov, and radio operator Ernst Krenkel. Shirshov and Krenkel were veterans of the *Chelyuskin* camp. There was also a dog (Vesydy – Happy), the polar bear guard. The team were landed 25km (15 miles) from the pole and drifted until February 1938 when they were rescued from a melting floe close to Scoresbysund in east Greenland.

The team lived well in an insulated, but cramped, tent, electricity for the radio generated by an 'exercise

Above **The last photograph of Roald Amundsen, taken as he was about to board the Latham for his last flight on 18 June 1928.**
From F. Behounek *Männen på isflaket*, courtesy of the Swedish Polar Research Secretariat

cycle' which powered a generator. The drift station was entirely successful, the men remaining well throughout, and excellent data were obtained. It is also a memorable trip for one claimed incident (based on truth, but probably apocryphal) which has gone down in the annals of Russian polar science. Papanin was a devoted Communist. The two scientists were also party members, but Krenkel was not. Regular party broadcasts were received but Krenkel, who took them down, was not allowed either to hear them read by Papanin or to discuss them. He was therefore required to walk around the tent while the party members held their meeting. Papanin was not a scientist and so had no allotted task (other than as leader, which was hardly taxing as there were few decisions to be made). He apparently spent most of his time dismantling and reassembling his pistol. Krenkel, aggravated by his enforced retirements to the cold Arctic wastes and driven to distraction by Papanin's constant activity with the pistol (Papanin would work blindfolded and

behind his back to vary the work) took revenge on the ship home. After Papanin had again dismantled his gun, Krenkel added a likely looking item to the pieces and retired. It is said that two days later Papanin had to be rescued from his cabin after he was heard beating his head on the wall in frustration at not being able to reassemble the gun.

The 1939–45 war ended the projected Soviet drift-station programme, but it began again in 1950, a series of stations being set up and manned through to the 1980s. As a prelude to the 1950 stations the Soviets also landed an aircraft at the pole on 23 April 1948. The pole team comprised scientists led by Mikhail Somov – the others were Pavel Sen'ko, Mikhail Ostrekin and Pavel Gordienko – and they became the first men to be confirmed as having stood there. On 4 August 1958 the US navy submarine USS *Nautilus*, commanded by W.R. Anderson, reached the pole on a sub-surface crossing of the Arctic Ocean. The submarine's name recalled that of Sir Hubert Wilkins' craft in which he had also tried to reach the pole underwater in 1931, failing to do more than descend beneath a single ice floe: it is believed his *Nautilus* had been damaged by sabotage, perhaps understandably as the technology of the time made the projected trip dangerous if not foolhardy. On 12 August 1958 James Calvert, commander of the submarine USS *Skate*, surfaced at the pole. Not until 18 August 1977 did a surface ship reach the pole, the nuclear-powered Russian ice-breaker *Arktika*.

Over the ice to the pole

The first overground expedition to reach the pole was in April 1968 when a Canadian/US team led by Ralph Plaisted used snowmobiles to travel from Ward Hunt Island, off Ellesmere Island's northern coast. Four men reached the pole on 19 April and were then taken out by aircraft. The same year a team of four set out to cross the Arctic by way of the pole. The British TransArctic Expedition, comprising leader Wally Herbert, Allan Gill, Kenneth Hedges and Fritz Koerner, set out from Barrow on Alaska's north coast on 21 February 1963 with 40 dogs and four sledges. Despite the winter start they were forced to retreat early in the trip when a pressure ridge of ice heading south threatened to overwhelm them. Sustained by air drops of supplies the team pushed on, sometimes making lengthy detours because of leads. By the time Plaisted reached the pole Herbert's team were about 500km (300 miles) from Barrow. By the beginning of July, Herbert noted, they had sledged 1,900km (1,180 miles), but were still only at 81°33'N.

On 14 July the four established a summer camp and waited for autumn to bring easier sledging conditions. Polar bear and seal meat were added to the menu during their summer 'holiday', by which time ice drift had moved them 1°30' closer to the pole. On the 8th Allan Gill stumbled and injured his back. They returned to their summer camp intending to have Gill evacuated, but the weather and ice conditions would not allow an aircraft to approach or land. They therefore had to remain at the camp site throughout the winter, though the statements on local ice conditions being too difficult for a landing – made by Herbert – caused dissension with the expedition's organising committee in London who wanted the injured man taken off the ice as soon as possible. Gill remaining with the team was seen as Herbert's preferred option and a not-altogether sensible one.

In the event Gill recovered and was able to start with the team on 24 February 1969. Winter drift had taken them north, but also east, and it was still a long way to the pole. The winter cold was intense (below –50°C) but progress was steady and the pole was reached on 5 April, 407 days after leaving Barrow. The remainder of the journey was rather less fraught, though one of their two-man tents caught fire on the first day south of the pole. A new tent dropped to them had a 'No Smoking' sign fixed inside it. On 23 May the team sighted land. They reached it ('Little Blackboard Island' off Nordaustlandet, Svalbard) on 29 May and after a further 13 days of difficult travel over broken ice were picked up by a relief ship.

Later trips to the pole filled in the perceived gaps in human endeavour. In 1978 the Japanese Naomi Uemura set off from Ellesmere Island on 5 March solo, but with a dog team, and reached the pole on 29 April. He was then taken by air to Cape Morris Jesup on Greenland's north coast and sledged the island's length between 10 May and 22 August. In 1986 the Frenchman Jean-Louis Etienne made a solo ski journey to the pole, with air resupply every ten days. The first unsupported journey was made in 1986 when a team of eight (one of whom was evacuated when his ribs were broken by a sledge) led by Will Steger and Paul Schurke used dog teams hauling 3 tons of equipment. Steger's team included Anne Bancroft, the first woman to reach the pole. On day 32 of the 47-day journey the team met Etienne on his solo ski trek. It was this chance meeting that led to Steger and Etienne (and others) organising the TransAntarctic Expedition.

Right **On 1 April 1959 the USS *Skate*, the first submarine to have surfaced at the pole, repeated the trip so that the ashes of Sir Hubert Wilkins could be scattered there. Wilkins had not only attempted the first submarine crossing of the Arctic Ocean but was a pioneer polar airman.**
US Navy Historical Centre

In 1990 the Norwegians Erling Kagge and Børge Ousland made an unsupported ski trek from Ward Hunt Island. They had started as a threesome, but on the ninth day Geir Randby had injured his back and had to be evacuated. Despite all his equipment and food being taken out with him the purists maintained this invalidated the journey. The discussion was rendered academic when Børge Ousland made a solo, unsupported journey from Cape Arktichesky at the northern end of Severnaya Zemlya in 1994. Ousland had chosen a Russian start because although it was 200km (125 miles) further to the pole the ice was usually less disrupted. Ousland pulled a sledge constructed of inner and outer shells which could be locked together with skis to form a catamaran which he used to cross leads. Starting on 2 March 1994 Ousland covered an area of very broken ice, but then maintained a steady average of 15km (10 miles) daily. This increased as he neared the pole, which he reached on 22 April.

Steger's intention when he set out in 1986 was to journey to the pole and back unsupported, but he had been unable to complete the return trip. The out-and-back, unsupported journey was not completed until 1995 when it was achieved by Canadian Richard Weber, who had been part of Steger's team in 1986, and the Russian Mikhail Malakhov. Weber rightly noted that the early pioneers had not had the advantage of air evacuation from the pole and that the pair's journey would therefore be closer in spirit to them. The two had already tried the trip once before in 1992 when they started from Ward Hunt with a team of three on 13 March. But on 22 April (day 39) Bob Mantell realised he would not make the trip and returned to Ward Hunt alone, reaching it on 7 May. Weber and Malakhov were eventually forced to accept defeat in June at 89°38'N. During the trek they saw whales at 89°N, the furthest north ever. In 1995 Weber and Malakhov started on 14 February, hauling one sledge at a time because of their weight (each man had two sledges, each weighing more than 50kg/110lb, as well as a heavy backpack) and so covering double distances. On 28 February they established a depot at 83°50'N, returning to Ward Hunt for more supplies. Starting out again they experienced temperatures down to –58°C. They reached their depot on 17 March and, now with sledges weighing 140kg (309lb) and 20kg (44lb) backpacks, they started for the pole. They reached it on 12 May and, with lightened loads, returned to Ward Hunt, reaching it on 14 June 107 days after setting out. They had covered 1,500km (almost 1,000 miles).

The next landmark was the unsupported crossing of the Arctic Ocean, achieved by the Norwegians Rune Gjeldnes and Torry Larsen who had already completed the unsupported south–north traverse of Greenland. The pair set out from Cape Arktichesky on 16 February 2000, starting in the Arctic twilight as the sun did not appear until the 29th. They crossed ice so thin that they had to keep moving as to stop might mean to fall through it: with survival time measured in minutes and no chance of rescue by his team-mate this concentrated their minds wonderfully. They reached the pole on 29 April after 74 days of travel. Progress towards Canada was slow and on 13 May, at 88°N with 550km (344 miles) to go, they made the bold decision to leave their pulks behind, continuing on ski with everything in backpacks. Their packs weighed 45kg (99lb), so heavy that a fall meant waiting for assistance, and the possibility of a broken leg. With time, food and fuel running out their crossings of leads became increasingly audacious (or foolhardy). Inevitably Gjeldnes fell through the ice of one lead and was lucky to be wedged by his pack rather than pulled down by it; he was rescued by Larsen after several minutes' partial immersion. The pair ran out of food and fuel 45km (28 miles) from Ellesmere Island's Cape Discovery and were then stopped by an open lead. Had this been continuous around the coast it would have been disastrous, but they forced a way across, landing on 3 June after a trek of 109 days.

Gjeldnes' fall through the ice clearly demonstrated the hazards facing any solo trekker, but Børge Ousland was back on the ice in 2001 intent on repeating the Gjeldnes/Larsen crossing of 2000, but solo and unsupported. He also started from Cape Arktichesky, on 3 March. After one week his sledge cracked. Despite efforts to repair it a new sledge had to be brought to him by helicopter. Continuing against a headwind and across extremely broken ice Ousland reached the pole on 23 April, where he found a collection of people, including an Arab in full national costume. Ousland accepted a meal from Weber and Malakhov (see above) who were on a commercial pole trip. He then continued alone. The wind was occasionally favourable and he was able to use a sail (wing) to assist him, on one day covering a record 72km (45 miles) and several times covering more than 50km (30 miles). Ousland also used a drysuit to swim across leads and so reduce the time to bypass them, towing his sledge behind him. In all he used the suit 23 times. Ousland reached Ward Hunt Island on 23 May after covering 1,996km (1,250 miles)

in 82 days. Purists will argue that the replacement sledge and chilli con carne at the pole invalidates Ousland's claim of a first solo, unsupported traverse of the Arctic Ocean, but the fabled man-in-the-street will likely have little sympathy for such arguments and will view the journey as a success.

Today the North Pole is regularly reached by commercial trips on Russian ice-breakers. Each year the Russians construct ice runways at 89°N to fly in adventure seekers who ski the 'last degree' and are then taken back to 89° base by smaller planes. The pole has been reached by motorcycle, hot-air balloon and relay teams. Yet despite this commercialism journeys to it from Canada or Siberia (or any other starting point) are extremely hazardous. The broken nature of the ice, the open water (a Japanese explorer drowned in a lead during Ousland's solo crossing) and the risk from polar bears (stealthy hunters whose approach can go unnoticed and which represent a particular hazard to the tent-bound, sleeping trekker) are added to the problems of cold and bad weather, making the Arctic a more daunting challenge than Antarctica. The substantial thinning of the sea ice noted by Ousland in 2001 – he carried out thickness measurements as he had in 1994 – makes matters worse. For man the effect of global warming on the fragile ecology of the Arctic is a tragedy. For a man the effect could be lethal.

Top right **Børge Ousland, the outstanding polar traveller of the present generation.**

Above right **A self-portrait taken during Ousland's solo, unsupported North Pole Trek.**

Right **During his unsupported Arctic traverse, Ousland used a drysuit to swim across leads.**
Børge Ousland

Antarctica

Before the heroes came

The Ice Ages of the Quaternary era of geological time squeezed the ancestors of modern man into a narrowing belt of the earth. Paradoxically, the quantity of water locked into the glaciers and ice sheets of the polar regions lowered the levels of oceans by as much as 100m, opening land bridges that meltwaters later covered, closing the door to further migration. The Aborigines walked across the Torres Strait that now separates New Guinea from Australia, but further exploration of the islands of the south Pacific required ocean-going boats. About 2,500 years ago the peoples of New Guinea began a slow advance eastwards across the islands of Melanesia. They settled Vanuatu, Fiji, Tonga and Samoa, then crossed the vast and empty Pacific, reaching the Marquesas Islands by about AD300. From there the settlers headed north and south across the islands of Polynesia, reaching Hawaii in about AD800, New Zealand a century or so later. A stepping stone to New Zealand were the Cook Islands. In about AD650 Ui-Te-Rangiora pointed his canoe *Te-Ivi-O-Atea* southwards from Rarotonga, one of the southerly islands of the group. After days at sea Ui-Te-Rangiora and his crew discovered either sea ice or an island covered in ice.

Though often dismissed as pure legend the remarkable feats of seamanship required by the colonisation of Polynesia make the journey feasible, at least theoretically. Exactly what Ui-Te-Rangiora discovered is the subject of a debate that is unlikely to be satisfactorily resolved. As with the story of Pytheas' journey to the Arctic, Ui-Te-Rangiora's voyage implies achievements by early travellers which are at odds with the accepted wisdom that exploration of the polar wildernesses awaited the rise of Western civilisation, an assertion which owes as much to an arrogant view of history as it does to lack of evidence. That said, it has to be accepted that while the existence of the Arctic could well have been known from quite early times, it is unlikely that Ptolemy included *Terra Incognito* on his map because rumours of the Cook Islander's voyage had reached Greek ears.

The Greeks reasoned the earth was spherical. To Pythagoras, the 6th-century BC mathematician and philosopher, only a sphere would satisfy the purity he believed underwrote the cosmos. More pragmatically, Eratosthenes, who died in 194BC, had during his time as head of the great library of Alexandria calculated the circumference of the earth by measuring the length of the shadow of a stick at noon at two different places (Aswan and Alexandria) and pacing the distances between them. This simple, beautiful method gave him an answer of staggering accuracy. To the Greeks it was obvious that to balance this spherical earth, the lands of the north, those defined by Arktos, the constellation of the bear, must be balanced by lands to the south, the Antarktos. Not only did a southern land mass obviously exist but, as the Greeks assumed the balance of the earth extended to climate as well, it must also be inhabited.

By the early years of the 16th century the assumed southern continent was taking shape as discoveries by Portuguese and Spanish sailors, driven by the need to find trade routes to Asia free from the control of the city states of Italy and hostile Muslims, extended the frontiers of the known world. It had been assumed that Terra Australis, as it had become known, might be an extension of Africa, but Bartolomeo Diaz and Vasco de Gama showed that it was not. Ferdinand Magellan and Sebastian del Cano negotiated the straits between the South American mainland and Tierra del Fuego, then crossed the Pacific to reveal that the land of the south was not connected – as had also been considered likely – to Asia. Magellan named Tierra del Fuego – the Land of Fire – not from volcanic activity as is still commonly believed (and occasionally written) but from the camp fires of the indigenous people. Magellan believed Tierra del Fuego was an island, though back in Europe most believed it to be the tip of the southern continent. Not for another century would the Dutch explorers Willem Schouten and Jacob Le Maire in the ships *Hoorn* and *Eendracht* show that Tierra del Fuego was indeed an island, though Drake's observations of the passage which bears his name had hinted as much 40 years before. To add to the excitement of discovering Cape Horn, the Dutch also collided with a creature of unknown species which they confidently recorded as a sea monster.

In 1642 Abel Tasman sailed around Australia, proving it was not part of a southern continent, and in the years that followed expeditions beyond latitude 50°S showed that the Southern Ocean was an empty place, pushing back the possible shores of the expected land mass. It is an intriguing aspect of the search for the southern continent that it ran the normal reel of discovery backwards. The Americas were unknown, unsuspected by everyone except those with an intimate knowledge of the Norse sagas, their discovery leading to expeditions which investigated and mapped their extent. The southern continent was suspected. It was pencilled in on maps, however tentatively or imaginatively, expeditions progressively shrinking its projected extent until it was finally discovered.

Furthest south

The record for man's 'furthest south' probably starts with Englishman Francis Drake, though there are still references to the claim of the Florentine-born merchant Amerigo Vespucci who, in 1502, sailed southwards along the western shore of South America, discovering the Rio de la Plata and continuing to a point where, he claimed, the night was 15 hours long. It was 7 April when Vespucci measured the night hours: on that date a night of that length would mean he had sailed to 72°S, placing him south of the Antarctic Circle. He would have sailed along the Antarctic Peninsula, reaching either the Weddell or Bellingshausen Seas. No credible historian believes that Vespucci had actually gone south of 54°S.

More credibly, in 1578, during his circumnavigation of the world, Francis Drake sailed through the Magellan Strait and headed north-west across the Pacific. On 9 September a strong north-easterly wind pushed his flotilla of three ships southwards to about 57°S. After the loss of the *Marigold* the wind eased, allowing the two remaining ships to regain Tierra del Fuego. Here the master of the *Elizabeth* declined to follow Drake any further and returned through the Magellan Strait leaving Drake to continue alone in the *Pelican* (later renamed *Golden Hind*). On 24 October he again reached 57°S before continuing across the Pacific.

It is unclear how long Drake's record stood. In September 1599 the Dutchman Dirck Gherritz claims his ship was blown to 64°S and that he spotted what are now the South Shetland Islands. Four years later the islands were again spotted, also by a Dutch ship, the *Blijde Bootschap*, the Good News, a wholly inappropriate name as it had been commandeered by pirates and then driven south by a storm. However, both these southerly claims date not from the early 17th century but from 1819, just after the American War of Independence. They were made by Edmund Fanning, a Connecticut sealer who had worked out of South Georgia and was about to embark on an expedition to find the southern continent when the war intervened.

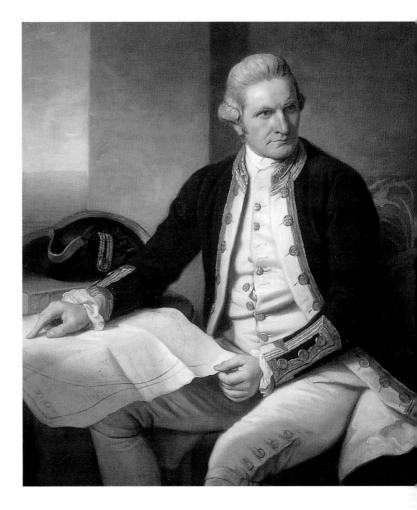

Above **Nathaniel Dance's portrait of James Cook, the Yorkshireman who has a claim to being the greatest seaborne explorer of all.**
UK National Maritime Museum

Fanning was presumably far from enchanted by the British or by their claim on the rich sealing grounds of the South Shetlands, and wished to see William Smith's claim to have discovered the islands nullified. Fanning not only put forward the earlier claims of the Dutch ships, but also another by the possibly fictitious Captain Frazer who, Fanning claimed, had not only seen the islands in 1712 but named them South Iceland. There were also claims by several pirates that they had passed 60°S while in the grip of the Southern Ocean's notorious weather. Jacob l'Hermite declared he had passed 60°S in 1624, while much later, in 1687, the delightfully named Lionel Wafer, a surgeon turned pirate, claimed to have spent Christmas Day at 62°45'S. Though all of these claims have their doubters, it is generally agreed that George Shelvocke, a British Royal Navy captain turned privateer, reached 61°30'S in the *Speedwell* during the austral summer of 1719–20.

Shelvocke's expedition was also notable for two other events. Firstly, on 1 October 1719, William Camell fell overboard and drowned. Camell was probably the first man to drown south of 60°S, a fact which was doubtless of no comfort as the chilly waters of the Southern Ocean closed over his head for the last time. Secondly, after passing through the Le Maire Strait (between Tierra del Fuego's eastern tip and Staten Island) the *Speedwell* was followed for several days by a solitary black albatross 'hovering above us as if he had lost himself'. Thinking this was a sinister omen Simon Hatley, Shelvocke's second captain, killed the bird with a shotgun after several attempts in the hope that its death would bring an end to the 'contrary tempestuous winds, which had oppressed us ever since we got into this sea'. In 1728 Shelvocke published *A Voyage round the World by way of the Great South Sea*. In 1797 the book was read by William Wordsworth who suggested to his friend Samuel Taylor Coleridge that he use the incident in the epic poem he was writing (and that the 'tutelary spirits of these regions take upon them to avenge the crime'). Coleridge substituted a more romantic crossbow for the shotgun and used the killing as the central theme of the *Rime of the Ancient Mariner*. Interestingly, the Arctic has a claim to be the basis of the poem, an indication of the hold the polar regions had on the 19th-century English mind.

James Cook

Not until 1773 was the Antarctic Circle crossed, during the second of the momentous voyages of James Cook, the Yorkshireman who has a claim to being the greatest seaborne explorer of all time. In 1768 Cook explored the southern Pacific at modest latitudes, charting the east coasts of New Zealand and Australia. In terms of defining the extent of the elusive southern continent that voyage is of limited interest, but Joseph Banks, the botanist who accompanied Cook, set down the first known expression of enthusiasm for reaching the South Pole merely for the sake, the fun, of doing so. It would, Banks said, be 'Glorious... to set my heel upon the Pole and turn myself 360° in a second!'

In 1771 Cook proposed searching for land at higher latitudes and set sail with two ships, *Resolution* and *Adventure*, and orders from the British Navy Board for 'prosecuting your discoveries as near to the South Pole as possible'. Cook crossed the Antarctic Circle at about 1.15pm on 17 January 1723, eventually reaching 67°14'S (at 40°46'E, about 145km/90 miles off Kronprins Olav Kyst) before being stopped by ice which stretched to the horizon. In February Cook and the *Resolution* were separated from the *Adventure*, commanded by Tobias Furneaux. The two ships did not meet while wintering on New Zealand and so Cook was alone when he headed south again. He crossed the circle again on 20 December 1773, reaching 67°31'S (at 142°30'W between the Amundsen and Ross Seas, about 720km/450 miles from land) on the 22nd. Christmas Day was 'spent in jollity', though on 26 December two men were 'put in irons for being drunk, and threatening the second lieutenant'. When the two had sobered up they expressed their sorrow and were released.

Encouraged by warmer weather and fewer icebergs (or 'ice islands or hills' as the crew called them) Cook headed south again. On 30 January he noted in his journal that at 'a little after 4am we perceived the clouds to the South near the horizon to be an unusual Snow White brightness which denounced our approach to field ice.' What Cook was seeing is now called ice blink, the reflection of unseen ice in the sky. The ship reached the edge of the sea ice at 8pm. It 'extended East and West in a straight line far beyond our sight; as appeared by the brightness of the horizon; in the Situation we were now just in, the Southern half of the horizon was enlightened by the Reflected rays of the Ice to a considerable height.' Because of this bright ice blink 'the clouds near the horizon... were difficult to distinguish from the Ice hills... The outer or Northern edge of this immense Ice field was composed of loose or broken ice so close packed together that nothing could enter it; about a Mile in began the firm ice, in one compact solid body and seemed to increase in height as you traced it to the south.' The crew counted 97 ice hills rising from the sea ice, but saw no evidence of land.

The *Resolution* had reached 71°10'S at about 107°W. The difficulty of fixing the ship's exact longitude – Cook and Charles Clarke, second lieutenant and a gifted navigator, differed by 4° in their best estimates – means it is not easy to say exactly how close Cook came to land. At worst he was some 160km (100 miles) from Thurston Island, at best he was only about half that distance and so was tantalisingly close to seeing Mount Coldwell at the western end of Thurston's Walker Mountains.

While Cook was making his furthest south Tobias Furneaux was sailing the *Adventure* east from New Zealand, staying below 60°S all the way to Cape Horn and beyond to avoid the notorious cape waters. Because of fog and haze he missed seeing Elephant Island, though he was probably within 37km (20 nautical

miles) of it. He also narrowly avoided seeing the South Orkneys (just beyond his range of vision, though again there was fog) and South Georgia (within range, but obscured by haze). On his own return journey Cook landed on South Georgia, naming it for King George III in whose name he claimed it for Great Britain. It was, he said, 'a land doomed by nature to perpetual frigidity, a terrain savage and horrible... not a tree nor a shrub to be seen, no not even big enough to make a toothpick'. Though this was the first landing on the island it had been seen before, the London merchant Antoine de la Roche probably sighting it in 1675 when his ship was blown off course after rounding Cape Horn, and the Spaniard Gregorio Jerez seeing it again in 1756 (when he named it San Pedro, but did not land).

Cook had sailed all the way around Antarctica. He had not proved conclusively that the southern continent existed (though he conjectured, correctly, that the presence of icebergs implied land) but he had established that if it did it was unlikely to be either inhabited or habitable. He wrote, 'The disappointment I now met with did not affect me much; for to judge of the bulk by the sample it would not be worth the discovery.' And, 'should anyone possess the resolution and the fortitude to elucidate this point by pushing yet

Top **In this watercolour by William Hodges, Cook's ships *Resolution* and *Adventure* are taking on ice from an 'ice hill' for water.**
Mitchell Library, State Library of New South Wales, Australia

Above **The waters of the Southern Ocean are notorious for their storms, nowhere more so than off Cape Horn. Here a ship battles with a force 8 wind and sea close to the cape.**
Richard Sale

Above **Thaddens von Bellingshausen, probably the first man to sight Antarctica.**
Scott Polar Research Institute, University of Cambridge, UK

further south than I have done, I shall not envy him the fame of his discovery, but I make bold that the world will derive no benefit from it.' Despite the denials Cook was an ambitious man and it is possible to detect disappointment in this apparently sanguine acceptance.

Not for almost half a century would Antarctica, the true southern continent, be seen, and then, as is occasionally the case for things which take an age to arrive, it was sighted from two different ships in the space of three days.

The continent sighted

Faddey Faddeyevich Bellingshauzen was born in 1778 in Ösel, now called Saaremaa or Sarema, an Estonian island in the southern Gulf of Riga. At the time of his birth Estonia was a recent acquisition of the Russian Empire. In the west Bellingshauzen – itself an approximation to the Cyrillic original – has been given the Germanic name Thaddens von Bellingshausen, following the translation of his account of his southern voyage into German in 1902, the noble 'von' presumably added as a mark of respect. In 1819 Czar Alexander I appointed Bellingshausen commander of an expedi-

tion of two ships, *Vostock* and *Mirnyi*, both considerably larger than Cook's *Resolution* and *Adventure*. The expedition was to discover the South Pole (and hence, by inference, the southern continent) and a southern base for the Russian Pacific fleet.

Bellingshausen sailed in July 1819. He visited South Georgia, meeting a pair of British sealing ships and charting the southern coast, and then sailed to the South Sandwich Islands which had been seen, but not visited, by Cook. Bellingshausen confirmed that South Sandwich was an island group and not part of a larger land mass. He next crossed the Antarctic Circle, becoming the first man to do so since Cook, although the event does not seem to have mattered much to him as he did not record it. The exact date is also not helped by the fact that Russia still maintained the Julian calendar (not changing until 1918) whereas the other nations active in the Southern Ocean used the Gregorian. A further complication is Bellingshausen's use of three different times ('ordinary' time, ship time – in which the day changed at noon – and 'astronomical' time) and made no allowance for time zones as he journeyed across the ocean. Exact dates are therefore likely to be wrong by half or one day. However, by general agreement Bellingshausen crossed the circle on 26 January and on 27 January was at 69°21'28"S, 2°14'50"W when he observed 'a solid stretch of ice running from east to west'. Lt Lazarev on the *Mirnyi* wrote that the ships had encountered 'continental ice', a phrase Bellingshausen himself used in a later letter. It is very probable that the Russians were seeing the ice shelf (the western edge of the Fimbul Ice Shelf) extending from the Princess Martha and Princess Astrid coasts. It is, however, a moot point whether Bellingshausen actually knew what he was looking at. His description implies that he knew he was not observing pack ice, but ice shelves were unknown at the time so his use of the word 'continental' may have been fortuitous. What can be said is that he obviously knew he was seeing something unknown. If the ice shelf is considered to be part of Antarctica then Bellingshausen had become the first man to see the southern continent. If the definition of a continent requires that a man sees land, then the true discovery had to wait a little longer.

Unlike the Russian admiral, the Englishman William Smith was a working sailor, probably starting in the coastal coal trade before serving on Greenland whalers. In 1811 he was master of a colliery vessel, the following year becoming master of the *Williams*, an ocean-going

ship in which Smith made several journeys to South America. In January 1819 Smith took the *Williams* out of Buenos Aires bound for Valparaiso, but the wind would not allow him to round Cape Horn, forcing him southwards where he sighted the South Shetlands (naming them New South Britain). The rest of the journey was uneventful: he arrived at Valparaiso in March and left again for Montevideo in May. Smith had been careful to keep news of his discovery secret as he had seen a lot of whales near the South Shetlands. But when he reached Uruguay he was shocked to discover that news of his find had already arrived; the careless words of his crew in Valparaiso had quickly carried across the Andes. Smith returned around the Horn in June 1819, returning in October, this voyage allowing him to survey the northern coasts of the South Shetlands and to land. He planted the Union Jack and claimed the islands for King George. The acquisition seemed important as Smith believed he saw pine trees growing on one island implying (as a British newspaper formally announced in August when the news finally reached London) a temperate climate, though this unlikely 'discovery' was soon shown to be false.

When he arrived in Valparaiso Smith's ship was chartered by Captain William Shirreff, the senior British naval officer in the Pacific, who wished to continue the survey of the new lands and to formalise the British claim. In an effort to prevent further news of the discovery leaking out Shirreff ordered the *Williams* anchored offshore, though it is likely that sealers had by then already landed on the islands, making a nonsense of both the secrecy and the British claim. When the *Williams* sailed in early December 1819 Smith had been joined by Captain Edward Bransfield, a Royal Navy officer, installed by Shirreff to give the expedition legitimacy.

The ship reached Livingston Island in the South Shetlands on 19 December, the first landfall being named Cape Shirreff by the dutiful Smith and Bransfield. The pair resurveyed the northern coastlines, then headed south, proving the new lands were islands and discovering Deception Island, the flooded volcanic caldera now popular with tourists to Antarctica. One day later, on 30 January 1820, having sailed south from Deception, Smith and Bransfield saw

Tower Island and, rising beyond it, the peaks of what they called Trinity Land. Today this is the Trinity Peninsula, the northernmost part of Graham Land on the Antarctic Peninsula. If land is the criterion for identifying the true Antarctic continent then Smith and Bransfield are the discoverers, just three days after Bellingshausen had observed the continental ice shelf. Smith and Bransfield then sailed eastwards through what is now the Bransfield Strait, seeing Trinity Land again before heading north where they discovered Elephant Island (named the following year by American sealers because of the abundance of elephant seals) before returning to Valparaiso.

One last name must be mentioned when considering who can be attributed as the discoverer of Antarctica, that of National Palmer. Palmer was born in Stonington, Connecticut, in 1799. At the age of 12 he was sailing as a blockade runner during the American War of Independence and was master of his own ship by the age of 19. In 1819/20 Palmer was part of a sealing expedition to the South Shetlands and in 1820/1 was master of the *Hero* on a similar trip. During this voyage he met Bellingshausen in an extraordinary incident on 6 February 1821 during which the two Russian ships *Vostock* and *Mirnyi* were separated in thick fog in the Bransfield Strait. When the fog lifted, to the Russians' astonishment the *Hero* lay between them. Bellingshausen invited Palmer aboard and was later escorted by the American ship to the safe anchorage of Deception Island (which Palmer had almost certainly been the first to discover: he was probably also first to land on Deception). There are several accounts of the meeting and the American version of these have formed the basis of the claim that Palmer was the first to see Antarctica. In fact he had first seen what is now called Graham Land (part of the Antarctica Peninsula: in deference to the American the southern section of the peninsula is now called Palmer Land) on 17 November 1820, ten months after Smith and Bransfield. Palmer was, however, the first to discover the South Orkney Islands when, as master of the *James Monroe*, he accompanied the British ship *Dove*, under George Powell, on a sealing trip. The discovery was on 6 December 1821, but finding no seals Palmer sailed away leaving Powell to claim the islands for Britain. Powell went ashore on an island he named Coronation in honour of the recently enthralled George IV.

After the chance meeting with Palmer, Bellingshausen completed his voyage. In all he sailed over 240° of longitude (two-thirds of the way around the world)

south of 60° and crossed the Antarctic Circle half-a-dozen times. It was a masterful enterprise, but Bellingshausen had found no southern continent, no useful bases, and sealing grounds that were already overrun by British and Americans. The Czar was not impressed and declined to authorise the cash needed to publish Bellingshausen's maps.

Finally the southern continent had been discovered, though its shores had still to be mapped, an exercise that occupied sealers and scientists for decades, and its true nature was unknown. As late as 1895, just 15 years before Amundsen's polar trek, Nansen was suggesting that Antarctica might comprise a group of islands rather a single land mass.

Hunters in the south

Sealers

The killing of fur seals on a commercial basis began on the Falkland Islands in 1766 and would, as the seal population collapsed, inevitably have led the sealers to seek out new breeding grounds even if the early explorers had not, unwittingly, done it for them. When James Cook took possession of South Georgia for the British Crown he noted that fur seals were 'pretty numerous', his comment being enough to trigger the arrival of British and American sealers once the Falkland Islands' population had been decimated. In 1800/01 there were at least 17 sealing ships at the island, their catch totalling over 100,000 animals. By 1822 James Weddell was calculating that well over a million animals had been taken. By then the South Georgia population had been hunted to the edge of extinction: indeed, it was actually believed that not only were the fur seals commercially extinct but that they had been entirely wiped out on the island. It is thought that a few – perhaps no more than ten animals – survived, probably on Bird Island off South Georgia's north-western tip.

The extinction of the seals on South Georgia led to the sealers exploiting the South Shetlands. The rapid spread of the news of William Smith's discovery is an indication of the sealers' enthusiasm for new stock. It is also possible that those sealers shrewd enough to have foreseen the collapse of the South Georgian seal population had already sought new land. If sealers discovered the South Shetlands before Smith they would certainly have kept quiet about it, a fact which has led many to wonder whether not only the South Shetlands but also the Antarctic Peninsula were known before (though probably not long before) the official discoveries. It is estimated that the sealers took over 300,000 seals from the South Shetlands in the period 1820–2. By the 1822/3 season the catch was so poor that visiting the islands was no longer commercially viable: new lands had to be sought.

Smith's crew had little incentive to stay quiet about what they had seen around the South Shetlands as the *Williams* was a freighter. For the sealers the incentive was huge. In the early years of the 19th century a top-quality fur-seal pelt fetched $5 in the USA and even a tiny ship could hold 10–20,000 skins. In the 1820/1 season – a season which lasted from late November until mid-January, a total of just seven weeks – the Fanning–Pendleton expedition from Stonington, Connecticut, operated on the South Shetlands. The five ships of the expedition – one of which was Nathaniel Palmer's *Hero* – took back 51,000 skins, netting perhaps $250,000 for the 70 men who crewed them. One ship, the *Hersilia*, carried 18,000 skins and this was merely the number of top-quality pelts. It is possible that as many again were rejected. The five ships of Fanning–Pendleton were joined on the islands by a further 25 American ships and an equal number of British. There may also have been smaller numbers of ships from Australia, South Africa and France. Although it was not until 1822/3 that the seal population of the South Shetlands was deemed commercially extinct, even during the 1821/2 season ships of the second Fanning–Pendleton expedition had found a reduction in numbers. That was the reason Nathaniel Palmer and George Powell sailed east and discovered the South Orkneys. Though Palmer was not impressed, there were seals on the islands. The population was small and was rapidly annihilated, the South Orkneys having no seals for over 100 years until a single animal was spotted on Signy Island (an island named for his daughter by the Norwegian whaler Petter Sørlle, a later visitor) in 1947. The population has now increased to several thousand.

Though greed was the driving force for the slaughter, the behaviour of the seals contributed to their downfall. Devoid of fear because of the absence of a land predator in Antarctica the seals were curious about these new creatures and happily waddled up to them, only to be clubbed or shot. The numbers killed were so great that clubbing was the preferred means of dispatch, the sealers walking along the crowded beaches swinging without pause, stopping only as a result of exhaustion or complete annihilation. The sealers

Above **Since they have been protected elephant-seal numbers have increased, creating ironic images as they recolonise areas of South Georgia such as Grytviken.**
Richard Sale

preferentially took breeding females and young males as their skins were of better quality, leaving the breeding bulls, whose skins also took more salt to cure, alone. The effect of this targeting, together with the sheer numbers killed, ensured that the stock would collapse. Late in the season, when there were fewer seals and those that were found rapidly fled into the sea, the sealers would often pursue them in boats and shoot them. Dead seals sank quickly, so the success rate in gathering them was unlikely to exceed one in five, while wounded animals might escape only to die later.

Often the sealers were left on shore while their ship went off to drop men at other sites, the men living in poor-quality tents, crude huts or in rock shelters, with little protection from wind and cold. It would seem that only the exceptional pay made the job bearable. After the seals had been skinned, the carcasses were left on the beaches to rot or to feed the petrels and skuas. Very young pups would not be killed as their skins were valueless, but without mothers they starved to death. The salted skins were packed for transport, though even here the stupidity of the exercise is apparent. It is reported that on one large ship returning to London with 100,000 skins on board, the poorly preserved skins became so overheated during the equatorial part of the voyage that they started to rot. By the time London was reached the whole cargo had degenerated into a stinking heap that had to be dug out of the hold and was fit only for spreading as fertiliser.

After the virtual destruction of the fur seals commercial interests turned to elephant seals whose hides made an excellent leather and whose rendered blubber was as good as whale oil for lighting lamps and lubricating machinery. The huge bulls, too dangerous to club (they are surprisingly quick at turning a ferociously-toothed mouth to anyone approaching, and have a neck whose flexibility and extension is equally surprising) were lanced with a long spear or shot. Bulls yielded 150–300 litres (33–66 gallons) of top-quality oil, enough to fill one or two barrels. Some idea of the seasonal slaughter is gained by noting that a single ship could carry 15,000 or more barrels away from South Georgia. The story of the exploitation of the southern elephant seal follows that of the fur seals, with massive over-killing resulting in commercial extinction.

Whereas catches of elephant seals were still reasonable at the end of the 1870s, in the 1885/6 season only two animals were taken, and they yielded just a few tens of barrels of oil. Ironically the populations of fur seals on some islands had by then recovered sufficiently for sealing to begin again, on the Falklands and certain sites on the Antarctic Peninsula. But the same greed and lack of foresight prevailed, and fur-seal populations again fell disastrously, leading to regulations being introduced by the British to control the numbers taken. The elephant-seal population on South Georgia also recovered sufficiently for sealing to begin again in the early 20th century, over 250,000 bulls being slaughtered in the 50 years to 1960. The elephant seal is now protected.

The return of the fur seal to South Georgia is one of the great recovery stories of the animal world. From the handful left after exploitation there were still probably less than 100 in the early 20th century, this growing to several thousand by the 1950s and, perhaps, a million today. Ironically, this satisfying recovery of an endearing species is largely the result of an excess of krill, on which the seals feed, as a result of the slaughter of the krill-feeding baleen whales by commercial whalers.

Whalers

The first phase of Antarctic whaling coincided with the seal hunts, many of the companies involved operating both whalers and sealers. The whalers sought the right whale, southern cousin of the Arctic species, and brought it to the edge of extinction just as they had the northern species. The right was so-named because it was the right one to kill. It was slow, swimming at a maximum of 6 knots, and so vulnerable to the rowed whaling boats, and it was so heavy with blubber that it floated when killed. The latter was both convenient, for obvious reasons, and a commercial boon: more blubber meant a higher oil yield. By contrast rorquals (blue, fin, sei, humpback, Bryde's and minke whales) are fast, occasionally reaching speeds of over 15 knots (sei whales have been recorded at speeds of over 25 knots), too quick for a rowed boat to catch. If chance allowed a rorqual to be harpooned it was not a forgone conclusion that it could be taken. There are numerous stories of harpooned rorquals dragging boats, and even ships, for up to a day. In many such elongated hunts the line parted before the whale died.

In the early years of whaling, with men hand-throwing harpoons from rowing boats launched from sailing ships, the catches were not huge. The hunt was also dangerous. Boats could be overturned and men drowned, either during the occasionally lengthy period when a stricken whale towed the whalers – the infamous 'Nantucket sleigh ride', named for America's principle whaling port – or when a wounded whale attacked. Ships were also rammed and sunk by whales. The whale 'hero' of Herman Melville's *Moby Dick* is said to have been based on Mocha Dick, a white sperm whale which wrecked two boats, killing two men, from a Bristol whaler operating close to the Falkland Islands in May 1841. The sperm whale was a favoured species of early whalers because of the spermaceti wax found in its head and the ambergris found in the intestine. Ambergris was used in perfume manufacture and was, literally, worth its weight in gold. The production of ambergris is not well understood: it is believed that it is produced by the whale as a means of coating the non-digestible beaks of giant squid so as to prevent them from damaging the whale's gut. It is often expelled by the whale and is found floating on the surface. Ironically in view of its use in perfume, the substance is probably excreted by the whale, and some scientists have even suggested it is a by-product of sperm whale constipation. In about 1860 the population of sperm whales crashed because of over-exploitation for spermaceti and ambergris.

The contract the whalers sailed under held almost as many dangers as the whaling itself, though these were less obviously life-threatening. Many (almost all when the whales were plentiful) sailed for a percentage of the profit, emphasising the need to kill more whales, but meaning that there was no pay in the event of a man surviving a disaster. The share was known as a lay and was expressed as a fraction, for example 1/100 (1 per cent). First-time sailors were given a long lay, that is a big number. As many first-timers did not understand the system (or, probably, fractions) they attempted to get a bigger number, unscrupulous ship owners being only too willing to accommodate them. Many sailors, needing to buy clothes and so on for a voyage, were given an advance on their lay which had to be repaid from their share. Some owners – particularly the Nantucket Quakers, a singularly rapacious and whale-bloodthirsty lot for being Christian pacifists – charged hefty interest on the lay advances, and since some whaling trips lasted two or three years, this could seriously reduce a sailor's pay. For those few who were allowed, or opted for, a wage, the situation was hardly better: their pay usually ceased in the event of a shipwreck, and if they survived they were required to make their own way home, and pay their own fare.

The killing rate of the great whales was probably, in terms of the population, manageable at first, but the prize for capture of these huge rorquals was considerable. Baleen (whalebone) was needed for women's corsets and umbrella stays, and fetched prices of up to £10,000 per ton when whales were scarce in the late 19th century. With such rewards it was inevitable that the technology to hunt the great whales would not be long in arriving. The problem was solved in the 1860s by the Norwegian Svend Foyn who designed the first steam-powered whale boat, and also invented the explosive harpoon.

Foyn's new technology also allowed more whales to be killed, small killing ships hauling their catches quickly to larger factory ships on which the carcass was

Above **Grytviken. The name means Pot Cove, the pot being the three-legged tri-pot in which blubber was rendered to oil, though the pots in question were discovered there, having been left behind by elephant sealers.**
Richard Sale

rendered to oil, or to shore stations. The boom time of Antarctic whaling was the 20th century. In 1906 a Norwegian–Chilean enterprise anchored a factory ship in the Deception Island caldera. Then in 1908 the British formally claimed the island and leased it to a Norwegian whaling company, a move aimed at cleansing the caldera of the 3,000 or so whale carcasses that had accumulated there. Contrary to the belief that only the blubber can be rendered into oil, as much as 50 per

Left **Sir James Clark Ross by John R. Wildman.**
The Ross Ice Shelf, named for Sir James, is one of the wonders of the natural world. Though by its nature variable in size it generally occupies an area from 76°–86°S, 155°W–160°E, the largest body of ice in the world. It reaches almost 1,000km (600 miles) inland, an average of about 300km (200 miles) across the sea. It is up to 700m (2,400ft) thick and its 60m (200ft) frontal ice cliff is 650km (400 miles) long. The ice shelf covers an area of over 600,00 sq km (about 230,000 sq miles), roughly the area of France. The Ross shelf advances into the sea at a rate of about 670m (2,200ft) annually.

It is from such ice shelves – others are the Ronne and Filchner in the Weddell Sea, the Larsen on the eastern side of the Antarctic Peninsula, and the Amery, West and Shackleton on the Kerguélen side of Antarctica – that the great tabular icebergs, such a feature of Antarctica, break free. In an average year over 700 cu km (about 140 cu miles) of icebergs are created from the continent. In 1956 one was seen which measured 333km (208 miles) by 100km (60 miles), making it a bit bigger than Belgium.
UK National Maritime Museum

Below **Mount Erebus, which James Clark Ross named for one of his ships.**
P.S. Kristensen, courtesy of Quark Expeditions

The British

The contrast between the Wilkes' expedition and that of James Clark Ross could hardly be more extreme. Ross was already a veteran of polar travel having spent many years in the Arctic, searching for the North-West Passage with Parry, then reaching the North Magnetic Pole with his uncle, Sir John Ross. His expedition was also well funded and prepared, and his two ships, *Erebus* and *Terror*, were shallow-draughted and strengthened so as to be able to navigate ice. Ross sailed in September 1839, exploring the Kerguélen Islands before reaching Hobart. At the time Sir John Franklin was governor of Van Diemen's Land (as Tasmania was then called). Ross later named an island he discovered for Franklin, but the true irony of their meeting was that when Franklin disappeared in the Arctic on what is arguably the most famous of all polar voyages, he was in command of *Erebus* and *Terror*, the same two ships. In Hobart Ross heard about the Dumont d'Urville and Wilkes expeditions and was annoyed at their impudence in invading 'his' territory. Wilkes had left charts for him, and Ross' disparaging remarks about them led to the American's court-martial (though it didn't stop the Englishman from making use of the data).

Ross sailed south in November 1840 pushing through the pack ice to discover the sea which bears his name. Ross saw and claimed Victoria Land (named for the queen), then continued south to discover the volcanoes which he named for his ships. Mounts Erebus and Terror are on Ross Island, though at the time Ross believed the island to be part of the mainland (it was Robert Falcon Scott in 1902 who found it was an island). On 22 January 1841 Ross set a new furthest south record, reaching 78°9'S. Ross also discovered what he called the Victoria Barrier, 'a mighty and wonderful object far beyond anything we could have thought or conceived'. Later the Victoria Barrier was called the Great Ice Barrier and, eventually, the Ross Ice Shelf. Ross sailed over 550km (350 miles) along the ice shelf, marvelling at its unyielding 60m (200ft) ice cliffs which offered neither a passage through nor any glimpse of what lay beyond.

After Ross' expedition the world lost interest in Antarctica: clearly there was no habitable land; the animal life had been exploited to exhaustion if not extinction; and any mineral wealth was locked beyond or beneath impenetrable ice. Besides, Franklin's loss in the Arctic was much more interesting to both governments and the public. One exception was the scientific expedition aboard the *Challenger* sponsored in part by Britain's leading scientific institution, the Royal Society, and with Sir Charles Wyville Thomson as chief scientist, which explored the area in 1872–6. When *Challenger* crossed the Antarctic Circle on 16 February 1874 it was the first steam ship to do so, and the first since Ross 33 years before. The expedition was extraordinary: it covered over 110,000km (nearly 70,000 miles) and its report ran to 50 volumes.

The first landing

Twenty years later the first official landing on the continent was made. Svend Foyn's invention had, not surprisingly, made him rich and he organised and funded an Antarctica whaling expedition in 1893. The *Antarctic* (originally the *Kap Nor* but renamed by Foyn) left Norway in September, captained by Leonard Kristensen, but with Henryk Bull as Foyn's agent, a co-leadership that led to antagonism and ill-feeling which seems to have affected the entire crew and, consequently, the trip. The ship visited the Kerguélen Islands where an entire population of about 16,000 fur seals were slaughtered. Bull, who had never seen a seal hunt, was horrified and later called for international control of sealing. In Melbourne the seal pelts were sold and the *Antarctic* spent the southern winter unsuccessfully hunting whales around Campbell Island. They also took on new crew to replace two who jumped ship and several who were dismissed for refusing to sail to Antarctica. One of the newcomers was Carsten Borchgrevink, born in 1864, probably in Oslo, to a Norwegian father and English mother. Borchgrevink studied and travelled in Europe then, after the death of his father, emigrated to Australia in 1888, eventually becoming a teacher. He attempted to join the *Antarctic* as a scientist, but was accepted as a deck hand. The ship sailed south in September (but was forced to land in New Zealand after it collided with an iceberg), eventually crossing the Antarctic Circle on 25 December 1894, the first to do so since the *Challenger* 20 years before.

On 18 January 1895 the crew landed on Possession Island where Borchgrevink found lichen growing in sheltered areas, the first discovery of vegetation in Antarctica and one which dumbfounded many leading botanists who had claimed that the climate was too hostile to sustain plantlife. Six days later, on 24 January 1895, the expedition landed at Cape Adare, on the mainland itself. Who was first ashore, and whether they were, in fact, the first to land on the continent, remains a mystery – but an appealing one, so bizarre was the landing.

Above **Carsten Borchgrevink claimed the first landing on Antarctica though his claim is disputed. Later Borchgrevink led the first expedition to overwinter on the continent.**
Canterbury Museum, New Zealand

There had been persistent rumours of landings on the mainland for years, the absence of documented trips being easily accounted for, without any need to dismiss them as nonsense. In the period from Cook's voyage to the *Antarctic*'s arrival at Cape Adare well over a thousand sealing and whaling ships had sailed Antarctica's water, probably 50 times as many as had visited purely for exploration. It seems inevitable that some of those ships would have seen the continent (though almost certainly none before the sightings of Bellingshausen, Smith and Bransfield). If land was spotted sealers invariably went ashore in the hope of finding breeding grounds. If they found nothing they might not bother to tell anyone, if they found seals they had an interest in not telling. On 7 February 1821 John Davis, an American sealer from New Haven, Connecticut, and master of the *Cecilia*, put men ashore near Hughes Bay, an inlet of the Antarctic Peninsula near Trinity Island. His men searched the coast for about an hour. Davis himself did not go ashore. Opinions differ over whether the landing was on the

mainland or on an offshore island, but many believe it was actually on the peninsula. It is also possible that Davis' men were not the first; John McFarlane, a British sealer, master of the *Dragon*, was in the South Shetlands in November 1820 and sailed south at some stage, landing men at an unknown destination. There are a handful of later claims too, so the exact status of the *Antarctic*'s shore party is unclear: it represents only the first authenticated landing.

As the ship's boat neared the mainland the *Antarctic*'s captain, Leonard Kristensen, was at the prow, Borchgrevink at the stern. As the boat beached Kristensen stepped ashore, while Borchgrevink leaped into the water and rushed forward to beach the craft. At the same time, Alexander Van Tunzelman, a Campbell Island youth who had joined the ship in New Zealand, jumped ashore to hold the boat for his captain. Later, all three would claim to have been first man ashore and the argument would reach the correspondence column of *The Times* of London.

The *Antarctic*'s party collected more lichen and some penguins from a nearby rookery and returned to the ship. Despite the landing the crew felt the voyage had been a disaster; no catch to speak of and having to endure the constant bickering of Bull and Kristensen. To make matters worse, when the ship docked in Melbourne they heard Svend Foyn was dead. Almost the entire crew jumped ship and found other vessels for the journey home.

Winter in the south: *Belgica*
In the wake of the Antarctic voyage Borchgrevink and Bull teamed up to try to launch another expedition, a short-lived venture. Bull soon left in disgust at Borchgrevink's continuous claims to have been a leader of the 1894–5 trip and to have been first man ashore, and Borchgrevink's disgust at Bull's excessive drinking. Borchgrevink therefore organised his own trip and sought finance and sponsorship. He planned an over-wintering at Cape Adare, suggesting the use of skis, dogs and a tethered balloon for observation (in all of which, events were to prove him right). Borchgrevink secured backing from a commercial company (one with the remarkably honest name of Commercial Company) who agreed to drop his team at the cape, to go whaling, and to return the next year. Initially Britain's Royal Geographical Society were keen to be involved, but became nervous about the commercial aspects and pulled out, deciding instead to back a national expedi-tion. Undeterred, Borchgrevink continued with his plan.

At the same time, the American Dr Frederick Cook began to seek backing for his own trip, but when this fell through he applied for the job of medical officer on another expedition, and was accepted. The expedition was organised by Adrian de Gerlache, a Belgian naval officer. While the British were still trying to raise £100,000 to finance their own expedition, de Gerlache raised about one-tenth of that. He bought a Norwegian steam whaler (*Patria*, renamed the *Belgica*) for 60,000 Belgian francs. The ship was three-masted and steam-sail powered, 33m (about 110ft) in overall length, 8m (26ft) wide and 4.5m (15ft) draught. She was built of oak, the bow and stern sheathed in greenheart, an American tree of the laurel family renowned for its hardness – special tools were needed to work it – and also for its elasticity, a combination which offered excellent protection against ice rubbing. Under sail, but with the addition of the 150hp engine, she could manage 7 knots. The boat was crewed by Belgian and Norwegian sailors under a Belgian captain, Georges Lecointe.

De Gerlache invited a number of scientists, his final selection creating an international expedition. Emile Danco was Belgian, Henryk Arctowski was Polish (the Polish base on King George Island is named for him), Antoine Dobrowolski was Russian, while Emile Racovitza was a Romanian. Most interesting of the initial appointments was Roald Amundsen, who at 25 was on his first polar expedition. Then, after the first-appointed medical officer pulled out, another was selected without interview, and joined the ship in Rio de Janeiro. He was Frederick Albert Cook MD, already a veteran of Arctic expeditions and the man who had failed to put together his own trip south. So when the *Belgica* finally reached Antarctic waters she had on board Amundsen, later to be the first man to set foot on the South Pole and, arguably, the first to see the North Pole, and Cook, whose claim to have reached the North Pole would become infamous, but has never been discredited.

In Rio, Cook noted, the locals were more interested in the ship's absence of luxuries than in what the expedition was hoping to find or do. This, and the view of one visiting cabinet minister – 'well on in the winter of life,' as Cook delicately put it – that if there were no women on board he wouldn't want to go, led Cook to conclude that 'so long as beautiful women, good wine, fine cigars and delicate foods are not found at the south pole, Latin Americans will probably not aspire to reach it'. Equally indiscreet was Cook's comment on the seasickness which afflicted everyone when the rough southern waters were entered. It seemed, he noted, 'to

Above **Henryk Arctowski, Dr Frederick Cook and Roald Amundsen photographed in a Patagonian studio before the *Belgica* trip. Clearly the photographer asked them to strike as natural a pose as they could manage.**
USA Library of Congress

be in evidence in direct proportion to the mental development of the personnel'. The captain was the first to succumb, and the seaman 'of lowest mental development' the last 'to loosen the gastric bonds'.

After exploring Tierra del Fuego – Cook's book on the expedition contains extremely interesting passages on the native Fuegans – the ship headed south. It was now mid-January 1898, late to be setting out for Antarctica, a fact that has led many to speculate that it had been de Gerlache's intention all along to have *Belgica* locked into the polar ice for the winter. The ship had supplies for three years, more than normal prudence would require, and many of those on board suspected the plan. It must have been even more apparent after time was spent surveying the Hughes Bay area: not until 15 February was the Antarctic Circle crossed. It was not an auspicious day: ice encased the ropes, cutting one man's hands, and plated the deck causing several, including the cook, to slip, losing the day's soup. Steering towards the narrow, dark bands whose appearance, like spectral lines on the ice blink, indicates the presence of open water, the *Belgica* continued south. Finally, on 23 February de Gerlache asked the crew how they felt about overwintering. To a man they opposed the idea. At this point in his account Cook claims that the officers and scientists were also against the plan, but that they had become resigned to

de Gerlache's unspoken intention despite their misgivings. In his book on the expedition Cook notes that to attempt to overwinter with only one ship would be foolhardy, particularly as no one knew where they were or that they were staying. If the *Belgica* were crushed by the ice the crew would have little hope of rescue, and 'death by freezing or starvation would be our lot'. Apparently swayed by the arguments de Gerlache agreed to head north for the winter and to return south the following spring. The way north was blocked by pack ice, so *Belgica* headed west, but as soon as she was clear of the pack de Gerlache changed his mind again.

Despite the austral winter beckoning, he decided to try for a new furthest south record, an ambition which the scientists opposed, but not vociferously enough to halt the ship's progress. Forced to seek shelter from a ferocious storm by going into the pack ice, the *Belgica* found leads heading south, but by 3 March the ship was surrounded by ice. After a futile week attempting to free the ship, it became clear that the expedition was trapped, at 70°20'S, 85°W in the Bellingshausen Sea. Man's first experience of the Antarctic winter had begun.

By Cook's account the *Belgica*'s crew rapidly became

Above **The Lemaire Channel. The channel was first sailed by the *Belgica* and was named by Adrian de Gerlache in honour of the Belgian explorer Charles Lemaire.**
Richard Sale

Right **The *Belgica* trapped in the ice.**
Byrd Polar Research Centre, Ohio State University, USA

not only resigned, but excited by the prospect of overwintering, though the fact that the ice was drifting (westward through 7° of longitude in the first two months) caused consternation – where would they be next spring? Was it possible the ship could be dragged over shallow rocks and have her bottom ripped out? Later a new fear arose: movement of water beneath the ice, caused by a storm, created ridges on either side of the ship, which seemed to threaten her survival.

Eventually the crew settled down to a reasonably ordered life. The scientists pursued their studies and there were regular trips out to observe ice and icebergs – the expedition had already become the first to ski on Antarctica, and now did so regularly – and to kill penguins and seals. At first the killing was chiefly for

scientific purposes, though later the men would be glad they had been so diligent. King Leopold of Belgium's birthday was celebrated in style on 9 April, a liberal supply of wine adding to the enthusiasm for a 'Grand Concourse of Beautiful Women' in which points were allocated for the best attributes of pictures of women from a Parisian magazine someone had brought along.

On 16 May the men realised – by fixing their position from the stars – that the sun had disappeared the previous day. At noon that day the northern sky brightened, but the sun had truly gone. With the long Antarctic night came a 'curtain of blackness' which seems to have entered the souls of many of the officers and men, the brief reappearance of the sun due to refraction the next day merely heightening its loss. The melancholy even affected Nansen; the ship's cat, who became lethargic and aggressive when roused, eventually died. The men might have too, as besides suffering from deep depression they were all becoming ill with scurvy. Cook, as medical officer, persuaded them to eat seal and penguin as from studying the reports of Arctic expeditions he knew this was a cure for the disease. It was a difficult task: by Cook's own admission penguin 'seems to be made up of an equal proportion of mam-

mal, fish and fowl. If it is possible to imagine a piece of beef, an odiferous codfish, and a canvas-back duck, roasted in a pot, with blood and cod-liver oil for sauce, the illustration will be complete.' Danco, there to study the earth's magnetic field, did not heed the advice. He would, he said, rather die than eat penguin, a prophetic comment as on 5 June he did die (though as much due to an existing heart complaint as the debilitation of scurvy). His was the second death on the expedition, Carl Wiencke, one of the sailors having fallen overboard on the journey south. Cook describes this in a very affecting passage. Cook threw Wiencke the log line and hauled him to the ship, but those on board were unable to complete the rescue before Wiencke, exhausted in the freezing sea, lost his grip.

One advantage of the fresh-meat diet was that the food was plentiful. When there was open water near the ship there was always an abundance of penguins and seals, and Cook had also lain in stocks prior to winter's arrival. Cook notes that a cornet blown to tell men on the ice that meals were ready also brought penguins waddling right up to the ship and seals out on to the ice, their curiosity being their downfall.

To the diet, Cook added a 'light' cure, making sure

that the men had a dose of heat and light from the fire each day. This was enough to dispel the gloom of perpetual night though it could do little for the permanent sense of isolation. Two sailors went insane, Engebret Knudsen (whose condition was temporary, though he died shortly after the expedition was over) and Adam Tollefsen. Ironically, Tollefsen's insanity occurred later in the year, his mind finally unbalanced, according to Cook, as much by the permanent daylight of the Antarctic summer as by the isolation.

On 22 July (after ten weeks of night) the sun came back. By 28 July they could feel the sun's warmth, but it was some time before they could expect the ice to melt and free the ship. At first they hoped to be free by late October, then late November, but it soon became clear that the *Belgica* could be held for a second winter. Eventually, in early January 1898, Cook suggested hacking a channel to open water. The attempt to use tonit (an explosive: the *Belgica* carried almost a ton of it, Cook having noted in Rio its potential usefulness in freeing the ship if it became 'embraced by the Frost King') was unsuccessful, but several weeks of labouring with picks and saws was. On 14 February the *Belgica* broke free and sailed for Punta Arenas, arriving on 28 March. There Cook discovered that in the time they had been away from the world the Spanish–American war had been fought. The scientists left the *Belgica* and made their way home, as did Amundsen. Aggravated by what he saw as de Gerlache's pro-Belgian attitude, he escorted the insane Tollefsen home independently.

The expedition had proved that man could survive the Antarctic winter, though the lowest recorded temperature, –43°C, was no lower than the Inuit had been coping with for centuries. It had also provided Roald Amundsen with his first polar experience and laid the groundwork for his later trips. Cook was impressed by Amundsen 'who was the biggest, the strongest, the bravest, and generally the best dressed man for sudden emergencies', particularly by his ability to ski and his willingness to be involved in everything. But Cook's admiration for Amundsen was nothing in comparison to Amundsen's for Cook. Amundsen later wrote, 'I came to know Dr Cook intimately and to form an affection for him and gratitude to him which nothing in his later career could ever cause me to alter. He, of all the ship's company, was the one man of unfaltering courage, unfailing hope, endless cheerfulness, and unwearied kindness. When anyone was sick, he was at his bedside to comfort him; when any was disheartened, he was there to encourage and inspire. And not

only was his faith undaunted, but his ingenuity and enterprise were boundless.' And as the pair, roped together, explore a crevassed landscape '...the experienced polar explorer walks in front, I follow... It is interesting to see the practical and calm manner in which this man works.' It was Cook who kept the men healthy, Cook who suggested the way of extricating the *Belgica* from the ice (though the idea of cutting channels in the ice had been practised by the British navy in their search for the North-West Passage for almost 100 years, though usually to reach rather than leave a harbour). Cook improved clothing, sleeping-bag and tent design: Amundsen's tent, which Scott found at the South Pole, was sewn to Cook's design, and Amundsen had used Cook's snow goggles on his trek. Cook was also the pioneering polar photographer, Amundsen recognising the value of photography in providing a record of achievement that disarmed sceptics (a true irony, given the use of Cook's own photographs to challenge his later claims).

Cook was not only a remarkable leader and polar pioneer, but was also an excellent writer. His account of the *Belgica* expedition is a superb read, his boyish enthusiasm jumping from every page. He is also lyrical, poetic even, in his description of a land he clearly loved. Given his sense of place and his real achievements it is deeply sad that his reputation has been so soiled.

Winter in the south: *Southern Cross*

As the *Belgica* sailed south, Carsten Borchgrevink was still trying to organise his own expedition back in Britain. Having lost official support, in part because of his dealings with a commercial company, he had now lost the commercial backing as well. He therefore approached George Newnes, a self-made man whose fortune was based on *Tit-Bits*, a magazine which had captured the fancy of the British public from its first edition in October 1881 by offering fun and entertainment at a time when the majority of popular reading was worthy, but dull. Much taken with Borchgrevink's enthusiasm and experience Newnes gave him £40,000. At one go the Anglo-Norwegian had obtained double the money the Royal Geographical Society had raised for a national expedition over several years of trying.

To transport his expedition Borchgrevink bought *Pollux* from Norway, a ship built by Colin Archer, the genius designer who had built the *Fram* for Nansen. The ship was of oak with a greenheart sheathing, the total over 3m (almost 11ft) thick at the bow and a metre (3ft) thick along the sides. Borchgrevink re-registered the ship as the *Southern Cross* and installed Bernhard Jensen (of whom Borchgrevink noted 'a man he looked and a man he was') as captain. Most of the officers and crew were also Norwegian. As scientists Borchgrevink chose the young physicist Louis Bernacchi, Belgian-born, of Italian descent but now Australian; William Colbeck, an English navigator and surveyor; and Nicolai Hanson, a Norwegian zoologist. Another Norwegian, Herlof Klövstad, was the medical officer. The ship's complement was completed by Norwegian Anton Fougner, Hugh Evans, born in England, but resident in northern Canada, and two Lapps. All the men except Bernacchi had polar experience, most were expert skiers and the Lapps were expert with dogs, brought specifically to handle Borchgrevink's Siberian and Greenlandic dog teams. Borchgrevink also took kayaks, but not the observation balloon he had originally intended. Despite criticisms at the time and later, the expedition was well thought out and organised.

During the journey south many of the crew were ill, probably from drinking contaminated water on the Cape Verde Islands, accentuated by the stench of the dogs as the equator was approached. Hanson was the sickest, and never fully recovered. The ship was late reaching Tasmania (where pigeons were taken on board, in part to satisfy the enthusiasm of local racing enthusiasts, in part to act as message carriers: the former was of little success, the latter none), and lost more time when Borchgrevink attempted to clear the pack ice too far to the east, despite Colbeck's warning. *Southern Cross* spent six weeks getting nowhere before Borchgrevink agreed to move further west. When he did the ship pushed through the pack into open water in just six hours. As a result of the delays it was 1 March by the time stores had been unloaded at Cape Adare. The *Southern Cross* headed north immediately. The next day Robertson Bay (enclosed to the west by Cape Adare) froze over: the ship had been just one day from being frozen in. The unloading had taken 12 days: when the dogs had been landed they had immediately slaughtered the local penguin colony. Later, when a storm forced the two Lapps to remain onshore for a night, the dogs crawled into their tent and curled up with them.

Borchgrevink had chosen Cape Adare simply because he had been there and he knew it was possible to land, but it proved to be an unfortunate choice. The expedition's site was windy and the cape was difficult to climb, making access to the 'true' continent difficult. This made life awkward for the scientists and probably exacerbated the animosity between them and Borchgrevink which

Top **The *Southern Cross*, in which the first team to overwinter on Antarctica headed south.**
Canterbury Museum, New Zealand

Above **Cape Adare.**
P.S. Kristensen, courtesy of Quark Expeditions

had arisen during the journey south. Borchgrevink was a short-tempered man and, occasionally, an arbitrary leader. On the journey he had refused to let the men write letters home in case any information reached the newspapers and compromised Newnes' intended scoop. The ructions this caused led him to reluctantly reverse the decision, but left a bitter taste. Now the windswept site was another cause for complaint – perhaps the men realised that without the leader's senseless loss of six weeks messing around in the pack ice the *Southern Cross* could have gone further south and found a better site. When the ship returned and they explored McMurdo Sound they found this to be true.

Camp Ridley (as Borchgrevink called it in honour of his English mother: he claimed Ridley ancestry which

Above **Herlof Klövstad, William Colbeck, Hugh Evans, Anton Fougner and Nicolai Hanson standing in front of Camp Ridley. The flag was presented to the team by the Duke of York, the expedition's patron. The photograph was taken by Louis Bernacchi.**

Canterbury Museum, New Zealand

Below **During the austral autumn of 1899 the *Southern Cross* team made the first tentative sledge journeys onto the sea ice off Cape Adare. Carsten Borchgrevink is photographed heading out towards Possession Island.**

Courtesy of Nicolai Vogt

included Nicholas Ridley, the Protestant bishop burnt as a heretic in Mary Tudor's reign) consisted of two huts linked by a canvas-covered storage area, home to its ten occupants for the next 11 months. The huts were anchored to the ground – literally, with anchors from the *Southern Cross* from which ropes were attached to the huts – and were adequate for the winter-long campaign. The only problem occurred when a lighted candle set fire to a mattress and threatened the entire hut; fortunately the fire was quickly put out. Because of the difficulty of moving inland, the intended sledge journeys were much curtailed, though explorations did prove the advantages of dogs.

But the journeys also provided further evidence of Borchgrevink's unsuitability as a leader. On an early trip the sledge party was caught by a storm which broke up the sea ice, resulting in waves crashing into the camp. Borchgrevink's behaviour in the ensuing chaos was, according to Bernacchi, disgraceful: he saved himself, leaving the rest to rescue the supplies. Bernacchi thought him 'thoroughly incompetent and a miserable coward'. In his account of the incident Bernacchi refers to Borchgrevink throughout as a 'booby': later he refined his ideas and changed the reference to 'disreputable beggar'. Part of the problem lay in Borchgrevink's frequent claims to be a scientist: he professed to be a practised surveyor, but couldn't use

a theodolite; he often claimed to be a naturalist, but on one occasion identified a range medusa (jellyfish) as an octopus. Borchgrevink said he had discovered gold on Duke of York Island (which he named for the expedition's patron, who had presented the expedition with a Union Flag which was flown at Camp Ridley). The scientists believed (rightly) that his find was iron pyrites, but Borchgrevink ignored them and continued to talk of the importance of his find and the commercial exploration he and Newnes would undertake. Later, in an attempt to bring the scientists to heel (having realised their opinion of him) he claimed he had a contract which prevented all expedition staff from criticising him: if they did it was mutiny, punishable by 15 years' imprisonment when they returned to civilisation. At this point Bernacchi confided in his diary his view that Borchgrevink was insane, confirming an opinion he had probably come to a little earlier when the leader had informed him, quite seriously, that he could read people's minds.

These actions, together with frequent long-term disagreements with individual men in which he tried to get others to take his side (one row, with Colbeck, lasted most of the trip and was at times both bad tempered and irrational) led to tensions. But these may well have alleviated some of the depressive problems that afflicted the *Belgica*'s crew by providing a focus for fears and frustrations. It is also true, of course, that while the men may have been nervous that the *Southern Cross* might not return, leaving them to face another Antarctic winter, they did not suffer the constant worry of their ship being broken up by ice and so leaving them completely helpless.

Several on the expedition had near misses, but the only death was that of Hanson whose condition worsened steadily. Some have suggested he had scurvy, but none of the others showed any sign of the disease and Hanson's symptoms were not characteristic. He died on 14 October after bidding farewell to the other nine and saying that 'it is not so hard to die in a strange land, it is just like saying goodbye to one's friends when starting on a long journey'. Hanson had been looking forward to the arrival of the Adélie penguins which nested at the cape: two days after his death over 250,000 of them arrived, a continuous stream of birds that took two weeks to come ashore. At his own request Hanson was buried in the shadow of a huge rock on top of Cape Adare, the first man to die on the continent, and the first to be buried there.

By January 1900 the men were anxious to leave, but the *Southern Cross* did not arrive until the 28th. Ironically, all but one of them, who had taken to scanning the horizon for any sign of the ship, were asleep in the huts when she finally turned up, and were woken by Captain Jensen hurling a sack of mail on to the table and shouting 'post'. Back on the ship, the expedition explored the Ross Sea and then sailed along the ice shelf, finding the harbour that would later be called the Bay of Whales (the starting point for Amundsen's journey to the pole). Here two teams of men landed, one using sledges, the other skis. Borchgrevink led the sledge team and claimed to have established a new furthest south record of 78°50'.

The British claim Antarctica

Back home in Britain, the expedition was heralded for having established the position of the South Magnetic Pole by careful measurement of the earth's magnetic field and for the first discovery of insect life on Antarctica. A dispute arose over Hanson's notebooks: many said the zoologist had given Borchgrevink personal charge of these, but he claimed never to have seen them. The argument, never fully resolved, reached the letters page of *The Times* and the staff of the British Museum's National History Department. The staff, which included Edward Wilson, later one of Scott's team, took the side of Hanson, who had been a staff member before the trip: they were particularly vehement in his support after Borchgrevink's outrageous reference to the dead zoologist as 'my late taxidermist'.

As a consequence of the ructions over Hanson's notes and the latent hostility of the Royal Geographical Society, Borchgrevink did not receive the honour and glory to which he believed he was entitled and which he craved. He turned his back on an ungrateful (as he saw it) nation and spent the rest of his life in Norway. Thirty years later, when he was in failing health and suffering from the illness that would kill him – though it would take four more years – Borchgrevink was belatedly awarded the Patron's Medal of the Royal Geographical Society.

The main reason for the society's antagonism was Sir Clements Markham, the president. Markham was born in 1830, just 25 years after Trafalgar. He joined the Royal Navy at 14 and while still a young man was on Horatio Austin's Franklin search expedition of 1850/1. This taste of the Arctic appears to have given him a lifelong enthusiasm for polar exploration, one he was able to indulge when he became president of the society in 1893. His lack of enthusiasm for Borchgrevink's offer to lead a

Above **The return of the southern party. Scott and Wilson are greeted by Reginald Koettlitz (the expedition's surgeon/doctor who was known as Cutlets to his colleagues) while, some way behind (see figures far right), the sick Shackleton is helped in.**
Scott Polar Research Institute, University of Cambridge, UK

But despite the friction the trek continued, the men now forced to feed their dogs with dog meat. Wilson was the unhappiest about this: no means of killing the dogs had been brought and so he had to use a scalpel. Both men and dogs were also hungry, their inexperience in polar travel allowing the British to unwittingly put their heads into a noose. By 24 December Scott and Shackleton, both weak with hunger, were exhibiting symptoms of scurvy. Wilson wanted the trek to end, but Scott insisted on them pushing on reach 82°S, which they reached on 28 December. Scott and Wilson continued to 82°17'S, by definition a new furthest south record, while Shackleton was left at camp at 82°15'S, nominally to look after the dogs.

The weather, which had been remarkably good up until then, turned and the three were very lucky in finding their first food dump on the return journey. They killed the last of the dogs and began a slow and difficult journey manhauling back to the ship. Weakened by hunger and plagued by bad weather the noose now tightened. Had they missed any of their dumps they would almost certainly have died, and

given the occasional limited visibility they were fortunate not to; even so they were still lucky to make it to the ship. Shackleton became very ill on 18 January, and Wilson thought he would die. A lesser man probably would have, but Shackleton's ferocious will kept him going. On 3 February, after 93 days on the ice, the exhausted trio reached the *Discovery*.

At the ship Scott found that a relief ship (the *Morning*, captained by the William Colbeck who had had so many problems with Borchgrevink on the *Southern Cross*) had arrived. Scott also heard that Albert Armitage, his deputy on the expedition, had led a sledge trip on to the Antarctic ice cap. Armitage was therefore the first man to have set foot on the ice cap, reaching an altitude of 2,740m (9,000ft). His team had travelled 385km (240 miles) and reached 78°S. But Scott also found that the *Discovery* was firmly iced in and that a second overwintering was inevitable. Many of his crew went home on the *Morning*, as did Shackleton, Scott clearly deciding that Antarctica was not big enough for both of them.

After an uneventful winter Scott used the second summer to retrace Armitage's route across Victoria Land (but, pointedly, without taking Armitage). Sending some of his men back when they could not keep up with his punishing manhauling schedule Scott travelled about 1,100km (680 miles) achieving a 'furthest west' mark. The two seamen who accompanied him to this point were William Lashly and one who was later to achieve immortality on the continent, Edgar Evans. The *Discovery* was finally released from the ice on 14 February 1904, Scott returning home to the hostility of his navy superiors but the adulation of a nation. He wrote a best-selling book, but in it showed that he had learned little from his near-disastrous trip south and his equally fraught westward push with Lashly and Evans. Each journey had teetered on the brink of oblivion because of the use of manhauling and the narrow safety margins against poor weather and conditions. Yet Scott wrote that the use of dogs 'does rob sledge-travelling of much of its glory... no journey ever made with dogs can approach the height of that fine conception which is realised when a party of men go forth to face hardships, dangers, and difficulties with their own unaided efforts, and by days and weeks of hard physical labour succeed in solving some problem of the great unknown. Surely in this case the conquest is more nobly and splendidly won.' Markham, his benefactor, agreed: 'The sledge journeys without dogs are quite unequalled.' Markham was right

of course, the journeys *were* unequalled; and given the limited experience of Scott and his men they were remarkable, Scott also showed astonishing powers of endurance and great courage. But his failure to heed the lessons of both his own and others' experience were to prove fatal.

Drygalski

Nine days after the *Discovery* departed from England the *Gauss* left the Elbe estuary, carrying the German Antarctic Expedition, led by von Drygalski. Though the Germans had been active in the Arctic in a relatively minor way, this was their first foray south. It rankled that despite the fact that Karl Gauss had made the most important contribution to the study of terrestrial magnetism it had been other nations that had followed up the work with practical science. Now with other nations

again heading south after the brief lull in activities it would be, as von Drygalski notes in his book on it, 'a matter of national honour and duty not to lag behind'. Even so, little was actually done until de Gerlache sailed south in the *Belgica*. For Germany to be upstaged by Belgium, a much smaller country with a short coastline, limited seafaring tradition and equally limited resources, was a shock. The response was an upsurge of nationalist fervour: 'Germany too should become actively involved, unless she were once again prepared to stand humbly by, leaving the glory to other nations' and '…it is important to show the flag, to demonstrate Germany's might and power… and bring honour to the fatherland'.

Despite the patriotic drive for an early expedition, the Germans, as would be expected, planned well. Erich von Drygalski, a 36-year old physicist with a particular interest in glaciology, had led a successful expedition to west Greenland in the early 1890s. The ship which carried the expedition was specially built, and named for Karl Gauss. The *Gauss* was captained by Hans Ruser, the total complement of 32 men (in Antarctica, others were left en route) including four other scientists. The

Germans therefore followed the model of previous successful expeditions, splitting leadership of the expedition from captaincy of the ship, that had been rejected by the British. The ship sailed to the Kerguélen islands to collect 40 dogs, then headed south, discovering Wilhelm II Land on 21 February 1902. However, late that day the ship became trapped in the ice and despite attempts over the next week to break free – including the use of explosives – it was apparent by early March that the *Gauss* was imprisoned for the winter at a position just north of the Antarctic Circle.

From its winter position the scientists did what work they could. The extinct volcano Gaussberg was observed and named – and later climbed – and von Drygalski went up to about 500m (1,640ft) in a captive balloon to observe it, finding the air at that height so warm he could remove his gloves.

The expedition zoologist, Ernst Vanhöffen, had a dredge line fitted below the ship to collect fish. When the line snapped, another was rigged by attaching it to the foot of an Emperor penguin. Two holes, one at the bow, one at the stern, were drilled through the ice and the bird was forced into one. The penguin made valiant efforts to get out, but eventually swam to the second hole. After a couple of abortive attempts when the line came free, the method succeeded. The penguins were also used in less scientific ways, their skinned bodies being used to feed the ship's boilers, the high oil content making them a good substitute for coal. In the context of the expeditions of the time, which overwintered almost exclusively on seal and penguin meat, and fed dog meat to dogs, it was a straightforwardly pragmatic solution to a fuel crisis. There were also several sledge journeys south, one reaching about 71°S, a slightly risky idea as the ship was moving in the ice currents.

The following spring it seemed that the *Gauss* was so firmly held that a second winter was likely, but von Drygalski noticed that the ice was melting more quickly where it was covered by the fall-out from the ship's funnel smoke. As a physicist he rapidly realised why heat from the sun is absorbed by dark objects, and laid out a channel – the 'dirt road' – which was made from boiler ash and any other dark rubbish to hand, causing the underlying ice to thaw. Saws and explosives were also used, but it was the dirt road that formed the escape channel, the ship finally being freed in late February.

It had been an interesting and, scientifically, successful expedition. From the collected data the meteorologist Wilhelm Meinardus was able to infer the existence of the Antarctic Convergence (the narrow confluence – 30–50km/20–30 miles wide – where the warm waters of the Atlantic, Indian and Pacific Oceans meet the cold waters of the Antarctic), though its existence was not confirmed for another 20 years. In all the scientific data filled 20 volumes, and took von Drygalski 30 years to write up. But the Kaiser and the German public were not impressed: little land had been discovered and the furthest south the team had reached was north of the *Discovery*'s winter base. When von Drygalski asked the Kaiser's permission to return to Antarctica his request was refused.

Nordenskjöld

The summer of 1901 saw yet another expedition preparing to leave Europe, led by the Swede Otto Nordenskjöld, nephew of Adolf Erik Nordenskiöld, the first man to sail the North-East Passage. The difference in spelling of the men's surname ('j' rather than 'i',) is modern and follows the currently preferred Swedish forms of the two names. Otto was a 32-year-old geologist who had organised the expedition privately, the Royal Swedish Academy of Sciences having objected when he sought government backing. Though he managed to raise the cash to get the expedition underway, Nordenskjöld was debt-ridden for years after and much of the proposed scientific work had to be abandoned while the scientists hunted for seals when food ran short. Nordenskjöld's ship, the *Antarctic*, was captained by a Norwegian, Carl Anton Larsen, a man with plenty of polar experience: he had been on the *Jason* which took Nansen to Greenland for his crossing of the ice cap, and had also been to Antarctica twice before, firstly in 1892/3 to search for whales, then again in 1893/4 when he explored the northern end of the Antarctic Peninsula. Larsen is credited with the first use of skis on Antarctica and with discovering petrified wood on Seymour Island. He also sailed along the edge of the ice shelf which now bears his name.

The *Antarctic* sailed late, in October 1901, and did not leave Buenos Aires until late December, so the plan of establishing a winter base at the southern end of the Antarctic Peninsula was soon abandoned: there was too much sea ice for the ship to penetrate far enough south, and the Larsen Ice Shelf lay between the expedition and the peninsula. Nordenskjöld therefore set up camp on Snow Hill Island which lies south of Seymour Island (and east of James Ross Island and the peninsula). As soon as the wintering hut had been erected, the ship departed leaving six men (Nordenskjöld and five others) behind.

The winter was a hard one, with frequent storms and low temperatures. When summer came Nordenskjöld and two men set out southwards by dog-sledge, hoping to meet the *Antarctica* at Robertson Island, but had to return when the ship did not arrive. It also failed to rendezvous at Snow Hill, forcing the six men to prepare for a second winter. The ship had attempted to sail the Antarctic Sound (between the peninsula and Joinville Island) but had been stopped by the ice. Realising it could not hope to reach the Snow Hill men, three men went ashore at Hope Bay (in late December 1902) intending to sledge to the camp and return with the winter party. The ship retreated north to escape the ice, then went east around Joinville Island and tried to go south again, but she soon became trapped in the pack. On 11 January 1903 a large ice floe was driven into the ship. With no hope of repairing the damage the crew salvaged what they could, but stayed with the ship until she sank on 12 February. The crew then trekked across the sea ice to Paulet Island.

The Swedes were now in three groups, none of them knowing the state of the other two. At Hope Bay the sledging trio headed for Snow Hill, but were unable to cross the dangerously part-thawed sea ice separating the winter camp from James Ross Island. They returned to Hope Bay and, when the ship failed to return, built a makeshift hut in which they overwintered. The windowless hut, sealed against the bitter polar winter, was heated by burning seal blubber. They also used blubber for cooking so by winter's end the hut walls, the men and their clothing were caked in black soot and grease. When summer 1903 came they sledged off towards Snow Hill again, and by an extraordinary coincidence met Nordenskjöld and Ole Jonassen who had sledged to James Ross Island. Approached by three black-faced men dressed in greasy rags Nordenskjöld was convinced he had found continental natives, his delight at meeting fellow expedition members being tempered by the loss of a momentous discovery. Jonassen was less thrilled at the prospect and took out his revolver just in case: the point where the two groups met, on Vega Island, named by Nordenskjöld for his uncle's ship, was named Cape Well-Met.

On Paulet Island the remnant *Antarctic* crew killed over 1,000 Adélie penguins and overwintered, one man dying after a prolonged illness. When spring arrived Larsen set out with five others in an open boat salvaged from the ship, going first to Hope Bay where a grimy

Top **The stone hut at Hope Bay. This was built by Andersson, Duse and Grunden after they had failed to make it to Snow Hill Island. The three men spent the winter of 1903 here.**
From O. Nordenskjöld *Antarctic II*.
Courtesy of the Swedish Polar Research Secretariat

Above **The three sledgers who, dirty and dressed in greasy, ragged clothing convinced Otto Nordenskjöld he had discovered Antarctic natives. From left to right the men are Duse, Andersson and Grunden.**
From J.G. Andersson *Antarctic*.
Courtesy of the Swedish Polar Research Secretariat

Above **Port Lockroy, named by Jean-Baptiste Charcot in honour of the French politician Édouard Lockroy who persuaded the government to support his expedition.**
Werner Stambach, courtesy of Quark Expeditions

note directed him to Snow Hill. At the same time, concerned because the *Antarctic* was well overdue, the Swedes sent a relief ship, as did the Argentineans. The Argentinean navy gunboat *Uruguay* arrived first, reaching Snow Hill Island where two of Nordenskjöld's men were spotted. The relieved pair and two Argentineans arrived at the camp just hours before Larsen arrived. Incredibly all three Swedish groups had met up, the remaining men on Paulet Island being taken off as the *Uruguay* headed north.

It might be assumed that the drama of the expedition detracted from the science, but Nordenskjöld's was arguably the best scientific trip of the time; the science report ran to six volumes and 4,000 pages. The Swedes had found numerous fossils, including that of a giant penguin, and made important discoveries on plantlife, oceanography and geology.

Charcot

The Argentineans had rescued the Swedes, getting south ahead of the Swedish relief ship and also ahead of the *Français*, which carried the French Antarctic Expedition under the leadership of Dr Jean-Baptiste Charcot, son of Jean-Martin Charcot, a world-famous neurologist who is said to have influenced Freud. On his father's death Jean-Baptiste inherited a small fortune in cash and art and used it to buy a ship with the intention of exploring the Arctic (an idea which, judged by later events, was not greeted with loud enthusiasm by his wife, a granddaughter of Victor Hugo). When Charcot heard that Nordenskjöld was missing he decided to sail south instead, and when government and public money was donated in response to this humanitarian decision, it meant that he led a national expedition. It did not start well. The *Français* with its crew of 21 (Charcot, Captain Ernest Cholet and 19 others) and pet pig Toby left Le Havre on 15 August 1903, but the expedition was less than two minutes old when a hawser snapped, one flying end killing a seaman named Maignan. The funeral and enquiry delayed the new departure for 12 days. When the *Français* finally left Adrian de Gerlache, leader of the *Belgica* expedition, had joined the party (though he left in Buenos Aires, unable to stand the separation from his new fiancée).

Finding that the *Uruguay* had rescued Nordenskjöld, Charcot sailed for the western side of the Antarctic Peninsula, wintering on Booth Island, which forms the western side of the famous Lemaire Channel. Charcot's decision not to venture into the Ross Sea was to avoid any problems over British claims, a fact that Scott noted, calling Charcot 'the gentleman of the Pole'. The French team seem to have enjoyed a pleasant winter – there were early trials of a motorised sledge – apart from losing Toby, who ate a quantity of fish still attached to fish-hooks, and died a miserable death. The ship was moored in Port Charcot, a narrow inlet across the mouth of which a rope was slung to keep the pack ice out. The *Français* broke out easily in late December 1904, though then hit a rock and needed rapid repairs before limping back to South America where she was sold. When the French eventually reached home, Charcot's wife divorced him on the grounds of desertion.

Charcot remarried, insisting on a prenuptial agreement with his new wife which allowed him to go on expeditions. In 1908 he headed south again, in the *Pourquoi Pas?* naming Marguerite Bay for his accommodating wife and overwintering on Petermann Island: he also discovered and named Charcot Land – now known to be an island, Charcot Island – for his father. In 1937 he sailed the *Pourquoi Pas?* to Iceland where she was lost, with all but one crewman drowned.

Shackleton: the *Nimrod*

Back in Britain after his return from the *Discovery* Ernest Shackleton nursed a burning desire to return. He writes in *Heart of Antarctica*, his account of the *Nimrod* expedition, 'I had been invalided home...', but must

"Music hath Charms."
This Photo was taken off Coats Land, Lat. 74°01'S Long 22°W discovered by the Scottish National Antarctic Expedition.

Scott Polar Research Centre,
University of Cambridge, UK

There was one other team in the south during this time, that of William Bruce, the Scot who many believe should have led the *Discovery* expedition and who so infuriated Sir Clements Markham by organising a 'rival' trip. Refused government money, Bruce then sought the backing of Andrew Coats, the London-born, but Glasgow-based, clothing magnate. Bruce was a proud Scot, which appealed to Coats' nationalism. He backed the trip, allowing Bruce to buy the *Scotia*, a Norwegian whaler, in which the Scottish National Antarctic Expedition set sail in November 1902. The team wintered on Laurie Island in the South Orkneys, then carried out a remarkable amount of hydrographic and zoological research in the Weddell Sea during the summer of 1902/3 before overwintering on the ice-bound ship in 1903. When freed the ship returned to South America, leaving six men on Laurie Island where they made an impressive study of the local penguins. The *Scotia* returned with three Argentineans who joined two of the six men on the island, the others rejoining the ship which headed south to 74°S, discovering Coats Land. The Argentineans eventually took over the Laurie Island base, changing its name from Osmond House to Orcadas. The Bruce expedition may have made limited discoveries in terms of new land – though Coats Land was a significant find – but from a scientific point of view, and from consideration of Bruce's leadership, it has never received the credit it deserves. It is also rarely mentioned that it was on this expedition that bagpipes were first played on the Antarctic continent. The photograph of the piper serenading an apparently entranced penguin was made into a postcard. It is enchanting, but in order to keep the penguin close to the skirling pipes it had to have one foot tied to the ice.

have known – or been suspicious at the very least – that his health had not been the entire reason for his departure. He had already said when still on the *Discovery* that one day he would return and show himself a better man than Scott. This resentment was sharpened by the heroic reception Scott received and by the account of the southern journey in Scott's *Voyage of the Discovery* in which he referred to Shackleton as 'our invalid' and in other derogatory ways, and implied that the trek had failed because of Shackleton's 'sudden break-down'. The situation was probably not helped by the fact that Shackleton not only had a head start on the lecture circuit, having reached Britain first, but was a better speaker (which many suggest was due to his Anglo-Irish heritage: he was born in Kilkea in 1874), Scott's jealousy further fuelling Shackleton's resentment.

Almost certainly aware that there was little chance of his being invited on another Scott expedition, Shackleton decided to launch his own, working quickly to ensure a return to the south before any second Scott trip could be organised. The problem, as always, was finance, but this was solved in February 1907 when William Beardmore, a rich industrialist and shipbuilder based in Glasgow, for whom Shackleton was working as an early form of public relations officer, agreed to fund the trip.

Shackleton bought a 41-year-old Dundee-built sealing ship called the *Nimrod*. He intended to change her name to *Endurance*, a short form of his family motto *Fortitudue Vincimus* (By Fortitude – or Endurance – We Conquer) but in the end did not. He attempted to sign up several members of the *Discovery*'s crew, but many turned down the invitation. Of these the one that caused Shackleton's greatest pain was Edward Wilson: Wilson had taken on work and would not give it up. Worse was to follow when Wilson took Scott's side after a row broke out over the use of the Discovery base. Scott had decided to return to Antarctica – but not yet – and claimed 'squatter's rights' on the site. Indeed, he tried to claim rights to the whole Ross Sea. Shackleton was aghast, but under pressure from Wilson, who saw the dispute as an issue of morals, agreed to stay east of 170°W.

Shackleton visited Nansen who was now the ambassador in London for newly independent Norway. Though only in his mid-40s Nansen had acquired a (deserved) status as the Great Man of polar exploration. To the younger explorers of the time – Amundsen, Scott and Shackleton amongst others – he was a mentor, a polar guru, and God-speed from him had almost taken on the aura of a papal blessing. Nansen was amazed that Shackleton had learned so little from the *Discovery* trip. He was intending to walk not ski, and instead of taking dogs he was taking ponies. If the former, given Shackleton's own experience of skis on his journey with Scott and Wilson (when they had arguably saved his life on the return trip), was beyond comprehension, the latter was beyond reason. Ironically, after Nansen had met Frederick Jackson on Franz Josef Land following the *Fram* expedition they had discussed the use of horses in Antarctica. The incredulous Nansen had advised against it: now here, despite all the evidence in support of dogs, was another Briton with the same idea. An even greater irony is that Shackleton got his idea for horses from Jackson, who had tried both animals on his expedition to Franz Josef Land. The dogs were a complete success, the horses a constant problem: nevertheless Jackson had come down in favour of horses. History does not record Nansen's view, if any, of Shackleton's decision to take a motor car as well.

The *Nimrod* left London in July 1907, stopping in Australia where the geologist Douglas Mawson was added to the crew, and New Zealand where shortage of space meant that five of the Manchurian ponies which had already arrived there had to be left behind. Shackleton also now realised that to conserve coal he would need to be towed to the ice edge. He appealed for help and the Union Steamship Company of New Zealand offered a tramp steamer (the *Koonya*, six times the size of *Nimrod*), its cost defrayed by the company and the New Zealand government. The tow was a nightmare journey through the mountainous seas of a ferocious storm during which one pony was injured so badly it had to be destroyed: another injured animal was also put down later. Close to the ice edge the *Koonya* unhitched and turned for home, the *Nimrod* sailing on to the edge of the ice shelf in search of the inlet from where the *Discovery's* balloon launches had been made. The inlet was gone, presumably carved away, and a second inlet – christened Bay of Whales for obvious reasons – could not be reached because of the sea ice.

With the time until the *Nimrod* would have to depart for winter diminishing quickly, Shackleton was forced to break his promise to Scott and cross the 'forbidden' 170°W line for McMurdo Sound, an action that caused him great distress. Unable to reach Discovery Hut because of sea ice, Shackleton built a new hut near Cape Royds, about 35km (22 miles) to the north (and therefore further from the pole: the intended camp on the ice shelf was at least 100km/62 miles – straight-

line distance – closer). With everything unloaded the *Nimrod* left for New Zealand carrying secret orders from Shackleton for the dismissal of her captain, Rupert England. Shackleton had disagreed with England several times over what he saw as the captain's timidity when in the pack ice, and was deeply concerned that any over-caution in 1910 might lead to his team having to be relieved (worse still rescued) by Scott. That he could not allow. Ironically in view of his own departure from the *Discovery*, Shackleton cited England's poor health as the reason for the dismissal. Only when the *Nimrod* arrived back in New Zealand did England discovered he had been sacked. Subsequent details of his conflict led to livid headlines in British newspapers and from those Scott learned that Shackleton had broken his promise not to cross 170°W. The outraged Scott branded Shackleton a liar and swore never to have anything to do with him again, a promise unlikely to have broken Shackleton's heart.

To give his men something to do Shackleton suggested a first ascent of Mount Erebus, though he decided not to go himself when Eric Marshall, the expedition's surgeon refused to allow him to travel unless he was examined. Marshall clearly suspected Shackleton of being ill, and Shackleton refused to be examined, presumably because he was nervous of what Marshall might find, resulting in a conflict between the two. Six men – Marshall, Adams, Brocklehurst, David, Mackay and Mawson – set out in equipment that would have been censurable had not the peak been straightforward. In the absence of climbing equipment they improvised crampons with nails hammered through

Left **Shackleton's hut at Cape Royds.**
Frank Todd, courtesy of Quark Expeditions

Right **The interior of Shackleton's hut at Cape Royds.**
C. Carvalho, courtesy of Quark Expeditions

leather straps which they attached to their boots (though only some of them had time to make these as the decision to climb was taken at short notice). They towed a 270kg (595lb) sledge of equipment. Though gently sloping, Erebus is 3,794m (12,448ft) high, every metre of which had to be climbed from the sea-level hut. After two nights the six left the sledge as a dump. They also left the tent poles as too difficult to carry, so had to sleep under the fabric and cook in the open. One of their sleeping bags was enormous, constructed to accommodate three men, its vastness overburdening whoever carried it. Brocklehurst eventually stopped because of altitude sickness, but the other five reached the top. The five-day struggle was rewarded with a view into the deep, steam-filled crater.

During the winter some of the expedition novices were taught the very basics of snowcraft, involving little more than ski-less manhauling trips. The motor car was driven a few kilometres (a first for Antarctic mechanised transport, but of extremely limited practical use). In New Zealand Shackleton had found nine dogs, the descendants of Borchgrevink's 1900 team, and as an afterthought had taken them; but the winter training did not include any work with these. For the summer Shackleton decided on two objectives. He

Above **Among its many firsts, Shackleton's *Nimrod* expedition was the first to use a motor car on Antarctica. The car – an Arrol-Johnston, the gift of expedition sponsor William Beardmore – was not a great success.**
Richard Sale Collection

Right **Looking into the crater of Mount Erebus after the first ascent.**
Richard Sale Collection

would lead a team of four (himself, Jameson Adams, Eric Marshall and Frank Wild) south, while Edgworth David would lead Douglas Mawson and Alistair Mackay in an attempt to reach the South Magnetic Pole. Of the ten ponies only four remained (in addition to the two which had to be destroyed, four had died). Shackleton would take these. David's team therefore had no ponies and it was decided that they would not use dogs either.

Shackleton's party set out on 29 October 1908. At first they made reasonable time despite the ponies often sinking belly-deep into soft snow, but it soon became clear that ponies were not suited to polar work. They became chilled and had to have blankets draped over them when they stopped, snow walls built to protect them from the wind and their food required thawing. They also did not have the 'advantage' that dogs have of being willing to cannibalise their tracemates. But ponies do provide a large quantity of 'food on the hoof', early supply dumps being organised around a pony carcass, animals being shot in turn as

they weakened. The men fared better, with no real illnesses (other than Adams having a tooth pulled without anaesthetic, a miserable procedure not helped when Marshall's first attempt merely broke the tooth), though there were inevitable tensions. Marshall's view of Shackleton deteriorated and his concerns over Shackleton's health increased. By contrast, Wild's view of the leader steadily improved: it was on this trip that he first referred to Shackleton as 'the Boss', a nickname which stuck. Despite Wild's fear that they would be lucky to get to the pole and 'luckier still to get back' he was willing to follow wherever the Boss led.

The team passed Scott's furthest south mark and, hauling parallel to the coast, aimed for the 'Golden Gateway', an apparent pass in the mountains (now called the Transantarctic Mountains) ahead. It turned out to be only the entrance to a glacier (named Beardmore by Shackleton after the expedition's sponsor). The glacier was a nightmare; the men had no crampons and Socks, the only remaining pony, disappeared into a crevasse. As they climbed higher the thinning air also became a problem (the pole lies at the centre of a plateau lying at about 3,000m/10,000ft). As time was lost rations were reduced to maintain the possibility of reaching the pole, so the four were constantly hungry. Eventually Shackleton realised that reaching the pole would require an all-or-nothing dash. The four dumped what they could, but it was soon apparent that they were still going too slowly. By 3 January 1909 they were at 87°22'S, still 250km (about 160 miles) short of their goal. They were exhausted, cold (their body temperatures had fallen, a dangerous sign of hypothermia) hungry and dehydrated (fuel, too, being rationed). It was clear they had come to the end, more so when it was realised that even now it was possible that they might miss the *Nimrod* on their return. The weather, which had been excellent early in the trip, was now foul. But Shackleton would not give in. He asked who would continue with him and, with varying degrees of reluctance, all agreed. Shackleton was determined to get within 160km (100 miles) of the pole, so the men dumped half of what little they had and, on 4 January, continued in temperatures sometimes below −30°C, wearing just one layer of underwear, two sweaters and a thin windsuit (but no trousers beneath the leggings) and still hauling over 30kg (66lb) each. But now the weather worsened, a blizzard trapping them in their tents for 60 hours. When it blew over (9 January) the frost-bitten men pushed on one last time, finally reaching 88°23'S. They were 155km (97 miles) from the pole. His target reached, Shackleton bowed to the inevitable defeat and turned around.

The return journey was a nightmare, the four on the edge of starvation for almost the whole 1,170km (730 miles). Several times they ran out of food altogether and only luck allowed them to reach the next of their supply dumps: bad weather would inevitably have meant death. All collapsed at some point, Marshall taking the lead at one stage, Shackleton, who had been very ill, recovering at the end. Yet despite their poor health and limited food their willpower and stamina were phenomenal: one day they marched over 46km (29 miles). Eventually, after 123 days on the trek, and having left the sick Marshall, and Adams as nurse, at a last camp, Shackleton and Wild reached the base hut. The *Nimrod* and everyone had gone, but unbelievably the ship returned at just the right moment, intent on dropping off a wintering crew to search for the quartet's bodies. They had, after all,

Above **Adams, Wild and Shackleton at their furthest south.**
Richard Sale Collection

only 91 days supply of food and so must have perished.

With the return of the ship Shackleton found that the magnetic pole team had triumphed. David, Mackay and Mawson had started three weeks before Shackleton, travelling the first few kilometres of their journey by car before the vehicle became embedded in a snow drift. They then manhauled, starting with loads of 320kg (790lb) including the sledges. The team stayed on the sea-ice edge parallel to the coast, following a route chosen by Mawson who, of the three, had the best nose for a line, but always searching for a way to reach South Victoria Land. It was a precarious route as the sea ice was often fragile, threatening to tip the trio into the sea. Often, too, the ice was wet, making their boots wet and clinging to the sledges so that their daily rate of travel averaged only about 8km (around 5 miles). Mawson was concerned by this slow rate, claiming it was due, in part, to David's age – he was 51, the other two being under 30 – and that as the sea ice might have melted by the time of their return they might run out of food and fuel. He therefore suggested eating seal meat cooked on blubber oil in a biscuit-tin stove, lit with a calico food-bag wick. This saved their supplies, but the sledges remained heavy for a longer period and the change of diet caused acute diarrhoea.

The team's weather was reasonable: on one day it was so warm David gave his feet a snow bath. By 1 December they had reached the Drygalski Ice Tongue,

Above **Mackay, David and Mawson at the South Magnetic Pole.**
Richard Sale Collection

the ice shelf which defines the southern edge of Terra Nova Bay. Their first attempt to cross this failed, putting the expedition in jeopardy, but a second attempt succeeded, though it took eight days to cross the tongue because of hummocky ice. It took a further two weeks to find a route up the Larsen Glacier on to the plateau, though this included a three-day rest period (on one day of which the sun was so hot their food had to be shielded from it, while two days later there was a blizzard). On a glacier Mawson fell into a crevasse, but was rescued without incident – he even had the presence of mind to excavate some interesting snow crystals while in the crevasse.

Finally the trio emerged on the rising Antarctic plateau, the unbroken view ahead suggesting they were over the worst. They were now at an altitude of about 850m (2,800ft), some 1,350m (4,460ft) below the magnetic pole – though they did not know this – and about 300km (185 miles) from it. After making a dump of some of their supplies they covered this distance in

under three weeks, maintaining their target average of 16km (10 miles) each day despite the constant climbing. They estimated their height gain using a hypometer which calculates the boiling point of water and, therefore, the air pressure. The lower boiling point was a matter of contention in the party: how long should tea be allowed to boil before serving? The trip was not straightforward, however. The men had reduced their rations and were all hungry, and the occasional days of intense cold and biting wind had caused the skin of their faces to peel: Mawson's lips were sealed so tight each morning with congealed blood that he had difficulty opening his mouth.

On 16 January they arrived at the mean position of the South Magnetic Pole, as calculated by Mawson, the team's navigator. Because of the relative crudeness of his equipment Mawson was only able to establish the general area of the pole, but by taking several measurements the team were able to move across it. At what they considered the exact spot the three erected a Union Jack for the obligatory photograph and David spoke words given to him by Shackleton, claiming the area around the magnetic pole for the British Empire (an interesting idea given that the pole moves: at present it is offshore of Terre Adélie and regularly sailed over by tourist ships). At the time of the flag raising and photograph, for which the three went bareheaded, the temperature was –18°C.

On the return David hoped they might average 26km (just over 16 miles) daily, so as to meet the *Nimrod* close to the Drygalski Ice Tongue and avoid the potentially dangerous, perhaps impossible, return journey along the coast. At this point his account of the journey became dominated by food: its lack, its relative abundance, its form. He reports an argument when Mawson added sugar to the day's hoosh (what the British called the soup made by mixing pemmican – dried, ground meat and fat – and dry biscuit in boiling water). The variable weather continued, the three men being particularly plagued by strong winds which, with temperatures falling to –30°C, chilled them. But they maintained their target 26km (16 miles) average, in part helped by the fact that they were hauling downhill over reasonable ground and had rigged a mast and sail to the sledge to take advantage of the incessant wind. They reached their dump at the head of the glacier on 30 January, but the descent of the glacier was as arduous as the climb up it. The men fell into crevasses, the sledge overturned often, and Mawson broke through the ice on a glacial pool and went up to his waist in freezing water. On 3 February they arrived at the coast and were able to supplement their diet with seal and penguin meat.

The plan had been for the returning *Nimrod* to sail close to the shore looking for the men, but they had no way of knowing whether she had already passed the spot or was still many days away. Fearful of the possibly horrendous journey along the coast the exhausted David gave the leadership of the team to Mawson who, despite an injured leg, had shown himself the most capable of the three. Barely had this transfer been made when a gunshot announced the arrival of the *Nimrod*. On this expedition remarkable coincidences had become commonplace.

Though Shackleton felt the loss of the pole keenly, the expedition had been a major success. It was only 14 years since men had first (officially) stepped on Antarctica, only nine since the first overwintering, barely six since the first attempt to journey inland. Now *Nimrod*'s men had journeyed within 160km (100 miles) of the pole and stood on the South Magnetic Pole; and they had all returned safely. The achievement of David, Mawson and Mackay was overlooked in the praise of Shackleton's team, but it was every bit as magnificent. In 120 days they had travelled almost 2,000km (about 1,200 miles) without serious mishap. Apart from the first few kilometres in the motor car they had manhauled all the way. Irrespective of remarks that can be made about the lack of skis and dogs it had been a marvellous display of courage and willpower. That was true too of Shackleton. He had increased the record for furthest south by the greatest margin since Captain Cook's voyage, a margin that could never be broken. He had shown the way to the pole from McMurdo. If he had completed the same distance from the Bay of Whales he might well have reached the pole, a fact which Amundsen noted eagerly. Shackleton returned home a hero. The British are deeply suspicious of winners, but love a heroic loser; the only thing that could have improved Shackleton's stock was succeeding, but dying. He was knighted and produced a book, *The Heart of Antarctica* (ghosted by the New Zealand journalist Ernest Saunders) which won excellent reviews. Scott and other members of the British 'Antarctic establishment' were civil in public, bitter in private. They spread rumours about the true latitude reached. They could hardly argue with the last sun-spotted position of 87°22' (on 3 January), but raised doubts about later positions. They had a point. Shackleton's claimed position was based on dead

reckoning, no sun having been visible for days. Ironically later that day it was, but the theodolite had been left in the last camp to save weight and it was also only 9am when they stopped: by noon they had not yet reached their last camp and, in any case, no one had the strength left to bother to take a reading. The distances claimed for the last dash – 32 nautical miles (59km/37 miles) in ten hours at 3,000m (10,000ft) – do seem implausible. Perhaps Marshall wanted to give Shackleton his 'within 100 miles' so they could all go home. Who can tell? And, apart from Scott and his supporters, who would be churlish enough to deny the four their small victory?

Amundsen: the pole reached

Shackleton gave many lectures. At one, in Christiania (Oslo), Norway, the audience included Nansen and Amundsen. Nansen was secretly relieved that Shackleton had not made the pole as he wanted to make one last trip of his own – and he had decided to go south. In part the reason was that he had agreed to lend the *Fram* to Amundsen who wanted to try for the North Pole (though 'lend' is not really the correct term: the ship was owned by the Norwegian state and Nansen accepted Amundsen's first use). But news had just arrived that both Cook and Peary were claiming to have reached the North Pole.

As a young boy Roald Amundsen was a member of a gang who played in the nearby forests: another member of the group was Carsten Borchgrevink, the first man to officially set foot on Antarctica (perhaps). Amundsen claimed that reading about Franklin's Canada overland trip of 1819/25 made him want to be a polar explorer, a desire hardened by Nansen's crossing of Greenland which inspired a generation of Norwegian youth. Learning from Nansen's success Amundsen practised his skiing. He also recognised early on the advantages of dog-sledging demonstrated by the Peary/Astrup crossing of northern Greenland in 1892. Amundsen enrolled at Christiania (Oslo) University to study medicine, but failed his exams and left unqualified. In need of a job he joined several sealing expeditions, realising that another essential of polar travel was the ability to sail. His experience as a sailor in Arctic waters and his skill as a skier, coupled with his enthusiasm for the trip and his willingness to go without pay, got him a place on board de Gerlache's *Belgica*. There he learned at first hand about the polar winter and soaked up information from Frederick Cook whose Arctic trips made him one of the most experienced polar travellers of the time. On his return from Antarctica Amundsen decided to organise his own trip, choosing the North-West Passage and North Magnetic Pole (the first still to be sailed, the latter reached just once before by Ross in 1831), an objective which Nansen approved. Such was Nansen's status in Norway that just this nod of approval was sufficient to kick-start the expedition. The start of Amundsen's quest for the North-West Passage coincided with Sverdrup's return from his exploration of northern Canada in *Fram*. Sverdrup's experiences with dog-sledging reinforced Amundsen's opinion. He was determined to learn the technique from the Canadian Inuit, which he accomplished brilliantly while the *Gjøa* was overwintering during the passage transit.

Amundsen returned to a newly independent Norway and was heralded as its first hero (despite the massive shadow cast by Nansen). Encouraged to believe that a grateful nation might underwrite another trip he decided to try for the North Pole. He spoke to Nansen about use of the *Fram*, but found him less than keen as he still harboured ambitions to attempt the South Pole himself. Nansen believed (correctly) that Antarctica had an ice cap and that a trip to the South Pole would be merely a longer version of his Greenland crossing. Amundsen, probably surmising that Nansen's dream was just that – a dream – pressed him on the use of *Fram* and eventually Nansen agreed to give up his own priority in favour of the younger man's.

For his proposed North Pole expedition Amundsen chose his men wisely. One was Olav Bjaaland, a brilliant skier who had allied telemark techniques to standard cross-country skiing. He had Helmer Hanssen, who had been on *Gjøa* and was an excellent dog driver, and Hjalmar Johansen, Nansen's companion on the epic attempt to reach the North Pole from *Fram*. Interestingly, he had no doctor, preferring to send two of his men on short courses (and to use his own medical knowledge). The preparations for the trip were well advanced when word came that there were two claimants to the pole.

Amundsen's view of the Cook and Peary claims is strange. He sent his congratulations to his old friend Cook, but declined to confirm whether he believed him. He was equally evasive when asked about Peary's claim. Nevertheless, he was obviously sufficiently concerned to change his own plans, though he decided not to tell anyone until it was too late for them to stop him. He may have been worried about Nansen's reaction, and he was almost certainly nervous of the Norwegian government's

view of upsetting the British. Amundsen claimed that Peary's imputation of Cook was based, in part, on his assumed proprietorial rights over the North Pole, and he probably assumed, rightly, that Scott felt the same way about the South Pole; in a letter Scott wrote that he did not 'hold that anyone but an Englishman' should be first at the South Pole. For the same reason Amundsen decided against using McMurdo as his base, choosing instead to go to the Bay of Whales, which also had the advantage of being at least 100km (60 miles) closer to the pole. At his proposed daily rate of travel of 24km (15 miles) that difference amounted to eight days' travel, even if it meant he would be crossing new ground for his entire journey.

Amundsen had special larger skis made, and clothing similar to that of the Inuit in northern Canada. He was meticulous about all the other equipment too, and especially about food. His preparations also included an avoidance of Scott who several times tried to arrange meetings to discuss the sharing of scientific projects: Amundsen could tolerate being called a 'bad sport', but not a liar. On 6 June 1910 the *Fram* sailed from Bundefjord, Amundsen's home, leaving at midnight just as *Gjøa* had done when she set out for the North-West Passage. This was only a proving run; not until 9 August did the *Fram*, with 97 Greenland dogs on board, finally leave Norway. This time Amundsen slipped away in mid-evening rather than midnight, but to ensure that there would be no final farewells (potentially embarrassing because of his real plan, as well as being against his nature) he did not announce his departure and simply raised the anchor as soon as the last dog was loaded.

As the planned trip, sealing *Fram* in the ice just as Nansen had done, was to begin in the Bering Sea, the crew were not surprised to head south to Madeira even though Nansen had taken the North-East Passage: they assumed they were to round Cape Horn and sail north. They were, though, curious about certain aspects of the trip: why take dogs all the way to Alaska when there were dogs easily available there? What was this huge hut for – surely not for erecting on pack ice? It is possible that some of the more astute of Amundsen's team knew there was something going on; if they did, they were proved right at Madeira. There, after sending letters announcing his change of plan to Nansen, King Haakon and several others, Amundsen told the crew. None objected, though Amundsen did couch the change as an 'extension' to the original plan: getting to the South Pole would help finance the 'real' trip to the North Pole. What he did not tell them was where he was

Above **In the Bay of Whales on 3 February 1911, Lt Victor Campbell and *Terra Nova* found the Norwegians and was treated to a demonstration of dog-sledging that made all the British gasp – never had they seen sledges move so fast. It was a show put on specifically for the British by Amundsen, but for all that it was an indication of just what the dog-sledge was capable of as a means of transport.**
USA Library of Congress

Above **Framheim at the Bay of Whales. The Bay of Whales is a semi-permanent feature of the Ross Ice Shelf. The early expeditions knew this though at the time they did not know the reason for its existence. Amundsen surmised that it was actually land. It is not, being formed by Roosevelt Island which perturbs the flow of the shelf ice and so causes an indentation of varying size in the shelf edge.**
USA Library of Congress

planning to land, as he had no wish for this information to reach the British. The 19 Norwegians were now in a race with the 67 Britons on board *Terra Nova* which had left Cardiff on 15 June.

On the journey south the men honed their equipment towards perfection, a task they would complete during the winter on the Ross Ice Shelf. Amundsen was behind the British and though they were not – to Norwegian incredulity – using dogs and skis, they did have motor-sledges which might be quicker than dogs. All possible sources of delay must therefore be eliminated. Amundsen was 480km (300 miles) behind Scott when he entered the Ross Sea, and ten days behind him after unloading in the Bay of Whales and setting up Framheim (*Fram*'s home), his winter base.

In what remained of the austral autumn Amundsen laid out supply dumps southward, reaching 82°S: he was now, effectively, 240km (150 miles) ahead of Scott, and his dumps were better marked and, therefore, easier to find. The description of the Norwegian base

during the winter makes impressive reading. It was a hive of activity as the sledges, traces, skis, clothing and supplies were modified and perfected. The Norwegians were clearly in tune with their environment and with the job at hand in a way in which the British, who had brought England to Antarctica, were not. This can most readily be seen in one detail: Greenland dogs will, if given the chance, eat human excrement. The Norwegians made use of this as a means of keeping their base cleaner: the British stopped any dog that tried.

On 8 September Amundsen started for the pole against the advice of Johansen whose experience with Nansen had taught him the folly of trekking in extreme cold, and who had realised on the depot-laying tours that the cold of the Antarctic was even more brutal than that of the Arctic pack. But Amundsen feared an early move by Scott and insisted. With temperatures falling to –57°C the team soon began to experience frostbite and the dogs became exhausted and injured, blood from their paws staining the ice. The spirit compasses froze and were useless, the vacuum flasks broke into pieces in the cold, and even a reviving bottle of gin froze solid and cracked on thawing. Amundsen was forced to give up. The retreat, begun at 7am, was a shambles. Amundsen decided to go to Framheim in one go rather than the normal two-day trip, and set off on skis towed by Oscar Wisting's sledge. With them was Helmer Hanssen and his sledge. Behind them came the rest: Jørgen Stubberud and Olav Bjaaland, then Sverre Hassel (slowed by frostbite in a big toe). Behind again were Hjalmar Johansen and bringing up the rear Kristian Prestrud, a polar newcomer whose feet were frozen and whose dogs were now useless. Johansen caught Hassel and explained that someone had to wait for Prestrud. Hassel declined, probably fearing the state of his own feet, but gave Johansen a tent. When Prestrud eventually reached Johansen he was in a poor state. Without food or a stove to make drinks Johansen knew it was imperative that he get Prestrud back to Framheim. At times he had to carry him.

Amundsen's team of three reached Framheim at 4pm, the others trailing in between 6 and 6.30. Johansen brought Prestrud – now unable to walk and barely able to stand – in after midnight. In his book Amundsen notes this with the comment, 'Heaven knows what they had been doing on the way!'. What they had been doing was fighting for Prestrud's life, Johansen saving not only that but Amundsen's expedition as well, as there is little doubt that Prestrud's death would have precipitated its collapse. The following morning Amundsen asked Johansen why they had been so late arriving. Johansen's pent-up frustration erupted and he told Amundsen not only why, but exactly what he felt about a leader who abandoned his men without food or fuel in order to save himself. Johansen's view was that the retreat had not been an expedition but a panic, and that in addition to the charge of poor judgement for going too early Amundsen now stood accused of poor leadership.

Though there is good evidence that most of the rest of the team agreed with Johansen they were all too fearful of their position in the pole party to say so. Johansen was isolated. Amundsen noted in his diary that 'this was a sad end to an excellent unity, but I feel the only course after his [Johansen's] behaviour is to exclude him. We can accept no critical elements on our journey and coming from an experienced man like him it would be doubly dangerous.' Amundsen not only excluded Johansen from the pole party, but put him in a team which was to explore King Edward VII Land, a

team to be led by Prestrud. This quite deliberate snub led to further aggravation and, according to some sources, a fight.

Johansen noted in his own diary that Amundsen 'feels it as deadly insult because his qualities of leadership have been exposed as hollow... He is not the man I thought he was...' There is some evidence that Amundsen's spitefulness over the incident – which receives no mention in his book on the pole expedition – was not limited to removing Johansen from the team. Johansen left the team as soon as it reached civilisation and travelled back to Norway independently, and there is evidence that Amundsen forced this decision on him. It has also been said that Amundsen gave Johansen no money so that he had to beg cash for a passage home. However, it can be credibly argued that Johansen was given the money he was due and drank it away so that he was penniless when he arrived in Melbourne (from New Zealand). It is also claimed that Amundsen telegraphed to Norway ahead of Johansen's arrival (he arrived before the rest of the team) to ensure that he was not greeted as a hero. But again there is a credible alternative that it was Alexander Nansen, Fridtjof's brother and the expedition's lawyer, who wrote the telegram after hearing from Amundsen of Johansen's 'mutiny'. Whatever the truth it was an unpleasant end to an otherwise successful trip, and one with terrible consequences. Johansen, despite having been Nansen's companion and having saved Prestrud's life, never regained his reputation. His drinking, which had been a serious problem before the trip, increased heavily and he became depressed, eventually committing suicide in 1913 at the age of 46.

Amundsen, with Bjaaland, Hanssen, Hassel and Wisting, left again on 20 October, with 52 dogs pulling four sledges. Usually Bjaaland, the best skier, moved ahead of the convoy, giving the dogs something to chase. At the 80°S dump four dogs were released to make their way back to Framheim. When the team set out again on 24 October they were 240km (150 miles) ahead of Scott: his attempt set out that same day from his McMurdo base. Despite occasional requests from his men to go faster Amundsen set and maintained a daily distance target of 24km (15 miles) so as not to wear out the dogs. By 4 November they were at 82°S, their last dump. Here it was decided to create dumps every 1° south to progressively reduce the weight carried. To help locate the dumps on their return journey cairns were raised along the route. As the load reduced, so did the number of dogs, the weakest being shot to feed the rest.

Left **Amundsen's team on their way to the pole.**
USA Library of Congress

Above **Camp at 84°S on the pole journey.**
USA Library of Congress

Below **The Devil's Glacier, the most difficult part of the Norwegians' journey to the pole.**
USA Library of Congress

Ahead now lay a range of mountains Amundsen named after the Norwegian queen (the Queen Maud Mountains are part of the Transantarctic Range). Amundsen had hoped that the ice shelf rose gently to the polar plateau, but now he, like Shackleton and Scott, had to find a way through the mountains. His route took him to a glacier named for Axel Heiberg, steeper, but shorter, than the Beardmore: its ascent took four hard days. In a camp on the plateau at the top all but 18 dogs were shot, both men and the remaining dogs eating the carcasses. One sledge was left behind and the party moved on again.

Briefly the terrain became difficult – the Norwegians were crossing the start of the Devil's Glacier – then levelled again. The weather too was poor, but Shackleton's mark was passed on 8 December. The next day the last dump was made and marked. Now the weather was fine, the going easy, the only concern being whether Scott had beaten them: in fact, he was 575km (360 miles) behind them. On 14 December 1911

Amundsen was pushed to the front for the last few kilometres. At 3pm they reached what they thought was the pole: the snow was virginal, the Norwegians had won. The obligatory photographs were taken; ironically Amundsen's camera was damaged and took no shots, the iconic photograph being taken on a cheap camera brought by Bjaaland. Amundsen formally named the area around the pole King Haakon VII's Plateau. The pride the men felt at what they had achieved was mixed with a huge sense of relief that it was all over – now they could go home.

In fact the Norwegians stayed at Polheim, their polar camp, for three days, boxing the area with flags as they took readings from the sun to confirm their position. Amundsen's account remarks on the curious motion of the sun at the pole and he wonders if the Norwegians are the first to see it, which implies he believed neither Cook nor Peary had reached the North

Pole. It is estimated that on 17 December Bjaaland and Hanssen passed within a few tens of metres of the actual pole: Polheim was probably 2km (1¼ miles) from it. At Polheim Amundsen left a tent, a pole from which flew the Norwegian flag, and a letter for the Norwegian king with a covering note asking Scott to deliver it. (Scott was confused by the letter, not realising that Amundsen left it in case he failed to reach Framheim: a later author noted that by taking the letter Scott had, in one instance, gone from explorer to postman, which seems a gratuitously unkind thing to say.) The letter stated the Norwegian view that the polar plateau was 6,700m (22,000ft) high, about the only mistake Amundsen made on the entire trip, though as they had a hypsometer and took regular (and correct) readings it is more likely to have been a 'spelling' mistake.

On 17 December the Norwegians left, Amundsen still maintaining the 24km (15-mile) daily regime, the men sometimes spending 16 hours each day resting. Around 31 December the Norwegians and British were at the same latitude and probably less than 100km (60 miles) apart. Though they were well out of sight of each other it is interesting to speculate what would have happened had they spotted the other team. Would Scott have turned around?

The Norwegians had a comfortable journey back to Framheim: the dogs ran well, there was adequate food on the days between the dumps, and good supplies at the dumps. At the base of the Axel Heiberg Glacier another note on the expedition was left beneath a cairn: it was found in 1929 by a team led by Laurence Gould, part of Richard Byrd's expedition. Wisting had to have a tooth pulled – the only drama on the journey – and the weather deteriorated, but the daily target was consistently met. At 4am on 26 January 1912 Amundsen crept into the hut and woke the rest of his men by asking if there was any coffee. On 30 January the men boarded the *Fram* and sailed for Hobart where, on 7 March, the world was told of the success.

Scott: the race lost

On 7 March the four survivors of Scott's five-man team were struggling towards what they hoped would be a supply dump laid down for them by the other members of the expedition at McMurdo. Scott's second expedition had been brought to Antarctica by the *Terra Nova* which had accompanied the *Morning* on the second Discovery relief expedition in early 1904. Scott had asked Mawson and Wild to go with him on his second (the British Antarctic) expedition, but both had

Above **Sverre Hansen at the South Pole.**
USA Library of Congress

declined, though two others from Shackleton's *Nimrod* team had accepted. Wilson was going again: for the rest Scott had the pick of several thousand volunteers. The chosen party included Captain Lawrence Edward Grace Oates, ex-Eton, currently a cavalry officer serving in India. Oates was a sports enthusiast and was bored with the quiet of the sub-continent. He appears to have had little idea about Antarctica – when he heard he was likely to be accepted he wrote to his mother that 'the climate is healthy, but inclined to be cold' – but fancied the adventure. Oates' application was undoubtedly helped by the £1,000 cheque he wrote. Volunteers who paid for the privilege of joining were welcome: in addition to Oates there was one more who paid £1,000, Apsley Cherry-Garrard.

Chosen from the no-fee volunteers was Henry Robertson Bowers, a lieutenant in the Royal Indian Marine. He had sailing experience and an enthusiasm for the polar regions, though the latter was gained from books rather than direct experience. From the *Discovery* team came Crean, Lashly and Edgar Evans. The latter should not be confused with Lt (later Admiral Sir) Edward Evans (Teddy Evans) who was made second-in-command to Scott when news of his (Evans') intention to mount a separate expedition became known.

Shackleton, Scott's *bête noire*, had passed 88°S. Recognising this fact alone Scott decided to take ponies as Shackleton had. He also decided to use motor-sledges. When he met Nansen again, the great man was, yet again, aghast. There was nothing he could do about the sledging (though he did manage to cajole Scott into taking a few, token, dogs) but he did persuade Scott to take skis, even 'lending' him Tryggve Gran, a young Norwegian and an expert skier. This contact worked in changing Scott's mind, though not to the extent of him recognising that learning to ski was more than just a weekend's work.

On 15 June 1910 the *Terra Nova* sailed from Cardiff, but without the expedition leader: Scott left a month later, meeting his ship in Cape Town. *Terra Nova* and Scott reached Melbourne on 12 October. The next day he received a telegram from Christiania: 'Beg leave to inform you *Fram* proceeding Antarctic. Amundsen.' The sender was Leon Amundsen, Roald's brother. The story was front-line news in Norway that day and reached Britain soon after. In Britain some were astonished (Shackleton noted that since Amundsen had taken dogs not ponies he was unlikely to reach the pole as dogs 'are not very reliable'), and enraged others (Sir Clements Markham called Amundsen 'a blackguard'). On the *Terra*

Nova Tryggve Gran was embarrassed and perplexed – he knew nothing about Amundsen's plans – while Scott tried to persuade himself that Amundsen was heading for the Weddell Sea and would therefore be little threat.

In New Zealand the ponies were loaded on to the *Terra Nova*. Oates, the cavalry officer and horse expert, was not impressed with them. One team member who was rather more impressed with the stay in New Zealand was Teddy Evans. He had been keen to get rid of Edgar Evans for some time as he had no time for over-drinking unfit men. In this he had been thwarted by Scott who had a soft spot for the big sailor. But when Edgar Evans got drunk and fell in the sea at Lyttleton even Scott had had enough. To Teddy Evans' delight Scott dismissed Edgar Evans and *Terra Nova* sailed without him. But, to Teddy Evans' disgust, when Evans appealed to Scott, who had stayed behind in Lyttleton to tie up final loose ends, for one more chance, he was given it and travelled with Scott to rejoin the ship at Port Chalmers.

The team were subjected to the usual stormy crossing of the Southern Ocean (two ponies, two dogs and some stores were lost), McMurdo being reached on 2 January 1911. The ship was unloaded at Cape Evans (north of the Discovery Hut), one of the motor-sledges dropping through the thin sea ice and disappearing – not an auspicious start. After establishing a base Scott began to organise southern supply dumps, but was

Above **The interior of Scott's hut at Cape Evans.**
P.S. Kristensen, courtesy of Quark Expeditions

Above **The photograph of the *Terra Nova* through the opening of a grotto in an iceberg is one of Herbert Ponting's most enduring images from Scott's last expedition. This rarely seen shot, also by Ponting, shows the outside of the Grotto Berg.**
USA Library of Congress

start earlier than the ponies because they did not sink into the snow and the Norwegians were already closer to the pole. Had Scott, assisted by the show laid on by Amundsen for the *Terra Nova*'s crew, finally understood the value of dogs? Scott was also appalled by Amundsen invading his (Scott's) own territory, the more so as the British had intended to land an exploratory team at the Bay of Whales. To make matters worse, the team returning from the south – Scott had travelled ahead – lost seven out of eight ponies when attempting to cross unstable sea ice.

During the winter that followed Bowers, Cherry-Garrard and Wilson made a trip to Cape Crozier, on the east side of Ross Sea, to obtain the eggs of Emperor penguins, a round trip of some 240km (150 miles). Cherry-Garrard's description of the journey is the central theme of his book on the entire expedition. The chapter is called 'The Worse Journey', the book *The Worst Journey in the World*, which many have claimed to be the finest ever written on an Antarctic trek. The book also includes Cherry-Garrard's description of the early stages of Scott's polar trek and Lashly's account of the return of the final support team, as well as the harrowing description of finding the bodies of Scott, Wilson and Bowers.

Scott called 'the worst journey' 'one of the most gallant stories in polar history'. Considering that its objective was merely to retrieve penguin eggs it could also be termed one of the most ridiculous. Cherry-Garrard opens by noting that of the three men (Wilson, Bowers and himself) who waited to depart one was 'feeling a little frightened'. It was a sensible emotion as he soon discovered. He wrote 'the horror of the 19 days it took us to travel... to Cape Crozier would have to be re-experienced to be appreciated... it is not possible to describe it'. They averaged 2½km (1½ miles) each day. Their clothes froze so solid that it took two men to bend them to shape. Their balaclavas froze to their heads: once Cherry-Garrard raised his head as he stepped from the tent and his clothes solidified so quickly he could not look down for four hours. The temperature fell to −77.5°F (−61°C). Cherry-Garrard noting that temperatures in the minus fifties (about −48°C) seemed luxurious. They were so cold that the agonies of warming extremities became a daily occurrence. In the perpetual darkness they could not see the crevasses. Walking was like playing blind-man's-bluff as they frequently fell, saved only by their sledge harnesses, an experience that frayed the nerves.

Finally they arrived at Cape Crozier becoming the first men to see incubating Emperor penguins. They

only able to establish the One Ton Depot at 78°28½'S because the ponies found the going hard. Oates, the horse expert, wanted to kill the weakest (dumping them as food) and continue, but Scott refused: the frustrated Oates suggested presciently that Scott would regret the decision. Retreating from his southernmost dump Scott discovered that Amundsen was in the Bay of Whales. He was distraught: Amundsen's dogs could collected the eggs, but had a nightmare journey back to camp, Cherry-Garrard noting that by now the three were beginning to think of death as a friend. But worse was to come when they were struck by a storm so ferocious it was 'as though the world was having a bit of hysterics'. They had built an igloo beside their tent: the tent blew away, the roof blew off the igloo. They survived by staying in their sleeping bags for 36 hours and allowing snow to drift over them. Cherry-Garrard comforted himself with thoughts of peaches and syrup, and then, knowing that without the tent they were unlikely to survive the return journey, hoped for death. All three survived and then, miraculously, found the tent. The journey back was equally epic, but with less to haul much quicker. Once, when Bowers' balaclava froze so that he was no longer able to look down, he walked into a crevasse. At night – there was twilight now at midday, so they could differentiate night and day – they were so cold in their sleeping bags they could not sleep and often fell asleep as they walked. Finally they arrived back at base and 'thus ended the worst journey in the world'. It had been an amazing journey; and the penguin eggs were brought safely back.

On 24 October 1911 Scott's remaining motor-sledges started from Cape Evans as an advance party. On the same day the Norwegians were leaving their dump at 80°S. The motor-sledges lasted just five days before failing. Two days later, on 1 November, Scott and the main party set off. Within a few days Scott's concerns over the use of dogs must have been heightened considerably when his own teams (driven by Cecil Meares and Dimitri Gerov, a Russian 'acquired' by Meares when he bought the dogs in Siberia) covered his daily distance in considerably less time. But the die was cast, and with the ponies sinking into the snow Scott followed his own, then Shackleton's, route south. By 9 December at the bottom of the Beardmore Glacier the ponies were finished and were shot. Two days later the dog teams turned north, leaving Scott with 11 men. These, some on skis, manhauled up the glacier, back-breaking work, though at least the weather was fine. At the top four men (including Cherry-Garrard) turned and headed north, their job of hauling supplies for intermediate depots completed. The eight who continued were organised in two teams: Scott with Edgar Evans, Oates and Wilson; Teddy Evans with Bowers, Crean and Lashly.

When on 2 January 1912 the time came to choose the final pole party Scott chose his own four as a group. He then, surprisingly, picked Bowers to accom-

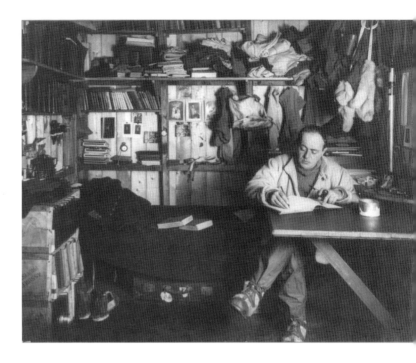

Above **Robert Falcon Scott at his desk in the hut at Cape Evans. The photograph was taken in October 1911 two weeks before Scott set out for the pole.**
USA Library of Congress

pany them. The reason seems to have been that no one in his own team was a competent navigator and Bowers was, though Scott's diary does not confirm this. The decision meant that the pole party had to sleep five in a four-man tent and share rations for four. More seriously it meant that Bowers had to haul on foot, while the other four were on skis because on 31 December Scott had ordered Teddy Evans' team to leave their skis behind. He does not explain why, but it has been speculated that he wished to slow the Evans team so that his decision to take his own would appear clearly justified.

The five men of the pole team continued south at a daily rate of about 14km (9 miles), a distance earned by hours of effort. Oates was hindered by an old Boer War wound to his thigh and Evans had an injured hand (cut while working on the sledges). But the men were driven by the thought that Amundsen was still behind them. Then, on 16 January the men detected something ahead: it was one of Amundsen's black flags, the surrounding snow etched with ski and sledge marks and paw prints. The British had lost the race. Scott's diary is matter-of-fact: 'The Norwegians have forestalled us and are first at the pole. It is a terrible

Above **Scott's team at the pole.**
Left to right: Bowers, Evans, Scott, Oates and Wilson.
The camera was triggered by string pulled by Bowers.
USA Library of Congress

Above **The British find the Norwegian tent.**
Left to right: Scott, Oates, Wilson and Evans.
USA Library of Congress

disappointment, and I am very sorry for my loyal companions', but the next day's entry when the British actually reached the pole is a more telling description. 'The pole, Yes, but under very different circumstances from those expected... none of us having slept much after the shock of our discovery... Great God! this is an awful place and terrible enough for us to have laboured to it without reward of priority.' Scott's words are as chilling a statement of defeat and failure as could be imagined. Lately it has become fashionable to depict Scott as an amateur bungler. There is truth in this (certainly in comparison to Amundsen's marvellously professional journey), but faced with Scott's pain at the enormity of his defeat it is hard not to feel sympathy for the man.

On 18 January, close to what they believed was the actual pole, Scott's team found Polheim and the letter for King Haakon. Other cairns and flags led Scott to note 'There is no doubt that our predecessors have made thoroughly sure of their mark'; there was not even the satisfaction of knowing that the British were the first to mark the exact spot even if they had come second in the main race. After the obligatory

photograph there was nothing left but to turn north for home. Scott noted in his diary (on 17 January) 'Now for the run home and a desperate struggle. I wonder if we can do it', a strangely downbeat comment even allowing for the disappointment.

But the homeward journey was indeed a desperate struggle. Food and fuel were short, as was time; yet despite this a gloriously fine half-day on the Beardmore Glacier was spent collecting 16kg (35lb) of rock samples which were then towed for the rest of the journey. The lost time equates to perhaps 8km (5 miles), the extra load perhaps as much again in terms of energy spent. And the last camp was 17.5km (11 miles) from One Ton Depot. The time loss is all the more surprising because Edgar Evans' condition was worsening. His cut hand was pus-filled, his mental health fragmenting. On 17 February Evans collapsed in the snow and was left behind. Later the four went back for him, and that night he died.

Oates was next. He had frost-bitten feet (the austral summer was fast drawing to a close and temperatures were falling), making walking agony and survival unlikely. His condition made hauling near impossible and probably slowed the rest. By 16 March, two weeks after first showing the others the appalling state of his feet (by now they were probably gangrenous, making death a near certainty) Scott says he asked to be left behind. The request was turned down and next morning Scott records that Oates famously said, 'I am just going outside and may be some time', before struggling into a blizzard. Wilson, writing to Oates' mother, does not mention these iconic words.

The last three struggled on until 21 March when they camped 17.5km (11 miles) from One Ton Depot. Scott was finished, his right foot probably gangrenous as he noted that 'amputation is the least I can hope for'. He says that the other two tried to go to the depot on 22nd and 23rd, but could not because of a blizzard. The next entry is 29 March and the gale has been blowing non-stop. Yet it is surprising that neither Bowers nor Wilson made one last effort to reach the depot. With no hope of rescue why do men sit and wait for death for nine days? During that time Scott wrote his poignant letter to the British public and composed the elegies for his companions. The tent, with the three still inside their sleeping bags, was discovered in November 1912 by a British search party. They were buried where they lay.

In his last letters Scott wrote 'we are setting a good example to our countrymen... by facing (hardship, death) like men' and 'we are showing that Englishmen can still die with a bold spirit, fighting it out to the end'. It is hard not to imagine that Scott, having no choice but to taste defeat rather than victory, chose death rather than dishonour, his words chillingly echoing the 'I wonder if we can do it' written at the pole. But even if it can be persuasively argued that Scott was resigned to death, would Bowers and Wilson have been so keen to follow his lead?

Within months many young men would follow Scott's display of dying with a bold spirit on the battlefields of France and Belgium. By then, and even more so after, his death had become a symbol of British heroism, the dubious details of the journey lost in jingoism. 'Great Scott!' became a British exclamation used to denote something supranormal (though the Scott of the expression is said to have been the novelist Sir Walter, the expression had a renaissance after Scott's journey). Scott, it was claimed, had died last – this was printed so many times it became a 'fact' (though it is likely to have been Bowers) – a model of leadership to the end.

Top **The final camp: the tent in which the bodies of Scott, Wilson and Bowers were discovered.**
Scott Polar Research Institute, University of Cambridge, UK

Above **The tent at the final camp had inner and outer fabrics. The inner was dropped over the bodies and a snow cairn was erected over it. The outer was brought back to Britain and erected in Earls Court. A Royal Navy honour guard stood beside it as thousands silently filed past.**
Scott Polar Research Institute, University of Cambridge, UK

Amundsen: victory denied

Amundsen heard of Scott's death soon after learning of Johansen's suicide. He was horrified, devastated. The idea that defeat had broken Scott's heart and spirit haunted Amundsen, as did the thought that had he left more supplies at the pole Scott might have survived. Logic told Amundsen that Scott's death had been both self-inflicted and avoidable, but logic is not as powerful as emotion. Norway, though enraptured with success, were nervous in victory. The British felt cheated and could hardly applaud Amundsen for giving them a hero, the more so as they saw Amundsen as a professional. Amundsen was in part the unwitting architect of this idea, a ludicrous suggestion and one which implied Scott was an amateur, which might have been closer to the truth than the British actually meant to suggest. Amundsen's story implied a comfortable, occasionally fun journey, whereas Scott's diary spoke only of hardship and woe, even before the race was lost. The British also thought Amundsen had used underhand tactics. Scott had manhauled, whereas the Norwegians had been pulled along. Amundsen claimed that at a dinner in London in his honour the president of the Royal Geographical Society had proposed three cheers for the dogs, but none for him. When he complained the Royal Geographical Society declared he had misheard and demanded an apology for his 'insult'. But the same muted praise was heard everywhere he went and, coupled with Amundsen's own doubts and fears, made him a bitter man. He had accomplished so much and so brilliantly, and it had all been taken from him. His death, when it came, was sad, lonely and unnecessary, with little of the glory Scott had found. Even now, despite the revisionist view of his expedition, everyone remembers Scott's name and even those of Bowers, Evans, Oates and Wilson.

Few outside Norway recall those of Amundsen's team. Sverre Hassel died in 1928 while visiting Amundsen, dropping down dead at his old leader's feet. In 1936 the 65-year-old Oscar Wisting asked to be allowed to spend the night on the *Fram* in his old cabin. The next morning he was found dead. Helmer Hanssen died in 1957 aged 87. Olav Bjaaland lived even longer; he was 89 and still living on his Telemark farm when he died in 1961. Not long before he had met Sir Vivian Fuchs, leader of the British 1957/8 expedition, the first Briton to reach the pole overland and return alive. There had been a great fuss over the expedition, but Bjaaland was unimpressed, reckoning that in all probability nothing much had changed there since his visit 45 years before.

Shirase and Filchner

When Amundsen regained his Bay of Whales base he discovered a Japanese expedition had arrived. Led by Nobu (sometimes given as Choku or Naoshi) Shirase, son of a Buddhist priest and a lieutenant in the Japanese navy, the expedition had arrived in the *Kainan Maru* (Southern Pioneer). Shirase had raised the cash for the trip in the face of public apathy and sailed in December 1910. Unable to locate a landing spot on Victoria Land, Shirase retreated to Australia where the expedition spent an unhappy winter camped in a garden, frequently harassed by the pro-Scott local press. Returning to Antarctica the Japanese landed in the bay in mid-January 1912, too late for their intended trip to the pole. A symbolic 'dash patrol' of Shirase and six others (using dog sledges) passed 80°S on 28 January. There they claimed the Ross Ice Shelf for Japan, calling it the Yamato Yukihara – Yamato Snow Plain. On their return to Japan they found the formerly apathetic public ecstatic at their success, though the Japanese government (not surprisingly) did not pursue the name or claim to the ice shelf.

Having encountered the Japanese on the ice shelf, Amundsen met Wilhelm Filchner, leader of the German Antarctic Expedition, in Buenos Aires, finding that he was primarily interested in discovering whether the Weddell and Ross Seas were connected, and that he intended to cross the continent. Filchner had come to some form of understanding with Scott which probably meant the Germans were not trying for the pole (though doubtless would not have been bothered if it lay in their path), but whatever the terms of the understanding they had become irrelevant. Leaving Buenos Aires the *Deutschland* (the renamed Norwegian ship *Bjørn*) reached the southern coast of the Weddell Sea (the Leopold Coast, named by Filchner for the German Prince Regent) and discovered the ice shelf that now bears Filchner's name. Filchner actually named it for Kaiser Wilhelm, but his majesty declined the offer and insisted on it bearing the expedition leader's name. The original Filchner Ice Shelf is now two separate ones, the Filchner and the Ronne – that latter named for the Norwegian Finn Ronne – separated by Berkner Island.

In the Weddell Sea the *Deutschland* became trapped in the pack ice and the Germans were forced to overwinter, their attempt to set up a base on the ice shelf almost ending disastrously when a vast tabular berg (with the base hut on it) cleaved. From the ship Filchner and two others dog-sledged across the ice in midwinter, a remarkable journey as the ship drifted

over 60km (about 40 miles) while they were away and they had to navigate by dead reckoning when their instruments froze. The *Deutschland* was released from the ice in November 1912 and made an uneventful journey home. There Filchner's attempts to raise money for another trip were thwarted by the looming European war.

Mawson: *The Home of the Blizzard*

A third expedition was also on the continent while Amundsen and Scott were striving for the pole. The Australasian Antarctic Expedition was led by Douglas Mawson who had declined Scott's offer of a place on *Terra Nova* in favour of leading his own trip. Mawson was hoping to fill in the gaps on the map between McMurdo and the German discoveries of 1902, a worthy objective for an expedition that was to turn into one of the great survival stories of polar exploration. The expedition left Hobart in December 1911 in the *Aurora*, an ex-Arctic sealer, captained by John Davis. Amongst other things, the ship was carrying the fuselage of a Vickers REP monoplane. The plane had crashed on its trial flight and, devoid of wings, was to be used as an 'air-tractor': it wasn't much better at that job either, managing little more than 30km (20 miles) before the engine seized.

Above **The cold, dense air of high Antarctica drops off the plateau, accelerating under the influence of gravity to speeds of over 300kmph (about 200mph), but the persistence of these katabatic winds (named from the Greek for 'going downhill') only became apparent to Mawson when it was too late. The expedition recorded an average windspeed of 69.4kmph (43.4mph) over a period of one calendar year. In July 1912 the wind averaged over 100kmph (over 62mph) for the whole 31 days. On 15 May the 24-hour average was over 145kmph (90mph). On one day in the winter of 1913 the wind blew at over 160kmph (100mph) for more than eight hours. The wind could hurl men and equipment about: it could also stop abruptly, leaving men who had been leaning into it to fall flat on their faces. It whipped up surface snow to create vicious white-outs, which led Mawson to call his base (and his book on the expedition) *The Home of the Blizzard*.** University of Adelaide, South Australia

Mawson's plan was to land close to, but to the west of, Cape Adare, but the unforgiving terrain forced the *Aurora* much further west, the expedition's chosen base being at Cape Denison (named for a Sydney patron) in Commonwealth Bay, almost 1,300 sea km (800 sea miles) west of Adare. Though apparently hospitable, Cape Denison was soon found to be a windy spot. In

fact, Mawson had inadvertently chosen one of the windiest places on the continent.

Mawson's landing at Cape Dennison was not without incident. Crucial stove parts, thought to be in a box which had fallen overboard into 1.5m (5ft) of water, had to be retrieved by Mawson stripping off and jumping in. The box contained only jam – the stove parts were found elsewhere – and Mawson 'established a new record for myself in dressing'. Then a huge sea elephant – rare on the continental mainland – threatened the dogs. It was shot, and measured at 5.3m (17½ft) long and 3.7m (12ft) around, a truly monstrous specimen which yielded a vast amount of dog food. After dropping Mawson (at the same time that Scott was heading north from the pole) the *Aurora* then left another team, led by Frank Wild – veteran of Scott's *Discovery* trip and Shackleton's furthest south – over 1,600km (1,000 miles) miles away to the west on an ice shelf Wild named for Shackleton. It was planned that Wild's team would explore towards Drygalski's discovered land.

The main party overwintered at Cape Denison, making forays to dump supplies to the south, many in Aladdin's Cave (an excavated ice cavern) on the rare occasions the weather was suitable. When summer came the party divided; the local coast was explored by three teams, while another went south to investigate the area close to the South Magnetic Pole. This team, which included the photographer Frank Hurley whose

record of Shackelton's *Endurance* expedition has brought him lasting fame, got to within 80km (50 miles) of the pole, manhauling against ferocious winds before retreating. Mawson, together with Lt Belgrave Edward Sutton Ninnis, a British army officer who had shown an aptitude with dogs, and Dr Xavier Guillaume Mertz, a Swiss lawyer, ski champion and mountaineer, headed east. The three left the base on 10 November 1912, a late start due to appalling weather, knowing that they had to be back by 15 January 1913 at the latest or the *Aurora* would leave without them. Their journey soon became difficult. Not only was the weather bad but they ran into the tortuous ice and crevasses of two huge glaciers (now called the Mertz and Ninnis Glaciers). Many times the dogs fell into crevasses, some being injured so badly they had to be destroyed, but the team's luck in surviving the falls was amazing. Eventually the luck ran out: on 14 December Ninnis, complete with his dog team and sledge, disappeared into a vast crevasse which Mertz had skied across and Mawson had sledged over. Peering down, Mawson and Mertz could see only a pair of dogs some 45m (150ft) down. Of Ninnis, his sledge, all the dog food and much of their own food, there was no sign.

The situation was immediately perilous. Mawson and Mertz were over 500km (320 miles) from base with food for about ten days, but no food for the remaining dogs. Mawson noted in his diary that they would have

to eat the dogs to survive, then wrote 'May God help us'. Feeding the weakest dog to the strongest the two men set off for base. Soon they were supplementing their own meagre rations with dog meat. The meat from the starving dogs offered little nourishment, but their livers were big.

Mawson and Mertz did not know that the Inuit and Nansen had warned against eating the livers of Arctic carnivores; as a result of their exclusively meat diet these animals store vast quantities of vitamin A in their livers. Earlier in 1912 the Polish-born biochemist Casimir Funk, working in London, had coined the word 'vitamine' (changed to 'vitamin' in 1920 by the Englishman Sir Jack Drummond), but not until the 1930s would George Wald understand the nature of vitamin A, and it was later still that the effects of excess vitamin A on the human body were recognised. Mawson and Mertz were not to know that their apparently life-saving diet of dog liver was poisoning them, causing dysentery and nausea, loss of hair and skin, chronic stomach pain and, eventually, delirium, convulsions and death. Ironically the younger, fitter Mawson gave his companion extra rations thinking it would help him, and in doing so, ensured his own survival.

As the two men became weaker they abandoned surplus weight. One item left behind was the rifle, forcing Mawson to kill the last dog with a spade. The glacier crossings were a nightmare: again they miracu-lously survived crevasse falls. By Christmas Day their skin was peeling, adding the pain of raw flesh to the other effects of vitamin A poisoning. The pair boiled down the bones and sinews of the last dog to a jelly, but by now Mertz could no longer face, or keep down, dog-based food. After harrowing days in which the delirious, convulsing Mertz could not leave his sleeping bag, he died on 8 January. Mawson buried him, then reduced the sledge, cutting it in half with a penknife. When he was ready to start moving again his condition was pitiful. The skin peeling from his thighs and scrotum meant he had to walk bow-legged, and the entire soles of his feet had come away forcing him to bandage them in place. His whole body seemed to be rotting away. To make matters worse, he was now travelling only 8–10km (5–6 miles) each day and would not make base before 15 January.

The crossing of the Mertz Glacier was a triumph of courage and will. Mawson fell into a crevasse, only held by the rope attaching him to his sledge. He hauled himself to the lip, but fell again. Luckily the sledge held and he hauled himself out at the second attempt. He then made a rope ladder to aid his climb in case the same thing happened again. By 15 January he was still 130km (80 miles) from base and his progress was down to 4–5km (2½–3 miles) each day. He walked at night because the snow was harder, and struggled on in conditions that many would have said were impossible. He

Above **Mawson after his arrival back at camp.**
University of Adelaide, South Australia

was knocked over by the persistent wind, but still he kept going. His hair was falling out and he feared he was dying of scurvy, but his will was undaunted, as was his hope that a rescue party would reach him. On 20 January he gained the plateau beyond the glacier. He could now sail his sledge so progress improved. On 29 January he stumbled on a new cairn; inside was food and a note with the news that Amundsen had reached the pole, and the bearing and distance of Aladdin's Cave. The note also said that a rescue party had left the cairn just six hours before: Mawson's last camp was only 8km (5 miles) from that of his rescuers. But there was no hope of catching them: they were three fit men, he was barely alive. Worse, he had abandoned his crampons when he reached the plateau, but the wind had polished it to hard ice. He improvised, knocking nails into pieces of wood which he strapped to his feet, leaving off the shed-skin soles that he had used to protect

his raw flash. The nails forced their way back, piercing his boots and flesh. He was now exhausted, both physically and mentally, the nearness of rescue bringing its own despair. It took him four days to reach Aladdin's Cave, but there were no crampons there and a blizzard imprisoned him for a week. When he could move again he saw the smoke of a disappearing ship and realised he might have to spend the winter alone. But then he saw men near the hut. He waved and they rushed towards him. The first to reach him was so shocked by Mawson's appearance that his first question was 'Which one are you?'.

Mawson's expedition was the first to use radio in Antarctica. The men called the *Aurora*, but the ship was unable to come close to shore because of the weather and finally had to abandon the attempt in order to pick up Wild's team who were not equipped to overwinter. Mawson therefore had to overwinter again, though the long months of inactivity helped him recover. Considering his ordeal, his return to full health was remarkable: he later led another Antarctic expedition, was knighted for his work, and died in 1958 at the age of 76.

Shackleton: *Endurance*

In Britain the national grief and euphoria that greeted the news of Scott's death had given way, at the higher levels of government, to a colder reality. There was the Irish crisis, there were the suffragettes: any anti-Norwegian feelings were a sideshow compared to the real unease felt about the rise of German naval power. The war clouds darkening the horizons of Europe were blocking out the view of Antarctica's snowy wastes. When Winston Churchill, the new First Lord of the Admiralty, heard about another southern expedition, he growled that 'enough life and money has been spent on this sterile quest', noting that polar expeditions 'are becoming an industry'. But Ernest Shackleton, the man behind the requests for government support, would not be denied. He was popular, the live hero the people wanted, the man who could restore some national pride, a fact that Chancellor of the Exchequer Lloyd George was more than willing to exploit. If Juvenal was right, that to keep the masses happy what was needed were bread and circuses, Lloyd George was more than willing to have Shackleton provide the circus at a time when difficult decisions needed to be made.

Shackleton's idea was to cross Antarctica from the Weddell Sea to the Ross Sea, going over the pole. He

needed two ships, buying the *Polaris*, a would-be cruise ship from a failed Arctic venture of de Gerlache, and renaming it *Endurance*, and borrowing the *Aurora* from Mawson. Shackleton would take the *Endurance* to the Weddell: he wanted the navy to take the *Aurora* to the Ross Sea from where supply dumps would be prepared for the arrival of the Weddell men, but Churchill vetoed that idea.

When the *Endurance* sailed under the command of Frank Worsley, on board were Frank Wild, the most experienced Antarctic polar explorer of the age and Shackleton's second-in-command, and the Australian photographer Frank Hurley, veteran of Mawson's expedition, whose photos were to help create the legend. It was 1 August 1914 when the *Endurance* left London. On 4 August Britain declared war on Germany. On 8 August when the ship finally left Plymouth for Antarctica it was only after Shackleton had offered to abort the trip and some men had left for active service. In the way of British legends Shackleton received a one-word telegram: 'Proceed'. In fact, it was the *Endurance* that proceeded, Shackleton not leaving Britain until 26 September on a ship bound for Buenos Aires. The news-

Above **The *Endurance* frozen in at 76°35'S. In addition to his famous series of black-and-white prints, Frank Hurley, the expedition's photographer, took a small number of Paget plates. These plates, created by Geoffrey Whitfield of London, used a series of dyed screens to produce a basic colour image. They were first marketed in April 1913. Hurley used an exposure of about 1/25th second at f4. An enlargement of the plate soon shows up the pattern of dye screens: that, and the cost, meant the plates had fallen out of use by the early 1900s. It is difficult to produce a colour image from Hurley's original plates, but they do offer a fascinating view of Shackleton's expedition.** Mitchell Library, State Library of New South Wales, Australia

papers claimed that the expedition had popular support and was perceived as every bit as dangerous as going to war, but there is evidence that the nation was not united in its approval, some believing that a fit, active man's place was on the battlefield.

The *Endurance* arrived in South Georgia on 5 November, choosing that island rather than the Falklands to hopefully avoid meeting the fleet of German Admiral von Spee which had recently destroyed

a British squadron off Chile's Cape Coronel. The whaling community of Grytviken was sceptical of Shackleton's chances of penetrating the Weddell Sea: they would have been even more so had they known he intended to freeze the *Endurance* into the ice there because he did not trust Worsley to get back to his base the following year. Shackleton sailed to the South Sandwich Islands, then turned south. His destination was Vahsel Bay. This had been discovered and named by Filchner in 1912. Richard Vahsel, a veteran of the *Gauss*, was captain of the *Deutschland*: when he died soon after the discovery, Filchner changed the name to that of one of his sponsors, but later explorers changed it back.

The *Endurance* made good progress towards Vahsel at first, but was then stopped by heavy pack ice. On 15 January 1915 they reached open water just 130km (80 miles) from the bay, but next day the ice closed around the ship. Despite desperate attempts to free her

Shackleton had to accept that they would never make landfall, throwing the transantarctic trek into doubt. Soon, as the ship drifted north with the ice it became apparent that the great adventure was over.

The men survived the winter well considering the disappointment of losing the trek and the makeshift nature of their quarters. The ship fared less well. Not built to ride the ice as *Fram* had been the *Endurance* was gripped by it, pushed, pulled and compressed. When spring came it was clear that a really powerful squeeze would destroy her timbers. On 15 October the ship broke free, but hope was short-lived. Two days later she was entombed again, ten days more and it was clear that irreparable damage had been sustained and Shackleton ordered his men on to the ice. To his disconsolate and fearful crew he now said, quite simply, 'So now we'll go home'. For all his faults – though he had taken dogs this time he had not learned to drive them or taken men who had; he had not learned to ski; his preparations were poor and hasty; his attitude towards his men sometimes divisive – when backs were against the wall Shackleton came into his own. Amundsen's careful preparation would probably keep

you out of trouble, but if trouble did come, Shackleton would probably get you out of it.

Shackleton decided to haul two loaded boats across the ice to Paulet Island, one of Nordenskjöld's bases which he knew was well stocked, or to Snow Hill Island which was closer; from either a small party could reach the whalers on Deception Island. Worsley disagreed: he was a sailor, not a manhauler, and wanted to wait for the ice to break up and then to use all three boats to head north, but he was overruled. Paulet was about 650km (400 miles) away, a journey of 65 days or more. The trek began on 30 October but was quickly abandoned. The optimism of hauling 10km (6 miles) daily was crushed by a 1.5km (1 mile) reality. A second attempt many weeks later proved equally futile. A camp was now set up on the ice and more equipment was salvaged from the *Endurance*. To save weight Hurley threw away many (perhaps 70 per cent) of his slides – in view of the quality of what he kept, the destruction is enough to make one weep.

On 21 November the crippled *Endurance* finally sank. The marooned men were now at the mercy of the elements and calculations showed food would likely run short. Tempers frayed and it took all of Shackleton's leadership skills to keep the group coherent. Eventually, as the floe on which they were camped was pushed north, penguins and seals arrived, supplementing the diet and allowing reserves to be built up. Finally, on 9 April 1916, after over five months on the ice, the men could take to the boats, heading north across an uneasy sea. The weather drove them south

Left **One of Hurley's night shots of the *Endurance* in the ice of the Weddell Sea.**
USA Library of Congress

Right **Men and dogs on the ice beside the stricken *Endurance*.**
USA Library of Congress

and east when they wanted to go north and west: they could not hope to reach Deception Island. If they headed north now they might be pushed past the South Shetlands into the Atlantic and almost certain death. Shackleton therefore decided to head for Elephant Island. It was close, but the weather made it an epic voyage. It was so cold that spray whipped up by the wind fell as ice: as two of the boats also leaked the men's feet were often immersed in freezing water. They landed on 15 April 1916, after seven days at sea (though they had been able to camp on floes early in the voyage) and 497 days since last touching land on 5 December 1914. (Shackleton has the landing on 15 April in his book *South*, but also states 'next morning (15 April)' implying the landing was on the 14th.) By then many of the men were in a state of shock or hypothermia. They had had no hot food or any drink for days, and wandered about as though inebriated.

Elephant Island teemed with seals and penguins (a source of food) but was otherwise inhospitable, so much so that the first landing place had to be abandoned for another along the coast – and that was little better. The weather was atrocious, soaking the men and

their sleeping bags before any shelter could be organised. To make matters worse, when they lay down to rest, the heat from their bodies melted the frozen penguin guano on the beach and it stank appallingly. By 19 April the situation was desperate, many of the men apparently so demoralised by finding themselves as badly off on land as they had been on the ice that they were almost ready to give up. Percy Blackborrow, who had stowed away on the ship in Buenos Aires as an adventure-seeking 19-year-old, had frostbite in his toes which threatened gangrene. Aware of the need for urgent action, Shackleton decided not to overwinter on the island, but to risk one boat and six men on a dash to South Georgia. The island was 1,300km (800 miles) away, the seas (as winter approached) likely to be mountainous, the navigational aids rudimentary. The only plus point was that the wind would be on the sailors' side, but it was a small positive against a mass of negatives. Many thought the trip was doomed.

Having decided to go Shackleton set the *Endurance*'s carpenter, Harry McNeish (sometimes written as McNish), to make the *James Caird* (the biggest and most seaworthy of the three boats: it was named

for a major benefactor of the expedition) as ready as could be. McNeish strengthened the keel with the mast of one of the other boats, and constructed a deck framework: as timber was short the decking was canvas. McNeish was one of the chosen crew, which consisted of Shackleton, Frank Worsley, Tom Crean (a veteran of both of Scott's expeditions), John Vincent, Tim McCarthy and McNeish. The choice of McNeish and Vincent is another indication of Shackleton's leadership skills. McNeish had wanted to build a ship from the wreckage of the *Endurance*, a reasonable suggestion Shackleton had vetoed: later the carpenter had 'mutinied', claiming loss of the ship freed him from any obligation to 'The Boss'. It had been a tricky moment, and there were others behind the physically strong Vincent, who was inclined to bully people. Shackleton's choice placed the two potential troublemakers where they would have other concerns to occupy them and could not disrupt the fragile accord on Elephant Island.

The weather was still atrocious, but improved slightly on 24 April. Shackleton launched immediately. Wild was left in charge on the island with orders to overwinter and then sail for Deception Island if rescue did not come. The *James Caird* had four weeks' supply of food – if they had not reached South Georgia in that time they would have died on the way – and bags of blubber oil to quell spiteful seas, an attempt to stop waves breaking over the boat. The 16-day voyage of the *James Caird* to South Georgia was one of the great boat journeys of all time. The crew were permanently soaked almost from the start. The cold was intense: occasionally ice had to be hacked from the canvas deck and the continuous pumping, which had to be done with bare hands, was a freezing nightmare. Sleeping in the claustrophobic space beneath the canvas, in wet, rotting sleeping bags on the boulders loaded as ballast, was near impossible. The sea was rough almost all the time, adding seasickness to the general misery: once a giant wave almost smashed the boat. On occasions the wind was so strong the boat had to be held into it making progress impossible: a hurricane-force blow endured at one stage sank a 500-ton steamer. To compound the agonies, one of the water

Top **The heroic nature of Shackleton's boat journey to South Georgia and his crossing of the island have inspired many subsequent adventurers to undertake sections of the journey again. This photograph was taken during a repeat of the island crossing by Conrad Anker, Reinhold Messner and Stephen Venables. Anker and Messner are descending the Fortuna Glacier towards Fortuna Bay.**
Stephen Venables

Above **Launching the *James Caird* from Elephant Island.**
USA Library of Congress

Above **Another photograph from the repeat South Georgia crossing of Anker, Messner and Venables. Here the team are starting their final descent to Stromness.**
Stephen Venables

kegs was spoiled by sea water so that the men had nothing to drink for the last three days. Navigation was by dead reckoning and from very occasional glimpses of the sun, Worsley's successful guidance of the boat to South Georgia therefore amounting to genius.

When seaweed and then seabirds were spotted, indicating that land was close, the men's elation was short-lived, a gale threatening to smash the boat against the sheer cliffs of South Georgia's south-western shore. Shackleton had deliberately made for this coast: though the whaling stations were on the north-eastern coast any failed attempt to reach that side meant the boat would have been pushed into open ocean. At least the southern side gave the chance of trying again on the north if the island had been missed. Only after hours of tacking, and a good dose of fortune, was the boat beached near Cape Rosa at the

entrance to King Haakon Bay. The grateful men found that they had landed near a stream. They slept in a handy cave, then added four albatross fledglings to their pot, the first substantial meal they had eaten in two-and-a-half weeks. Shackleton decided that another boat journey was too hazardous and that he would cross the island on foot. On 15 May after a few days of rest the *James Caird* was sailed to the back of King Haakon Bay where a clear pass split the mountains.

There were several whaling stations on South Georgia, the closest of which – at Prince Olav Harbour – was only 11km (7 miles) away, but unsure if it was manned in winter Shackleton decided to head for Husvik which he knew was. He chose Worsley and Crean to accompany him. Carrying food for three days, but no sleeping bags, and with salvaged screws in their boots as crampons, the three set off early on 19 May, after being stormbound at the bay's head for three days. In better weather than they could have hoped for they picked their way across the glaciated heart of South Georgia, sometimes retracing their steps when the terrain proved unyielding. After 36 hours during which they stopped only for short rests and meals they stumbled into Stromness, frightening the first people they met who mistook them for drunks. When the apprehensive whaling station manager asked, 'Who the hell are you?' the dirty, haggard, bearded man in the centre of the three said simply, 'My name is Shackleton.'

Worsley set off to rescue the three in King Haakon Bay – he also rescued the *James Caird* which can still be seen at Dulwich College, England – noting that the vicious storm which had blown up would have killed them on their walk, while Shackleton organised a ship to fetch the men on Elephant Island. The first two attempts failed because the rescue ships could not get through the winter ice. Then, incensed by the British government's decision to send the *Discovery* to rescue the men, which would entail a wait of many weeks, and not to have him as leader of the mission, Shackleton persuaded the Chilean government to lend him the *Yelcho*, an unsuitable steam tug. With Worsley and Crean, and a crew of Chileans, Shackleton set out on 25 August.

On Elephant Island the remaining two boats had been converted into a hut. In this the frost-bitten toes of Blackborrow's left foot were amputated using the last of the chloroform as anaesthetic. The winter was survived on a diet of seal and penguin. Wild had decided that when spring came he would take three men and one boat to Deception Island, but on 29 August the *Yelcho* anchored just 150m (500ft) offshore. The Endurance expedition was over.

The recent explosion of interest in Shackleton means that many could be forgiven for believing that the *Endurance* adventure was the whole story. Too often the *Aurora*'s men – Shackleton's Forgotten Men – are ignored. The *Aurora* left Hobart under the command of Aeneas Mackintosh, a veteran of the *Nimrod*. The ship was late leaving and also under-supplied because of financial problems. After making a base in Scott's hut at Cape Evans, Mackintosh and a party which included Ernest Wild, Frank Wild's brother, laid supply dumps to 80°S in dreadful weather. They returned to the hut to find that the *Aurora* had broken her moorings and drifted out to sea, leaving them and eight others marooned. They only survived because of stores left two years before when the survivors of Scott's expedition had been evacuated. Among the marooned men morale was low. They mistrusted Mackintosh who, as they (rightly) saw it, had abandoned his ship; they had no idea when they would be rescued; and they still had the responsibility of setting up supply dumps for Shackleton all the way to the Beardmore Glacier.

Freed from the ice in which she had become entombed after drifting out to sea the *Aurora* sailed to New Zealand, then, reprovisioned, returned to the Ross Sea. The captain was now John King Davis who had captained the ship for Mawson and been with Shackleton on the *Nimrod*. Shackleton himself, fit again after his Elephant Island/South Georgia exertions, went as a supernumerary officer. What the *Aurora* found was a group of men whose appearance shocked Shackleton as they looked far worse than the men rescued from Elephant Island.

After overwintering a team of six with those dogs that had survived set out to lay a dump at 83°S. It had been a harrowing trip: the men had no skis and the lack of dogs meant they had to manhaul. By the time they reached 83°S they were all suffering from scurvy and one man, the Rev Arnold Spencer-Smith, the first clergyman on Antarctica, had been left in a tent unable to move. Spencer-Smith was collected a week later, but was too ill to walk, the other five dragging him for over 300km (200 miles) to their 80°S dump. Leaving food for Shackleton the men were now dangerously short of supplies, but managed to reach a point just 16km (10 miles) from their next dump. A blizzard erupted, keeping them in camp for five days. Desperately short of food and fearing they would meet the same fate as Scott's team, three men – Joyce, Hayward and Richards – set off for base leaving Ernest Wild with Spencer-Smith and Mackintosh, both too sick to travel. The three miraculously found the dump in the blizzard and returned with food. Hauling Spencer-Smith and Mackintosh, the party set off again, but soon Hayward collapsed. Leaving Mackintosh in a tent Joyce, Richards and Wild hauled Spencer-Smith and Hayward south, but two days before reaching the Discovery hut Spencer-Smith died. He had been hauled almost 500km (300 miles). Leaving Hayward at the hut the three haulers went back to rescue Mackintosh.

The five survivors now waited for many weeks for the sea to freeze so they could reach Cape Evans. But on 8 May the now-recovered Mackintosh and Hayward, though discouraged by the others who were concerned the ice was too fragile, decided they could wait no longer. The others waited a further two months before daring to trust the ice, finally reaching Cape Evans on 15 July 1916, ten months after leaving it, to discover that Mackintosh and Hayward had not arrived.

The world that Shackleton and his men returned to had changed, almost beyond their imagining. The war which would be 'over by Christmas' was grinding on,

Above **Shackleton waving goodbye to England for the last time from the deck of the *Quest* at St Catherine's Dock, London in September 1921.**
USA Library of Congress

Right **Shackleton's grave, Grytviken, South Georgia.**
Richard Sale

countless bodies lying slaughtered on the Western Front. Shackleton's adventure was a momentary distraction for an exhausted nation. Within months of leaving Elephant Island many of The Boss' men were in action. Within four months of the *James Caird* landing on South Georgia, Tim McCarthy, one of the six crewmen, had been killed in action. Shackleton did not seem to understand the change. He had had a hero's reception in Chile, but a much less rapturous one on the Falklands where one islander commented that he should have 'been at the war long ago instead of messing about on icebergs'. When he joined the *Aurora* he was bluntly told that people were 'a little impatient with polar exploration...' and that 'when every man in uniform was either a real, or at least a potential hero, people were also a little impatient of explorers in general'.

Back in Britain Shackleton, too old for active service, was shuffled around the corridors of power, sent to Buenos Aires and then to north Norway and Murmansk to organise transport during the Arctic winter. Before he had a chance to do anything the war ended. In 1920 after dictating *South*, his book on the *Endurance* trip (written by Edward Saunders from the dictated notes and various diaries), and giving numerous lectures, Shackleton decided to head south again. With no clear idea of where he was going to go or why, but perhaps knowing that age and poor health were catching up with him – he had probably had a first heart attack in Tromsø in 1917 – and that he was ill-suited to a humdrum life, he found a ship, the *Quest*, gathered a few old colleagues, including Frank Wild, and set sail. The *Quest* reached South Georgia where, early on 5 January 1922, Shackleton had a massive heart attack and died. He was 47. At the request of his wife he was buried on the island. He was long outlived by many of the *Endurance*'s crew. Worsley, the last survivor of the *James Caird* crew died in 1943, Lionel Greenstreet, the last survivor of all died in March 1979. He was 89.

Over the years it has become *de rigueur* to denigrate Scott as an incompetent establishment man, to lionise Shackleton as the marvellous antithesis. The reality is too complex for such simple characterisations. Shackleton was a superb leader and a marvellous man in a crisis, but he was little better than Scott as a polar explorer. He took ponies on *Nimrod* and though he had dogs on *Endurance* he had no trained dog drivers.

Above **Percy Blackborrow and Harry McNeish's cat, Mrs Chippy. Blackborrow was refused a job on the *Endurance* when his friend, William Bakewell, was taken on in Buenos Aires. Bakewell helped Blackborrow stow away on the ship. When he was discovered Shackleton allowed him to stay – pointing out that he should remember that men on polar expeditions often went hungry and that stowaways were then the first to be eaten. Blackborrow's feet were frost-bitten and the toes of his left foot were amputated on Elephant Island. He returned to his native Wales after the expedition and worked on the docks in Newport. He died in 1949.**

As a carpenter Harry McNeish was a real craftsman, admired by almost everyone. But he was also an abrasive character which did not endear him to either Shackleton or Worsley. McNeish's cat, Mrs Chippy, was the expedition's mascot and the carpenter's true friend. When the *Endurance* sank Shackleton ordered that puppies and the cat should be put down as they could not earn their keep and food was likely to become scarce. McNeish never forgave him for it. After the expedition McNeish returned to his native Scotland, but then emigrated to New Zealand where, unable to work (because, he claimed, the trip had left his hands aching permanently), he became a fixture on Wellington docks, sleeping rough and maintained in drink by the dockers who considered him a hero for his work and voyage on the *James Caird*. It is said that McNeish could manipulate any conversation around to Shackleton and the death of his cat so that he could extol the virtues of the latter and berate the former. When he died in 1957 his coffin was borne on an army gun carriage before being taken to the grave by navy pallbearers.

Scott Polar Research Institute, University of Cambridge, UK

Neither had he learned to ski, nor taken any expert skiers. He had witnessed Amundsen's success, but not really learned from it. It is frequently stated that he never lost a man, yet the survival of the team on his furthest south expedition owed more to good luck than good management, and the deaths of the *Aurora* team members had their roots as much in Shackleton's poor organisation of the expedition as in the poor quality of Mackintosh's leadership. When Shackleton recommended the *Endurance* men for the Polar Medal he pointedly excluded four, including McNeish and Vincent who had been on the *James Caird*. In view of the enormous contribution McNeish made to the success of the boat journey this was a spiteful act whatever the perceived justification, and it outraged several who received the medal, as did the exclusion of Vincent whose only 'crime' was to have collapsed mentally towards the end of the *James Caird* voyage. That Shackleton was a great man is indisputable, but he was not quite as wonderful as he is now usually portrayed, any more than Scott was quite as bad.

Flying to the pole

In the aftermath of the Great War Britain, beaten in the race for the South Pole, and with the North Pole now won, turned its attention to the Third Pole: Everest. Many of the traits seen in the Antarctic trips can be glimpsed in the Everest expeditions of 1921, 1922 and 1924. After the Australian-born George Finch used a duvet jacket and enthusiastically promoted the use of oxygen in 1922 he was dropped from the 1924 team. In 1924 Mallory and Irvine died and became the new British heroes. Their deaths were heroic, like Scott's, and had the advantage that they might have reached the top and that defeat was not at the hands of a tiny, friendly nation of foreigners, but something huge, hostile and inanimate.

Trips south were now carried out in order to fill the gaps on the Antarctic map; but when the next explorers arrived they used aeroplanes. After the faintly ludicrous attempts with snowmobiles and motor cars the era of the engine had truly arrived. First of the 'new generation' was Sir Hubert Wilkins, an Australian who had been a member of the British Imperial Expedition of 1920/2 (a group of four despite its grandiose title, who had fallen out with each other and failed to cross Graham Land) and of Shackleton's *Quest* expedition. Early in 1928 Wilkins had made important Arctic flights and been knighted. Later the same year, backed by the American newspaper baron William Randolph Hearst, he decided to

In 1933 Richard Byrd returned with an even bigger expedition: 56 men, 153 dogs, 4 tractors, 3 airplanes and an autogyro. The base, Little America II, was on the site of the earlier one on the ice shelf and from it the tractors drove over 20,000km (12,500 miles) finally proving the worth of the internal combustion engine in Antarctic travel. The planes explored over 700,000 sq km (270,000 sq miles) of the continent, massively increasing knowledge of it. The expedition was an almost complete success apart from a bizarre incident which almost cost Byrd his life. Byrd built a hut (named the Bolling Advance Weather Station – Bolling after his mother's maiden name) at 80°8'S, some 190km (120 miles) from Little America II, sinking a prefabricated structure 2.5m (8ft) into the ice. Byrd had planned for three men to overwinter in the hut making meteorological observations, but the breakdown of a tractor bringing supplies meant that there was food for only two. Believing that two men, without recourse to a 'referee', would irritate each other beyond reason, Byrd decided to overwinter alone (though in constant radio contact with base). On 28 March he waved goodbye to the last of his team.

His early problems were associated with his daily walk outside the hut. Once he became lost, once almost fell into a crevasse and then, in a blizzard, found the trapdoor access to the hut iced over and was only just able to open it. Being alone was not only perilous outside: in the hut Byrd found the darkness and cold increasingly trying and became lonely and despondent. In May a fault developed in his heating/cooking stove burner which, combined with the hut ventilators being blocked with snow, made him ill from carbon monoxide poisoning. He spotted the problems in time, but soon after the petrol-driven generator developed a fault. The generator was in a small annex, but before he could return along an access tunnel Byrd had been near-poisoned again by fumes. This time the effect on him was irreversible, his health declining. With the worst of the winter to come – and he was the furthest south anyone had ever overwintered – Byrd attempted to prevent his colleagues from realising his condition in case they risked their lives in a rescue. But by early August his radio messages had become so strange the men at Little America II had guessed, and a rescue mission set out. After a false start due to mechanical problems, a tractor reached the hut where a weak, emaciated Byrd – he had lost 30kg (70lb) in weight – welcomed them with hot soup. It was two months before he was well enough to travel back to base. Of his solitary vigil Byrd claimed, 'I learned much, but I never want to go through that experience again.'

The next flyer on the continent was Lincoln Ellsworth, who in 1926 had flown across the Arctic with Amundsen and Nobile in the airship *Norge*. Ellsworth came south in 1933 determined to add a transantarctic flight to his Arctic record. He had his own ship, the *Wyatt Earp* (a renamed Norwegian herring boat) and aircraft (the *Polar Star*, a Northrup monoplane) and a team which included Hubert Wilkins and pilot Bernt Balchen. During this first trip the *Polar Star* was damaged when the ice sheet at the Bay of Whales split, dropping it into the crack. Ellsworth tried again in 1934 but could not find a suitable place for a runway on the Antarctic Peninsula. During the journey home the *Wyatt Earp* was overrun by rats which not only ate all the expedition's boats and snowshoe webbing but, ironically, also killed and ate the ship's cat.

In 1935, but now with a new pilot – Herbert Hollick-Kenyon, a British-born Canadian – Ellsworth tried for a third time. The *Polar Star* took off from Dundee Island, at the northern end of the peninsula, on 23 November and flew along it, heading directly for the Bay of Whales (and Byrd's Little America base). After 14 hours in the air, during which their radio failed (causing a rescue mission to be organised and frantic newspaper headlines written) Hollick-Kenyon landed the plane on the Antarctic plateau. After resting they took off again on 24 November, but were forced down by bad weather after just 30 minutes. The storm lasted three days, and when they took off again they managed only another 50 minutes' flying before bad weather returned, keeping them tent-bound for seven days as a blizzard raged. The plane took a day to free from the drifting snow (Ellsworth used a mug to clear snow from the inner tail section: his description of this notes that he lost all feeling in his left foot during the work but assumed it was just due to the cold!), but it snowed again before they could take off. Finally, after further digging, they took off on 4 December. They landed after four hours to check their position (by sextant): they were 200km (125 miles) from Little America.

Next day they continued, soon sighting the Ross Sea, but then being forced to land when the *Polar Star* ran out of fuel. They were 26km (16 miles) from Little America, though they did not reach it until 15 December after hauling the emergency sledge for more than five times that distance through bad weather. By then Ellsworth's frozen foot was giving him real trouble. The two men settled into Little America and on 19

Above **The *Polar Star* slipping through the ice during Ellsworth's first Antarctic expedition.**
USA National Archives and Records Administration

Right **Ellsworth's ship *Wyatt Earp* in the Bay of Whales during his second Antarctic expedition. The *Polar Star* has been unloaded onto the ice.**
USA National Archives and Records Administration

January 1936 a plane from an Australian rescue ship dropped them food and mail: three days later the *Wyatt Earp* arrived to pick them up.

After Byrd's pioneering flights, in 1929–31 Douglas Mawson led joint Australian, British, New Zealand expeditions to explore the coast between Wilhelm II coast and Coats Land. The team used the *Discovery*, Scott's old ship, but further flights by Ellsworth in 1938 emphasised Byrd's view that exploration and mapping of the continent was quicker and safer from the air. Mawson's expeditions represent the last of the 'old-fashioned' approach to discovering Antarctica. In 40 years Antarctica had gone from an unknown continent on which man had never set foot, one to which men voyaged in sailing ships, to one which had been mapped from the air. In 25 years man had gone from dreaming about reaching the South Pole to being able to fly to it in a matter of hours.

Crossing Antarctica

The 1939–45 war put an end to the Antarctic dream, though Richard Byrd led one more expedition (1939–41) as the Pacific sank towards despair. When peace returned interest in the continent was also revitalised. The Americans, Argentineans, Chileans and French all arrived to map, do scientific research and stake claims. Weather stations were set up: in 1954 the Australians set up Mawson, the first permanent year-round station on the Mac-Robertson Land coast.

All the expeditions were scientific – though it could not have escaped the notice of military planners that the 4,700 sailors involved in the US Operation Highjump would get cold-weather training that might prove valuable if the Cold War developed into Arctic warfare – and culminated in the work of the International Geographical Year (IGY). The IGY – 'the most significant peaceful activity since the Renaissance' to quote the hype of the time – involved tens of thousands of scientists from 60 or more countries. As part of the IGY the Americans set up a base at the South Pole, tactfully named Amundsen-Scott. On 31 October 1956 a DC3 (called the *Que Sera Sera*) piloted by Gus Shinn landed at the pole and Admiral George Dufek became the 11th man, and the first American, to stand there – and the first to have arrived there without days of cold, relentless effort. The following month Lt Richard Bowers – the second Lt Bowers to stand at the pole, but the first to arrive safely back at McMurdo – arrived to supervise construction of the base.

As part of the IGY the British decided to realise Shackleton's dream of crossing Antarctica from the Weddell to the Ross. Ironically the prime minister who committed the country to financing the plan was Winston Churchill, the man who had led the campaign against Shackleton's proposal. In charge of the project was Vivian Fuchs. His team would start from the Weddell

Above **Ed Hillary's team used tracked, but otherwise standard, Ferguson tractors. This shot shows Hillary helping to make a road in New Zealand as a way of getting to know the vehicle. He is watched by a suitably incredulous team.**
New Zealand High Commission

and, after reaching the pole, use supply depots laid by a New Zealand team working from McMurdo to continue to the Ross Sea. The New Zealanders were to be led by Sir Edmund Hillary who, three years earlier had, with Tenzing Norgay, been first to the summit of Everest. In January 1956 the *Theron*, a Canadian sealer captained by Harald Marø, took Fuchs and his team, together with Hillary, to the Weddell where, having reached Vahsel Bay, they established Shackleton base. The *Theron* had ice-spotter planes and radar, which gave her a superb advantage over the *Endurance*, but returning from the bay (eight men were left to overwinter) the ship almost became ice-bound in an eerie replay of Shackleton's trip.

In January 1957 the *Endeavour* took Hillary and his team to McMurdo where the ice-breaker USS *Glacier* helped her reach the continent. Hillary established Scott base at Pram Point from where, using planes, depots were established on the Skelton Glacier and the plateau beyond. Hillary chose the Skelton rather than

the Beardmore because, although a longer journey, it was an easier one for vehicles. To test his vehicles, which he secretly hoped to drive south, Hillary repeated the 'Worst Journey in the World' in March taking two days to reach Cape Crozier – where the ruins of the 1911 team's hut were discovered, a search revealing some of Edward Wilson's drawing pencils, a poignant find – and just 14 hours to return. On the other side of the continent Fuchs' team was establishing 'South Ice', an advanced base at 81°40'S, again using planes to transport all the base's supplies. The austral winter passed with teams at the Shackleton, Scott and South Ice bases.

When summer came Fuchs found the journey to South Ice – he was using a combination of dog teams and vehicles – much more difficult for his tractors than he had imagined, taking 37 days to cover the 644km (400 miles): he then flew back to Shackleton in two-and-a-half hours. He finally set out on the transantarctic journey on 24 November.

Fuchs' original plan had been to reach the pole on 25 December and even now he thought 31 December was possible, though this seems to have been a forlorn hope. In a note to Hillary before starting, Fuchs hints as much: using his calculations 10 January was the earliest he could arrive. Fuchs set out with US SnoCats

Above **A camp on the Skelton Glacier during the Trans-Antarctic expedition.**

Canterbury Museum, New Zealand

Above **Edmund Hillary, Vivian Fuchs and Admiral George Dufek at the South Pole, March 1958. Dufek was the 11th man to reach the pole. Hillary led the third team to reach it overland, while Fuchs was the first to complete the traverse of Antarctica.**

Canterbury Museum, New Zealand

and Weasels, reaching South Ice on 21 December and not leaving until 25 December. He then followed a trail forged by dog teams, catching these on 29 December, but continuing to follow them for several more days. Progress was mixed. On the ice shelf the heavy vehicles fell into crevasses the dogs could cross easily, much time and effort being required to extract them. On the plateau, which, in general, was much less heavily ice-ridged and crevassed, the vehicles were much quicker than the dogs. Fuchs had been unsure of the reliability of the vehicles and had been prepared to manhaul if necessary, but in fact lost only one tractor to mechanical failure.

On the Ross Sea side Hillary was establishing two further depots, at 770km and 1,100km (480 and 700 miles) from Scott base. Determined to try his tractors Hillary had driven south, discovering that they were not only reliable, but fast. By 15 December he had reached Depot 700 with three tractors. The plan had been for Fuchs to reach the pole by the 25th, then to travel to Depot 700 from where Hillary would guide him to Scott base. But now this plan was in tatters. Faced with a wait of at least a month and confident of his tractors Hillary decided to go for the pole. He crossed a crevassed area, then managed 65km (40 miles) daily for six days. Even though progress then slowed to just

1.5kmph (1mph) Hillary's team reached the pole at noon on 4 January 1958, the first men to do so overland since Scott in 1912. The next day Fuchs received a message from Hillary suggesting that because of the delay in his (Fuchs') plan a transantarctic journey was now unjustifiably risky and should be abandoned at the pole, then resumed in 1959. Hillary's message and Fuchs' sharp response were released to the press, doing nothing for relations between the two, which had clearly been strained by Hillary's pole dash.

The joint account of the trip glosses over these problems, but they are exposed by Hillary's account in his biography. He had been told that his job was to wait at Depot 700, then reluctantly allowed to continue, the pole dash causing exchanges at a very high level, the New Zealand prime minster supporting the trip, but the British clearly feeling Hillary was stealing Fuchs' thunder. Fuchs even sent a message telling Hillary not to go for the pole but to conserve fuel as he (Fuchs) was running low: this message annoyed Hillary and precipitated his suggestion that Fuchs abandon his journey at the pole. On his return flight from the pole Hillary flew low over Fuchs' team but only George Lowe (a fellow New Zealander and member of the 1953 Everest team) came out to wave. Hillary saw this as a deliberate slight. He was also very aggrieved when

Fuchs persuaded the Americans to fly his dogs from the pole to McMurdo as they were tired and slower than the vehicles: as the dogs could not enter New Zealand Hillary had to shoot them, a responsibility he fiercely resented. Overall, though, it is difficult not to see Hillary's dash as less a thumbed nose to the British, than a deliberate (and very successful) attempt to steal Fuchs' thunder.

From the pole Hillary flew to McMurdo, but returned to welcome Fuchs to the pole when he finally arrived on 19 January (20 January pole time, as Shackleton base and the pole station were on opposite sides of the Date Line and had times 12 hours apart). Fuchs left the pole on 24 January. One of his drivers was poisoned by carbon monoxide fumes from his engine and needed oxygen dropped by plane, but otherwise the trip was uneventful. Hillary joined the team at Depot 700 (on 7 February) and Scott base was reached on 2 March 1958 after a journey of 3,450km (2,158 miles) in 98 days, a daily average of 35km (22 miles). Shackleton's great dream had been realised.

With dogs, on foot – again
Fuchs, who at Scott base received the news that he had been knighted, had taken seismic readings every day on his journey to determine ice thickness – the ice shelf at Shackleton was found to be 400m (1,300ft) thick – though the journey had been as much for adventure as science. Future journeys to the pole and across the continent would be exclusively for adventure, though there are occasional, usually doubtful, scientific reasons given as side issues. In general scientific research is better handled by well-fed men landing in planes than by exhausted, under-fed ones arriving after days in the open. The other difference between the recent expeditions and the earlier ones is that nations no longer underwrite adventures, private finance being required. The need for sponsorship has led to increasingly audacious plans, but has also increased the antagonism between groups as unwritten (and, therefore, highly disputable) laws are transgressed – though to date there has been less aggravation and mutual mud-slinging in Antarctica than in the Arctic.

In 1980 the Trans-Globe Expedition, the three-man British team of Charles Burton, Sir Ranulph Fiennes and Oliver Shepard (none with previous Antarctic experience), landed on the Queen Maud Land coast, close to Sanae, the South African base, and the 0° meridian. The expedition was intending to circumnavigate the earth along (or as close as possible to) the prime meridian and, as part of that trip, was intending to cross Antarctica on open snow scooters, a feat which many claimed was not possible because of the extremes of cold and wind. The team also faced hostility from the British, New Zealand and US governments. The three landed from a chartered ship and overwintered in a double-skinned cardboard hut. They set out for the pole on 26 October 1980, towing sledges behind their scooters (ski-doos with 640cc engines) but being resupplied by air (a private twin-Otter piloted by Giles Kershaw). The three men reached the pole on 15 December and continued to Scott base on Ross Island, which they reached on 11 January. They had achieved the second crossing of the continent, covering 4,200km (2,600 miles) in 66 days, a significantly longer journey than the Fuchs traverse, and at almost double the speed. Trans-Globe was picked up by its chartered ship from Ross Island.

The next land journey to the pole, in 1985/6, recreated the journey of Scott's team. 'In the Footsteps of Scott' was the brainchild of Briton Robert Swan. The team sailed the *Southern Quest* from London to McMurdo following the route of the *Terra Nova*, then three of them – Roger Mear, Gareth Wood and Mike Stroud – overwintered, recreating the 'Worst Journey in the World' by manhauling to Cape Crozier, taking 30

Above **On the Ross Ice Shelf. Robert Swan following Gareth Wood during the 'Footsteps of Scott' expedition.**
Roger Mear

days for the trip. Then, almost exactly duplicating Scott's route three men – Swan, Mear and Wood – set off for the pole. They took no radio so as to recreate the same sense of isolation, but had sledges that weighed only half as much – in part because they were not walking out (they had their own air transport), in part because modern foodstuffs and equipment are lighter. Having set out on the same date as Scott they arrived at the pole on 11 January 1986, a week ahead of Scott's schedule. In an uncanny parallel with the disappointment of the 1911/12 expedition they also received bad news at the pole: the *Southern Quest* had been crushed by ice in McMurdo and sunk. They also met hostility from a proprietorial US government which declined to allow them to contact their base, refused permission for their support plane to fly in to meet them, and whisked them back to McMurdo for an immediate onward journey to New Zealand.

The official US line is that private adventures which go wrong can result in expensive rescues which endanger their personnel, a reasonable argument against the

deliberately foolhardy, but one which fails to stand up for the Swan expedition which was meticulously planned and superbly executed. As the team carried no radios and had no supply depots if they ran out of food they would die, though their air transport could have mounted a search if they were overdue. The loss of the *Southern Quest* was unfortunate, but hardly predictable.

Swan's team had two more links with the past, neither foreseen during the planning stage and one deeply ironical. In 1986 the Norwegian Monica Kristensen led a team attempting to recreate Amundsen's journey by dog-sledge from the Bay of Whales to the pole and back. Apart from Kristensen, the team was male; when asked how it felt to be a woman leading a male team she witheringly replied that she had no experience of being anything other than a woman. The team's start was

delayed until 17 December, much too late, especially as they had to make the return journey. By the end of January 1987 the team had to turn around, 440km (275 miles) short of the pole. If the British success contrasted with the unfortunate Norwegian effort, relations within the British team bore a marked similarity to those on the *Discovery* expedition trek, antagonism between Mear and Swan mirroring that between Scott and Shackleton. Indeed, Wood was only added to the team to keep the peace (Wilson style) between the two.

The 'Footsteps' expedition was the last which used a ship for transport (though by choice rather than a necessity). The air age had truly arrived with the discovery, at Patriot Hills near the south-western edge of the Ronne Ice Shelf, of a natural blue-ice runway which could be used safely by wheeled (as opposed to ski-mounted) aircraft. In 1988 one of the more amazing trips in Antarctic history saw the first commercial ski journey to the pole, a party of six paying 'tourists' being led by five guides of Mountain Travel from Patriot Hills to the pole. Starting on 3 December 1988 the party covered 1,200km (750 miles) in 49 days, a daily average of 24km (15 miles), arriving on 17 January 1989. The 'tourists' included the Americans Shirley Metz and Victoria Murdon, the first women to reach the pole overland.

Reinhold Messner, the world's greatest high-altitude climber, had pledged himself to climb the 14 8,000m (26,248ft) peaks without supplementary oxygen. When he achieved this feat in October 1986 he acceded to a promise made to his mother and stopped visiting the high hills. But the restless spirit, the relentless striving towards self-imposed goals or pure ambition – whatever it is that drives him – would not let him be, and he decided to attempt a crossing of Antarctica without mechanised transport. As partner he chose the German Arved Fuchs – no relation to Sir Vivian Fuchs – an expert navigator and Arctic veteran. The two wanted to start from the Filchner Ice Shelf, but an inadequate aircraft fuel supply at Patriot Hills – where Messner/ Fuchs met the Steger/Etienne group (see below) – meant a Ronne Shelf start. On 13 November 1989 they were landed at approximately 82°S, 72°W. From there they followed a route through the Thiel Mountains to the plateau, using specially designed parawings to assist with towing their sledges, the wings attached to them rather than their sledges (as Nansen, Shackleton and Scott had used them). The wings offered faster travel when the wind was in a convenient direction – on one day the pair travelled over 100km (more than 60 miles) – but were of limited value if sastrugi (wind-carved ridges of hard snow) lay across the line of travel. Then the sailor's skis could be caught causing tumbling falls. On one occasion Fuchs was picked up by a strong gust and was lucky to escape without breaking his leg. In addition to the sails the pair had global positioning system (a satellite signal-driven device which fixes the user's position to within a few metres) and radios, and were resupplied by air on the journey to the pole and at the pole itself.

They reached the pole on 30 December (or 31 December depending on which side of the Date Line they stood), Fuchs becoming the first man to have reached both poles on foot in one year. The pair then continued along the Shackleton/Scott Beardmore Glacier route, racing against time and hunger as they were not resupplied on this leg. They reached Scott base on 12 February 1990 after a trek of 92 days (during which they averaged 30km/19 miles daily) and sailed to New Zealand with an Italian expedition.

As with the Swan team, Messner and Fuchs were received with popular interest and admiration, tempered by official hostility at the US pole station. They also fell out, Messner becoming increasingly fed up with Fuchs' lack of fitness and slowness in the early stages of the trek. Though he later expressed admiration for Fuchs' willpower and commitment when hunger and fatigue threatened to end the trek, intemperate remarks by Fuchs after the trip, blown into a full-scale row by the media, discoloured what had been a fine, first, unmechanised traverse.

The Steger/Etienne team Fuchs and Messner met at Patriot Hills was multi-national. Joint leaders Will Steger, an American, and Frenchman Jean-Louis Etienne, had met when their tracks crossed (literally) on the way to the North Pole in 1986. They were joined by Victor Boyarsky, a Russian scientist, Qin Dahe, a Chinese glaciologist, and two dog experts, the Japanese Keizo Funatsu and Briton Geoff Somers. The route the team chose was the longest traverse that could be made, starting near the tip of the Antarctic Peninsula and going through the pole to the Russian Mirny Station on the shore of the Davis Sea, a distance of 6,000km (3,750 miles). Because they intended to complete the traverse in one continuous journey they had to start in midwinter, leaving the peninsula's tip on 27 July 1989 (with the temperature a surprisingly balmy –12°C) with three dog teams/sledges. On the journey to the pole the team moved between a dozen previously laid-down supply depots (though several were not located) and were also resupplied by air from Patriot Hills. Sick or exhausted dogs were also replaced. Nevertheless the trip was a great feat of endurance: September was a month of ferocious blizzards with temperatures down to –40°C and wind-chill temperatures much lower: days were lost as leaving the tents became near impossible and travel out of the question. But conditions improved when the peninsula was left behind: travel rates increased and the pole was reached on 11 December after 138 days. Their reception at the pole station was much the same as that of previous trekkers, with the addition of a 'no fraternising' rule that saw the team camp well away from the dome. They were refused facilities such as meals and showers, a situation which greatly embarrassed Steger, the team's lone American. He was appalled by the lack of warmth shown to his Chinese and Russian teammates, and even more so by the constant stream of 'official' visitors who arrived by air, bought souvenir T-shirts their plane had brought in, never went outside (except to get off and on the plane) and showed precious little interest in the scientific work of the station.

The difficult part of the journey now lay ahead. With limited air resupply possible the team had to make it to Vostok, the remote Russian station on the polar plateau across ground that was rumoured to be impassable because of deep powder snow. In reality the crossing was straightforward, Vostok being reached on 18 January 1990. Now the temperature began to fall, with many days continuously around –45°C, and the added hazard of wind. The weather frayed everyone's nerves and led to the most serious confrontation on the trip when Somers poured out his anger over Steger's handling of a sick dog whose death in October, nearly three months before, had, Somers claimed, been due to Steger's neglect. Then, within sight of success, just 25km (16 miles) from Mirny, Funatsu left his tent in a blizzard to feed his dogs, became disorientated and lost, and was forced to dig a ditch in the snow with a pair of pliers. The others, realising he had not returned,

Above **The Steger/Etienne Transarctic Expedition**
Will Steger

searched and shouted for him, all of them attached to a single rope, but without success. Eventually darkness and cold forced them to abandon the search. At dawn they began again, finding Funatsu soon after. In limited clothing he had survived 12 hours in appalling conditions, a tribute to both his fitness and his refusal to panic. The next day the team completed their journey to Mirny. They had trekked for 220 days at a daily average of 27km (17 miles).

Though the Messner/Fuchs and Steger traverses (and another, unheralded, traverse from the Weddell to the pole, then along Amundsen's route by the Norwegians Høibakk, Mehren and the Mørdre brothers) had been great achievements, the idea of an unsupported traverse – and even of an unsupported journey to the pole – was still a target. In 1992/3 the British pair of Ranulf Fiennes and Mike Stroud almost succeeded. Starting on 9 November 1992 from Berkner Island, between the Filchner and Ronne Ice Shelfs, they made it to the pole on 16 January 1993 hauling sledges that started out weighing 225kg (about 500lb). Reversing the Shackleton/Scott route down the Beardmore Glacier they reached the Ross Ice Shelf (and so were able to claim a sea-to-sea traverse), but had to

call for air evacuation on 12 February after 95 days and 2,000km (1,250 miles) of travel when their physical condition had deteriorated to the point where they could no longer manhaul. They were about 400km (250 miles) from McMurdo.

The following year the Norwegian Erling Kagge made the first unsupported, solo journey to the pole. Starting from Berkner Island on 18 November 1993 he reached the pole in 49 days and 13 hours, arriving on 7 January 1994. He had travelled 1,310km (819 miles), starting with a sledge which weighed 120kg (265lb), which included food for 66 days. Kagge's journey was remarkably uneventful: he had some minor injuries and was occasionally so cold that he had to keep moving so as to warm up rather than stopping to pitch his tent. These episodes depressed him, but overall he was in complete command of himself and the trek, and arrived at the pole fit and well, and almost sorry that the trip was over.

Three years later another Norwegian, Børge Ousland (who had already made solo, unsupported journeys to both the North and South Poles) completed the first unsupported traverse. Ousland started out at the same time as Ranulf Fiennes and the Pole Marek Kaminski who were also trying for the elusive first solo traverse. Interestingly his impression of Fiennes was an echo of the opinion of Nansen and Amundsen for their British competitors. He thought Fiennes' equipment heavy and poorly designed, and considered that all his expeditions had been ill-prepared and, consequently, too strenuous. Like the earlier Norwegian he was surprised how little Fiennes had learnt: on this trip he was following his 1992/3 route from Berkner, despite having found it difficult and dangerous then. Why not, he thought, follow the Norwegian-pioneered route which had been shown to be so much easier? By contrast Ousland's own preparations had an Amundsen-like thoroughness: he had a kevlar sledge, carefully designed equipment, and supplies considered to the gram so that his sledge weighed only about 180kg (400lb).

In the event Fiennes contracted kidney stones and had to be evacuated while Kaminski had a near-fatal fall on the ice shelf and, though he continued, had to stop at the pole. Ousland followed a similar route to Kagge from Berkner Island to the pole, reaching it on 19 December after 35 days, then followed Amundsen's route to and down the Axel Heiberg Glacier before crossing the Ross Ice Shelf to McMurdo. He crossed 2,840km (1,775 miles) of the continent in an astonishing 64 days – a daily average of over 44km (27½ miles).

This high figure was helped by some astonishing sail-skiing: on one day on the Ross Shelf he covered 226km (more than 140 miles).

Despite being a landmark journey, Ousland's solo trek has not marked the end of Antarctic adventure, despite the official frowns and the obvious hazards. In 1997/8 the Belgians Dixie Dansercoer and Alain Hubert followed the TransGlobe route from Queen Maud Land to the pole and on to McMurdo – 3,500km (2200 miles) in 97 days (they needed one resupply flight to replace a broken sledge) – then in 1998/9 the Japanese Mitsuro Ohba followed the same route to the pole before turning right (as it were) towards the Ellsworth Mountains. Sadly he didn't reach the sea: after a solo journey of 3,825km (2,390 miles), the longest in history, he was evacuated to Patriot Hills. Both the Belgians and Ohba were resupplied during their treks, but in the austral summer of 2000/1 the Norwegians Rolf Bae and Eirik Sønneland completed an unsupported journey of 3,800km (2,375 miles), the longest unsupported journey ever made. The pair started out from Queen Maud coast after overwintering at the Norwegian Troll station hauling sledges of 180kg (397lb). They journeyed to the pole, continuing to the Ross Ice Shelf by way of the Axel Heiberg Glacier (Amundsen's route). After 105 days they reached the McMurdo base, a phenomenal achievement.

Others can enjoy a less exacting journey, Adventure Network International offering 60-day ski trips to the pole from the Ronne Ice Shelf, or ten-day 'last degree' ski trips from 89°S. But whether solo unsupported or with the back-up of a commercial operation, Antarctica will continue to exert the same magnetic pull on the inner steel of adventurers that it has since Shackleton first felt compelled to return.

Below **Børge Ousland heads south on the first solo, unsupported traverse of Antarctica**
Børge Ousland

Selected bibliography

Albanov, Valerian. *In the Land of White Death* (Modern Library, NY, 2000)

Amundsen, Roald. *The North West Passage* (Constable, 1907)

Amundsen, Roald. *The South Pole* (John Murray, 1913)

Amundsen, Roald. *Nordostpassagen* (Gyldendal, Kristiania, 1921) (in Norwegian, has not been translated into English)

Amundsen, Roald and Ellsworth, Lincoln. *The First Flight Across the Polar Sea* (Hutchinson, 1926)

Amundsen, Roald. *My Life as an Explorer* (Heinemann, 1927)

Andrée's Story, the Complete Record of his Polar Flight, 1897 (Viking, NY, 1930)

Arlov, Thor. *A Short History of Svalbard* (Norsk Polarinstitutt, Oslo, 1989)

Astrup, Eivind. *With Peary near the Pole* (Pearson, 1898)

Barr, Susan. *Franz Josef Land* (Norsk Polarinstitutt, Oslo, 1995)

Barr, Susan (Editor), Ivar Fosheim. *Storvilt, Is Og Nytt Land* (Aschehoug, Oslo, 1994) (in Norwegian, not translated into English)

Barrow, John. *A Chronological History of Voyages into the Arctic Regions (1818)* (John Murray, 1818)

Baughman, T. H. *Pilgrims on the Ice* (University of Nebraska, 1999)

Beattie, Owen, and Geiger, John. *Frozen in Time* (Bloomsbury, 1987)

Beechey, Frederick. *Narrative of a Voyage to the Pacific and Beering's Strait* (Colburn and Bentley, 1831)

Beechey, Frederick. *A Voyage towards the North Pole* (Bentley, 1843)

Belcher, Edward. *The Last of the Arctic Voyages* (Lovell Reece, 1855)

Berton, Pierre. *The Arctic Grail* (Viking, 1988)

Bertrand, Kenneth. *Americans in Antarctica* (American Geographical Society, NY, 1971)

Best, George. *A True Discourse: George Best's Account of the Frobisher Voyages* (1578)

Bickel, Lennard. *Shackleton's Forgotten Men* (Thunder's Mouth Press, 2000)

Bickel, Lennard. *Mawson's Will* (Steerforth Press, Vermont, 2000)

Bobrick, Benson. *East of the Sun* (Heinemann, 1992)

Bockstoce, John, R. *Whales, Ice and Men* (University of Washington Press, 1986)

Bomann-Larsen, Tor. *Roald Amundsen, En Biografi* (Cappelen, Oslo, 1995) (in Norwegian, not translated into English)

Borchgrevink, Carsten. *First on the Antarctic Continent* (George Newnes, 1901)

Boyarsky, Victor. *Seven Months of Infinity* (Terra, Moscow, 1998) (in Russian, not translated into English)

Bruce, William. *Polar Exploration* (Williams and Norgate, 1911)

Bryce, Robert. *Cook and Peary* (Stackpole Books, 1997)

Byrd, Richard E. *Alone* (Putnam, 1938)

Capelotti, P.J. *By Airship to the North Pole* (Rutgers University Press, 1999)

Chapman, F. Spencer. *Northern Lights* (Chatto and Windus, 1832)

Charcot, Jean-Baptiste. *Le Français au Pôle Sud* (Ernest Flammarion, Paris, 1906)

Cherry-Garrard, Apsley. *The Worst Journey in the World* (Constable, 1922)

Chevigny, Hector. *Russian America* (Binford and Mort, Oregon, 1985)

Conway, Martin. *No Man's Land. A History of Spitsbergen from its Discovery* (CUP, 1906)

Cook, Frederick. *Through the First Antarctic Night* (Doubleday, Page and Co, 1909)

Cook, Frederick. *My Attainment of the Pole* (Polar Publishing, 1911)

Cook, Frederick. *Return from the Pole* (Burke, 1953)

Cookman, Scott. *Ice Blink* (John Wiley, 2000)

Crawford, Janet. *That First Antarctic Winter* (South Latitude Research Limited, 1998)

Cyriax, Richard. *Sir John Franklin's Last Expedition* (Methuen, 1939)

Delgado, James. *Across the Top of the World* (Checkmark Books, NY, 1999)

De Long, E. *The Voyage of the Jeanette. The Ship and Ice Journals of George W. De Long* (Houghton, Mifflin & Co, Boston, 1884)

Drygalski, Erich von. *The Southern Ice-Continent* (translated by Bluntisham Books, 1989)

Dupre, Lonnie. *Greenland Expedition: Where Ice Is Born* (NorthWord Press, Minnesota, 2000)

(One or two further volumes of the Dupre/Hoeschler Greenland Expedition will be published soon)

Erngaard, Erik. *Grønland, I Tusinde År, Sesam* (Viborg, 1982) (in Danish, no English translation)

Evans, Edward. *South with Scott* (Collins, 1919)

Fairley, T.C. *Sverdrup's Arctic Adventures* (Longmans, 1959)

Fiala, Anthony. *Fighting the Polar Ice* (Doubleday, Page & Co 1906)

Fisher, Raymond. *The Voyage of Semen Dezhnev in 1648* (Hakluyt Society, 1981)

Fox, Luke. *North-West Fox* (1635)

Franklin, John. *Narrative of Journey to the Shores of the Polar Sea* (John Murray, 1824)

Franklin, John. *Narrative of Second Expedition to the Shores of the Polar Sea* (John Murray, 1828)

Fuchs, Vivian and Hillary, Edmund. *The Crossing of Antarctica* (Cassell, 1958)

Geiger, John and Beattie, Owen. *Dead Silence: the Greatest Mystery in Arctic Discovery* (Bloomsbury, 1993)

Gjeldnes, Rune and Larsen, Torry. *Dead Men Walking* (Larsen and Gjeldnes, 2000)

Gould, Laurence McKinley. *Cold* (Brewer, Warren and Putnam, NY, 1931)

Greely, Adolphus. *Three Years of Arctic Service* (Charles Scribner's Sons, NY, 1886)

Grierson, John. *Challenge to the Pole* (G.T. Foulis and Co, 1964)

Guttridge, Leonard F. *Ghosts of Cape Sabine* (Putnam, NY, 2000)

Guttridge, Leonard F. *Icebound: the Jeanette Expedition's Quest for the North Pole* (Paragon, NY, 1987)

Hall, Charles Francis. *Arctic Researches and Life among the Eskimo* (Harper, NY, 1865)

Harper, Kenn. *Give Me My Father's Body* (Profile Books, 2000)

Hayes, Isaac. *An Arctic Boat Journey in the Autumn of 1854* (Brown, Taggard and Chase, Boston, 1860)

Hayes, Isaac. *The Open Polar Sea* (Hurd and Houghton, NY, 1867)

Henderson, Bruce. *Fatal North* (New American Library, NY, 2001)

Henson, Matthew. *A Negro Explorer at the North Pole* (Frederick A. Stokes, NY, 1912)

Herbert, Wally. *Across the Top of the World* (Longmans, 1969)

Herbert, Wally. *The Noose of Laurels* (Hodder and Stoughton, 1989)

Horwood, Harold. *Bartlett, the Great Canadian Explorer* (Doubleday, NY, 1977)

Huish, Robert. *The Last Voyage of Capt Sir John Ross* (John Saunders, 1835)

Huish, Robert. *A Narrative of the Voyage and Travels of Capt Beechey* (W. Wright, 1836)

Huntford, Roland. *Scott and Amundsen* (Macmillan, 1979)

Huntford, Roland. *Shackleton* (Hodder & Stoughton, 1985)

Huntford, Roland. *Nansen* (Duckworth, 1997)

Jackson, Frederick. *The Great Frozen Land* (Macmillan, 1895)

Jackson, Frederick. *A Thousand Days in the Arctic* (Harper, 1899)

James, Thomas. *The Strange and Dangerous Voyage of Capt Thomas James* (1633)

Jones, A.G.E. *Antarctica Observed* Caedmon of Whitby (1982)

Kane, Elisha Kent. *The US Grinnell Expedition in Search of Sir John Franklin* (Childs and Peterson, Philadelphia, 1856)

Kane, Elisha Kent. *Arctic Explorations: the Second Grinnell Expedition in Search of Sir John Franklin* (Childs and Peterson, NY, 1853)

Kaye Lamb, W. *The Journals and Letters of Sir Alexander Mackenzie* (Hakluyt Society, 1970)

Kish, George. *North East Passage* (Nico Israel, Amsterdam, 1973)

Kvam, Ragnar. *Den Tredje Mann* (Gyldendal, 1997) (a biography of Hjalmar Johansen: not translated into English)

Kushnarev, Evgenii. *Bering's Search for the Straits* (Oregon Historical Society, 1990)

Liljequist, Gösta. *High Latitudes* (Swedish Polar Research Secretariat, 1993)

Loomis, Chauncey. *Weird and Tragic Shores* (Macmillan, 1972)

Lyon, George. *A Brief Narrative of an Unsuccessful Attempt to Reach Repulse Bay* (John Murray, 1825)

M'Clintock, Francis. *The Voyage of the Fox in the Arctic Seas* (John Murray, 1859)

McClure, Robert. *The Discovery of the North West Passage* (Longman, Brown, Green, Longmans and Roberts, 1856)

McGhee, Robert. *Ancient People of the Arctic* (UBC Press, Vancouver, 1996)

McGoogan, Ken. *Fatal Passage* (Harper Flamingo, 2001)

McKinlay, William Laird. *Karluk* (Weidenfeld and Nicolson, 1976)

Mason, Theodore, K. *Two Against the Ice: Amundsen and Ellsworth* (Dodd, Mead and Co, NY, 1982)

Mawson, Douglas. *The Home of Blizzard* (Hodder and Stoughton, 1930)

Mear, Roger and Swan, Robert. *In the Footsteps of Scott* (Jonathan Cape, 1987)

Messner, Reinhold. Antarctica, *Both Heaven and Hell* (Crowood Press, 1991)

Mikkelsen, Ejnar. *Lost in the Arctic* (Heinemann, 1913)

Mirsky, Jeannette. *To the Arctic* (Wingate, 1934)

Nansen, Fridtjof. *In Northern Mists* (Heinemann, 1911)

Nansen, Fridtjof. *Farthest North* (Archibald Constable, 1897)

Nares, George. *The Official Record of the Recent Arctic Expedition* (John Murray, 1876)

Nares, George. *Narrative of a Voyage to the Polar Sea during 1875–6* (Sampson, Low, Marston, Searle and Rivington, 1878)

Newman, Peter. *Company of Adventurers* (Penguin Books, Canada, 1985)

Newman, Peter. *Caesars of the Wilderness* (Penguin Books, Canada, 1987)

(The Newman books are a history of the Hudson's Bay Company in two volumes)

Niven, Jennifer. *The Ice Master* (Macmillan, 2000)

Nobile, Umberto *With the Italia to the North Pole* (George Allen and Unwin, 1930)

Nobile, Umberto. *My Polar Flights* (Frederick Muller, 1961)

Nordenskiöld, Adolf. *The Voyage of the Vega around Asia and Europe* (Macmillan, 1881)

Oleson, Tryggvi. *Early Voyages and Northern Approaches* (McClelland and Stewart, 1963)

Ousland, Børge. *Alone Across Antarctica* (Ousland, 1997)

Ousland, Børge. *Alone to the North Pole* (Ousland, 1994)

Ousland, Børge. *Arctic Traverse* (Ousland, to be published)

Papanin, Ivan. *Life on an Ice Flow* (Julian Messner, NY, 1939)

Parry, William Edward. *Journal of a Voyage for the Discovery of a North-West Passage*(John Murray, 1821)

Parry, William Edward. *Journal of a Second Voyage for the Discovery of a North-West Passage* (John Murray, 1824)

Parry, William Edward. *Journal of a Third Voyage for the Discovery of a North-West Passage* (John Murray, 1826)

Parry, William Edward. *Narrative of a Journey to reach the North Pole* (John Murray, 1828)

Pasetskiy, B.M. *Russian discoveries in the Arctic, Volume 1* (Admiralteistovo, St. Petersburg 2000) (in Russian, not translated into English)

Payer, Julius. *New Lands within the Arctic Circle* (Macmillan, 1876)

Peary, Robert E. *Northward over the Great Ice* (Methuen, 1898)

Peary, Robert E. *Nearest the Pole* (Hutchinson, 1907)

Peary, Robert E. *The North Pole* (Hodder and Stoughton, 1910)

Ponting, Herbert. *The Great White South* (Duckworth, 1921)

Powys, Llewelyn. *Henry Hudson* (The Bodley Head, 1927)

Rasmussen, Knud. *Across Arctic America. Narrative of the Fifth Thule Expedition* (Putnam, 1933)

Richardson, John. *Arctic Searching Expedition* (Harper, 1851)

Ross, James Clark. *A Voyage of Discovery and Research in the Southern and Antarctic regions* (John Murray, 1847)

Ross, John. *A Voyage of Discovery under the Orders of the Admiralty* (John Murray, 1819)

Ross, John. *Narrative of a Second Voyage in search of a North-West Passage* (Webster, 1835)

Savoia, Luigi Amedeo di, Duke of the Abruzzi. *On the Polar Star in the Arctic Seas* (Hutchinson, London, 1903)

Savours, Ann. *The Search for the North West Passage* (St Martin's Press, NY, 1999)

Schley, W.S. and Soley J.R. *The Rescue of Greely* (Charles Scribner's Sons, 1889)

Scoresby, William. *An Account of the Arctic Regions* (Archibald Constable, 1820)

Scott, Robert F. *The Voyage of the Discovery* (Smith, Elder and Co, 1907)

Scott's Last Expedition (Smith, Elder and Co, 1913)

Shackleton, Ernest. *The Heart of Antarctica* (Heinemann, 1909)

Shackleton, Ernest. *South* (Heinemann, 1919)

Shelvocke, George, A Voyage round the World by way of the Great South Sea, J Senex, 1728

Simpson, A. *The Life and Travels of Thomas Simpson, the Arctic Discoverer* (Richard Bentley, 1845)

Simpson, Thomas. *Narrative of the Discoveries on the North Coast of America effected by the Officers of the Hudson's Bay Company* (Richard Bentley, 1843)

Spufford, Francis. *I May Be Some Time* (Faber and Faber, 1996)

Stefansson, Vilhjalmur. *The Friendly Arctic* (Macmillan, 1922)

Steger, Will, and Schurke, Paul. *North to the Pole* (Macmillan, 1987)

Steger, Will and Bowermaster, Jon. *Crossing Antarctica* (Bantam Press, 1991)

Struzik, Edward. *North West Passage* (Blandford, 1991)

Sverdrup, Otto. *New Land* (Longman Green, 1904)

Tyrell, James. *Across the Sub-Arctics of Canada* (William Briggs, Toronto, 1908)

Uemura. *Hokkyokuten Gurinrando tandokuk (Solo Journeys to the North Pole and across Greenland)* (Bungei Shunju, 1978) (in Japanese, not translated into English)

Urvantsev, Nikolai. *Severnaya Zemlya* (Arctic Institute, Leningrad, 1933) (in Russian, not translated into English)

Ushakov, George. *On Untrodden Land* (Molodaya Gvardiya, Moscow, 1953) (in Russian, not translated into English)

Vaughan, Richard. *North West Greenland: A History* (University of Maine Press, 1991)

Vaughan, Richard. *The Arctic, a History* (Alan Sutton, 1994)

The Voyage of the Chelyuskin (Chatto and Windus, 1935)

Weber, Richard and Malakhov, Mikhail. *Polar Attack* (McClelland and Stewart, 1996)

Weddell, James. *A Voyage towards the South Pole* (Longman, Rees, Orme, Brown and Green, 1825)

Wellman, Walter. *The Aerial Age* (Keller and Co, NY, 1911)

Wilkes, Charles. *Narrative of the US Exploring Expedition* (Lea & Blanchard, Philadelphia, 1845)

Woodman, David. *Unravelling the Franklin Mystery* (McGill-Queen's University Press, 1991)

Worsley, F.A. *Endurance* (Norton and Co, 1999)

Index